Exploring discourse and ideology through corpora

Linguistic Insights

Studies in Language and Communication

Edited by Maurizio Gotti,
University of Bergamo

Volume 276

PETER LANG
Bern · Berlin · Bruxelles · New York · Oxford

Miguel Fuster-Márquez
José Santaemilia
Carmen Gregori-Signes
Paula Rodríguez-Abruñeiras (eds.)

Exploring discourse and ideology through corpora

PETER LANG
Bern · Berlin · Bruxelles · New York · Oxford

Bibliographic information published by die Deutsche Nationalbibliothek
Die Deutsche Nationalbibliothek lists this publication in the Deutsche Nationalbibliografie; detailed bibliographic data is available on the Internet at ‹http://dnb.d-nb.de›.

We remain indebted to the Valencian Government (*Generalitat Valenciana*) for kindly giving financial support for this publication (project code 31/1769321).

This publication is the result of activities carried out within research project PID2019-110863GB-I00 ("Valores informativos e ideología: La construcción discursiva intercultural de género y desigualdades sociales en la prensa (digital) a través de lingüística de corpus"), funded by the Spanish Ministry of Science and Innovation. The editors belong to research groups CORPLING (GIUV2018-425) and GENTEXT (GIUV2015-230) of the *Universitat de València*.

GENERALITAT VALENCIANA
Conselleria d'Educació, Investigació, Cultura i Esport

ISSN 1424-8689
ISBN 978-3-0343-3969-8 (Print)
E-ISBN 978-3-0343-4235-3 (E-PDF)
E-ISBN 978-3-0343-4236-0 (EPUB)
E-ISBN 978-3-0343-4237-7 (MOBI)
DOI 10.3726/b17868

Wabernstrasse 40, CH-3007 Bern, Switzerland
bern@peterlang.com, www.peterlang.com

Contents

Miguel Fuster-Márquez, José Santaemilia, Carmen Gregori-Signes and Paula Rodríguez-Abruñeiras

Insights from corpus-assisted discourse analysis: Unveiling social attitudes and values

The exploration of discourse through corpus linguistics techniques is a rapidly expanding field. Indeed, Corpus-Assisted Discourse Studies (CADS), as introduced and defined by Alan Partington, has become a very popular methodology or approach for the critical and also non critical analysis of discourses. Publications have proliferated over the last decade, thus problematising their objects of study and increasingly widening their scope and focus. These trends have encompassed a wide range of interests and the proposal of applying specific corpus techniques, or combining different methodologies, or drawing on information from various relevant sources, as an appealing strategy. There is already a well-established tradition of disciplines that have benefitted from the potential application of corpus techniques, including applied linguistics, variationist studies, specialised languages, historical linguistics, pragmatics, forensic linguistics, learner language, translation and stylistic studies, among others. Additionally, young scholars who wish to engage themselves in corpus-related research, today have at their disposal handbooks and companions published by the most prestigious publishing houses, and also a large number of public corpora, web sources and software that will pave their way for their research. While some publications have dealt with corpus linguistics overviews others have, more specifically, focused on statistical methods. This is a helpful reminder that quantification is a crucial and distinctive aspect of most kinds of corpus research, perhaps inextricably bound to it. In contrast with earlier linguistic analysis which focused on single texts, or dealt with small amounts of data, dealing empirically with large amounts of text matter in corpora, not infrequently millions of words, and hundreds or thousands of texts, brings with it the need of solid and reliable quantification methods. The fact of exploring large amounts of data has meant a change of research priorities, and older alternative purely qualitative methods are simply not suitable. This also means that corpus linguistics, being more thoroughly empirical, has been moving away from the humanities to embrace methods, approaches which are regularly found in the social sciences.

It is increasingly evident that corpus methodologies have already greatly contributed to discourse analysis and shown their potential to unveil political or ideological attitudes, values, or social inequalities. The implementation of corpus techniques, which are increasingly refined every day, allow us access to document social attitudes, to expose injustice or sexism and –hopefully – to fight against discrimination by obtaining results which are more generalisable. Until quite recently, the study of social issues, identity politics or ideological values has favoured qualitative analyses of small collections of texts. Today, however, more and more researchers are convinced that the use of corpus linguistics for social analysis constitutes a very powerful instrument of social inquiry, especially if used in combination with other (qualitative) approaches which require close reading and the interpretation of particularly salient textual features. Corpus-Assisted Discourse Studies (CADS) enjoys today great popularity and academic appeal, partly because of its ability to move back and forth, in a complementary way, between qualitative and quantitative techniques in order to generate new hypotheses and to test existing ones.

Contributions to this volume deal with socio-ideological issues such as political and media discourses, gender-based studies or hate language, which have increasingly become the object of corpus linguistics research, as have their evaluative, emotive or attitudinal dimensions. Emerging trends in research have come from the application of CADS to the interactive discourses contained in social networks. Some contributions in this volume also bear witness to this trend. The contributions to this volume share a committed view on social reality. To meet their goals, on the one hand, they use corpus tools to guarantee a balanced quantitative and qualitative analysis of (large or small) corpora and, on the other, provide us with a critical approach to the ideological nuances present in texts. This book offers a wide range of analyses and insights into burning and/or conflicting social issues. Alan

Partington's chapter, entitled "Post-history, post-democracy, post-truth, post-Trump? Really? A corpus-assisted study of delegitimisation via argument strategies: 'dirty tricks', evaluation and hyperbole in modern political discourses," illustrates the balanced use of qualitative and quantitative approaches in the examination of a series of contemporary post-denominations (*post-history, post-democracy, post-truth, post-Trump*) in order to unveil the ideological delegitimisation of opposing groups or individuals. In this chapter, Partington quite insightfully addresses a number of crucial problems which have to do with the difficult synergy of Corpus Linguistics and more classical qualitative Discourse Studies. For this particular piece of research, Partington has made use of different corpora. In his view, researching 'macro' argument strategies (i.e. de/legitimisation) is a way of addressing one of the 'dusty corners' (Taylor/Marchi 2018) in corpus linguistics, which tends to favour a (sometimes decontextualised) scrutiny of large bodies of texts by focusing on 'micro' strategies. For Partington, macro level features should be " '*assisted*' by the researcher's intuitions" and world knowledge.

Tony McEnery, Helen Baker and Carmen Dayrell are in charge of the second chapter, "Analysing the impacts of 19th-century drought: A corpus-based study", where they turn their attention to the past in order to access information gaps through textual data about the weather that could be useful to historians and meteorologists, thus proving the usefulness and convenience of carrying out textual analyses of large amounts of historical media texts (in this case, a large sample of 19th century British newspapers reporting on climate conditions in different parts of the country) by means of corpus methodologies. The rigorous examination of discourses can become an indispensible contribution of corpus linguistics to non-linguistic fields such as the one dealt with here in relation to weather conditions in earlier centuries which cannot be accounted for directly through sophisticated modern standard methods. Nevertheless, the authors deem most appropriate to make use of triangulation, hence they use corpus methods in concert with other techniques (concordance geo-parsing and close reading analyses) with a view to reconstructing, as faithfully as possible, media narratives of the droughts and water shortages in different regions of the UK.

Political Discourse, one of the favourite targets of corpus-based analysis, is illustrated in this volume by Salvador Enguix-Oliver and Beatriz Gallardo-Paúls's study of recent political developments related to the extremist far-right Spanish party Vox during 2018 in their contribution "Coverage of the far-right in the Spanish written press: The case of Vox". With this aim in mind, the authors have selected a number of widely read Spanish quality written newspapers (*El País*, *El Mundo*, *La Vanguardia* and *ABC*) and digital dailies (*El Español*, *eldiario.es*, *Público* and *Infolibre*). According to the authors, these newspaper items belong to their own sub-corpus PRODISNET-201, which is part of the larger PRODISNET (Discursive Processes on the Internet corpus). The hypothesis explored in this chapter is that far-right parties like the Spanish party Vox have been, and are still, receiving largely undeserved media coverage in Western democracies, and this media attitude enhances their public visibility which results in unprecedented electoral success. The authors also resort to the use of quantitative methods such as sentiment analysis (using the software Lingmotif, which reveals a basically negative appraisal) and complementing their study with close pragmatic analyses of all texts, since the authors find, for example, that political evaluation in the media is often expressed implicitly. In their conclusion they highlight that negative political evaluations are most often carried out through presuppositions and anomalous implicatures of manner and quality.

In "Evaluation in Theresa May's political discourse: A study of the PM's seminal Brexit speeches", Ana Belén Cabrejas-Peñuelas and Rosana Dolón focus on a burning issue such as the Brexit process, as exemplified in three seminal speeches by the former British PM Theresa May. The speeches were delivered during key moments of Brexit negotations: the Lancaster House speech (January 2017), the Florence speech (September 2017) and the London Mansion House speech (March 2018). The authors home in on the verbal content of this corpus to show how evaluation of status (see Hunston 2000, 2008, 2011) is expressed in political texts, and reveals how corpus linguistics can meaningfully contribute to the study of evaluation and persuasion. The typological framework applied here has the earlier work by Díez-Prados & Cabrejas-Peñuelas (2018) as an acknowledged antecedent. Use has been made in this contribution of the freeware program called UAM Corpus Tool developed by Mick O'Donnell (2019). The corpus has been manually annotated to automatically carry out the inferential statistical analysis. According to the authors, a key persuasive strategy in Theresa May's speeches would be the use of rhetorical devices of "suggestion" against "proof", and of maintaining an apparently objective stance (Hunston 2011: 27). The linguistic choices made by the former British PM seem to have the projection of a down-to-earth and objective position as a specific persuasive intention.

Gender issues –and, specifically, violence against women (VAW) – feature prominently in the growing research that makes combined use of corpus linguistics and other methodologies, as shown in Leanne Victoria Bartley's chapter " 'Nobody is guilty in football. That's the first thing to understand': A corpus-assisted critical discourse analysis of the UK press coverage of the Ched Evans case." Bartley focuses on judicial events which took place in 2012 in the UK, when the famous footballer Ched Evans was convicted of raping a young woman in a hotel room in Rhyl, North Wales, after a night out together. In 2016, Evans' case was reviewed, his conviction overturned, and he also received a compensation of £800,000. Bartley explores the approaches of the British press (*The Daily Mail, The Guardian, The Mirror, The Sun*) during this period by means of a CADS approach, based on Martin and White's (2005) APPRAISAL theory slightly modified by Bednarek's (2008) recommendations concerning the subcategory of AFFECT. She makes use of UAM Corpus Tool (O'Donnell 2019), which allows users to employ this in-built paradigm for quantitative and qualitative analysis. Bartley investigates how both the perpetrator and his victim were represented in the British press at different stages of this controversial case. She finds that the media discourses changed over time – the view of the alleged perpetrator went from harsh criticism to a positive image. The focus on the victim, by contrast, went from understanding her inability to consent to sexual intercourse to criticising her inappropriate sexual activities.

In the following chapter, "News values in construing female victims of VAW discourses in the media: A view from CADS," Sergio Maruenda-Bataller also addresses a gender issue. The aim of this author is to explore how mainstream Spanish and British quality newspapers, during the decade from 2005 to 2015, have construed female victims of

VAW discursively. Classifying the news values that are used to depict female victims, he examines and compares the treatment that Spanish and British newspapers give to female victims in VAW news reports. For this purpose, the author makes use of a large purpose-built corpus where he applies the Discursive News Values Analysis paradigm as described by Bednarek and Caple (2017), but also relies on Potts et al.'s (2015) study for the use of corpus methods, where the authors also made use of a large corpus to investigate the representation of the Katrina Hurricane in the news. While more research is needed, it is the author's view that results appear to substantiate the uneven presence of two complementary discourses which are nevertheless inextricably linked: a discourse of death, violence and suffering (thus, predominance of news values such as NEGATIVITY and IMPACT) and another of institutional and social support, (which realises the news value of CONSONANCE).

Alfonso Sánchez-Moya also explores the gender issue of VAW in the chapter "How does violence-motivated online discourse differ from its non-violent counterpart? Insights from a CADS approach." He makes use LIWC, a sentiment software tool to analyse the discourse of female survivors of Intimate Partner Violence (IPV) in a corpus of online forum messages by women who are undergoing such violence, containing a total of 120,000 words. Insights into this phenomenon with a discursive approach are, in the author's words, scarce. Some of his conclusions are that, when compared to another neutral/non-violent corpus containing forum messages by women, the discourse in this IPV-related forum appears to be characterized by a narrative-oriented and personal style, focusing more on the here-and-now. Particularly, the sub-corpus dealing with abuse within the IPV corpus shows a severely pessimistic type of discourse. Also, the claims about IPV-related negative emotions and their discursive characterization are validated by this analysis.

In "'We'll watch TV and do other stuff': A corpus-assisted discourse study of vague language use in online child sexual grooming," Nuria Lorenzo-Dus and Anina Kinzel show the practical application of a CADS methodology for very serious sexuality-related issues – i.e. a recent escalation of cases of online child sexual grooming (OCSG) as "an Internet-enabled communicative process of entrapment" in the

UK. The authors' aim is to identify the linguistic and rhetorical tactics used by adults convicted of OCSG in order to provide collaboration to law enforcement agencies and educational institutions. The large corpus containing chat logs were compiled between 2004 and 2016. The corpus was uploaded to CQP Web, and VARD has been used by the authors to standardise the spelling. Among their conclusions they highlight the strategic use of implicitness and vague language for manipulative goals, and their results show that the main category used by groomers is that of quality-approximators, followed by vague identifiers and de-identifiers. Briefly, groomers manipulate communications with children as targets in ways which confuse them greatly.

Stefania M. Maci presents the chapter "The narrative of the anti-vax campaign on Twitter", on medical knowledge as disseminated by digital media. Maci describes the discourse strategies employed by US anti-vaccine activists in a small Twitter corpus of 16,768 tweets (75,960 running words) gathered in October 2018 after some children died from measles in New York City, their aim being spreading fake news about vaccination. The corpus has been semantically annotated by USAS to identify key semantic domains and WMatrix has been used for the automatic processing of the most relevant meanings. Maci also carried out a sentiment analysis, employing *Socialbearing.com* as its software. The results obtained reveal an overall strong, articulate anti-vaccine discourse displayed by these activists of the anti-vaccine movement in their tweets. Maci claims that, although apparently grounded on scientific truths, these activists favour a conspiracy theory between the government and the pharmacological industry.

And last but not least, Nouf Alotaibi and Jane Mulderrig are the authors of the chapter that closes this volume, "Debating Saudi womanhood: A corpus-aided critical discourse analysis of the representation of Saudi women in the Twitter campaign against the 'male guardianship' system." Again, gender politics features prominently here, as the chapter focuses on a highly controversial topic ('male guardianship') affecting the freedoms, and the whole lives, of millions of women in Saudi Arabia. The authors wish to analyse the Saudi women's attitudes towards the online campaign #سعوديات_نطالب_اسقاط_الولاية (i.e. '#EndMaleGuardianshipSystem' – #EMGC) that started in 2016, and is generating a polarization of Saudi women's positions into two groups – Pro-#EMGC and Anti-#EMGC. The paper seeks to answer three questions: "1) who were the salient social actors in the discourse of #EMGC?; 2) how did the *female* campaigners represent Saudi women as social actors?; and 3) what were their most prominent actions?" To that end they use a corpus-aided critical discourse approach, bringing together the potential of corpus tools (word list and concordance tools provided by the concordance software 'AntConc' – see Anthony 2017) to reveal key textual patterns and the insights drawn from CDA and the representation of social actors (van Leeuwen 2008). This chapter shows, as do the others in this volume, that a synergy between corpus and discourse analytical tools is crucial in identifying, analysing and even advancing social issues – i.e. in this case, the women's rights issue in Saudi Arabia.

Readers should notice that authors in this volume have relied on data contained in either small or large corpora. It is convenient to bear in mind that, in the same way as there is no specifically recommended methodology attached to the analysis of (critical) discourses, there is no agreed criterion either about the size of corpora suitable in research. Perhaps 'the bigger the better' is a good guiding principle to be seen in many published papers, since large corpora are more likely to yield generalisable findings and insights; however, small targeted corpora, as shown here, are perfectly suitable for many kinds of corpus research into discourse.

Also, although not a few analysts believe that the use of corpus linguistics tools is a thoroughly automatic process, where the "machine", not the analyst, decides the results obtained through quantification, this in fact constitutes a very poor understanding of the way corpus analysis is actually applied. Researchers need to use their intuition and knowledge to decide many aspects throughout their corpus research, not the computer software. For example, as shown in this volume, not a few authors have chosen specific annotation tools and, at times, annotation is also carried out manually. Other authors decide not to annotate their corpus. In any case, no two annotation systems are equal. Therefore, a variety of annotation tools can be used, in the same way as the "kind" and "size" of corpus is decided by the researchers according to their particular objectives. As to the corpus software, the contributions in this volume also show a variety of software tools, platforms, and the answer as to which ones to apply lie entirely in the researcher. As to quantification, different statistics are also displayed. All of these are decisions or choices which have to be made by researchers, and come to show the resourcefulness of corpus linguistics and why it is becoming more and more popular in discourse analysis research.

Finally, corpus linguistics has been enriched by the incorporation of larger social, historial, ideological and ethical considerations, brought about by critical approaches to discourse. Certainly, this volume is not the first one to be published around these issues. However, it attempts to provide readers with updated research from leading international scholars in Discourse Analysis. All CADS researchers found in this volume are quite aware of the strength which come from applying a methodological synergy that combines different kinds of quantitative and/or qualitative research. A critical attitude towards the choice of methods and the author's stance undoubtedly contribute to more fine-tuned analyses and to a more responsible and reflexive practice.

We believe this edited volume is an excellent example of this growing symbiosis between methods, types of corpora, disciplines, software programmes, discourse perspectives, and social and ethical concerns.

References

Anthony, Lawrence. 2017. AntConc (version 3.5.0), [Computer Software], <https://www.laurenceanthony.net/software>, accessed 10 February 2017.

Bednarek, Monika. 2008. *Emotion Talk across Corpora*. Houndmills/ New York: Palgrave Macmillan.

Bednarek, Monika/Caple, Helen. 2017. *The Discourse of News Values: How Organisations Create Newsworthiness*. Oxford: Oxford University Press.

Díez-Prados, Mercedes/Cabrejas-Peñuelas, Ana Belén. 2018. Evaluation of "Status" as a persuasive tool in Spanish and American pre-electoral debates in times of crisis. *Atlantis: Journal of the Spanish Association of Anglo-American Studies* 40/2, 169–195.

Hunston, Susan. 2008. The evaluation of status in multi-modal texts. *Functions of Language* 15/1, 64–83.

Hunston, Susan. 2011. *Corpus Approaches to Evaluation: Phraseology and Evaluative Language*. London/New York: Routledge.

Hunston, Susan/Thompson, Geoff. (eds.) 2000. *Evaluation in Text: Authorial Stance and the Construction of Discourse*. Oxford: Oxford University Press.

Martin, James Robert/White, Peter Robert Rupert. 2005. *The Language of Evaluation: Appraisal in English*. Basingstoke: Palgrave MacMillan.

O'Donnell, Mick. 2019. *UAM Corpus Tool: Annotation for the 21st Century*, <http://www.corpustool.com/index.html>, accessed 12 June 2019.

Partington, Alan. 2004. Corpora and discourse: a most congruous beast. In A. Partington, J. Morley & L. Haarman (eds.) *Corpora and Discourse*. Bern: Peter Lang. 11–20.

Potts, Amanda/Bednarek, Monika/Caple, Helen. 2015. How can computer-based methods help researchers to investigate news values in large datasets? A corpus linguistic study of the construction of newsworthiness in the reporting of Hurricane Katrina. *Discourse and Communication* 9/2, 149–172.

Taylor, C./Marchi, A. (eds.) 2018. *Corpus Approaches to Discourse*. London: Routledge.

van Leeuwen, Theo. 2008. *Discourse and Practice: New Tools for Critical Discourse Analysis*. Oxford: Oxford University Press.

Alan Partington

Post-history, post-democracy, post-truth, post-Trump? Really? A corpus-assisted study of delegitimisation via argument strategies: 'dirty tricks', evaluation and hyperbole in modern political discourses

1 Introduction

This chapter will cover a wide range of history, of themes and of linguistic approaches and notions. As the title implies, we intend to examine how *delegitimisation* of opposing speakers/authors and their stances is attempted, incorporating the use of techniques from the burgeoning area of Corpus-assisted Discourse Studies (CaDS; Partington et al 2013). We will draw on notions of persuasion first systematised by Aristotle, and also more recent theories which have largely arisen from the area of corpus-assisted linguistics, namely text organisation/structures (Hoey 1983, 1991; Partington/Taylor 2018), evaluation analysis (Hunston/Thompson 2000), lexical priming (Hoey 2005) and its subcategory, highly relevant to political discourse, of deliberately *forced* lexical priming (Duguid 2009a). Attempts to use corpus techniques to investigate argument structures is a much neglected 'dusty corner' (Taylor/Marchi 2018) of CaDS, given a historical tendency of corpus linguistics to focus on copious micro- rather than macro-structures and strategies.

2 Corpus-assisted Discourse Studies (CaDS): capacities and issues

Corpus-assisted Discourse Studies (CaDS) can be understood as 'the set of studies into the form and/or function of language as communicative discourse which incorporate the use of computerised corpora in their analyses' (Partington et al. 2013: 10). The advantages of including corpus linguistics techniques in discourse analysis are several. It provides availability of a wealth of data which enables the analyst, among other things, to perceive an overview of the data under analysis. These software techniques enable the researcher to reorganise the data in hand to analyse it in different ways (see for instance Marchi 2018 on how dividing a dataset in different ways can lead to radically different observations). The use of a variety of corpora facilitates the contrast and comparison of different but related datasets, not only for *differences* between them but also *similarities* (Taylor 2018). This contrastive virtue cannot be stressed sufficiently; it is only deontologically justifiable to make statements about the thematic contents and behaviours of participants in one dataset of discourse types if we can compare them with those of other discourse types. Finally, the ability to rearrange the data in various ways vastly augments the potential for serendipity, that is, of stumbling upon unexpected findings, some of which may even, as we shall discover here, be counter-intuitive.[1]

Naturally, as in all scientific endeavours, some ways of proceeding are more or less rigorous than others, more or less self-aware, not to mention more or less *honest.* Another of the added values of corpus techniques in discourse analysis can be summarised as the capacity of 'temporary alienation' of the observer from the object of observation. As is frequently repeated, complete objectivity of observation in the human sciences is unachievable – observers inevitably bring their personal primings into the experiment – but the *striving* towards a more accurate, defensible and powerful model of the object of observation is a

1 OED, s.v. serendipity, (n): 'The faculty of making happy and unexpected discoveries by accident'.

vital component of research. The temporary alienation in question is that of the abstraction or removal of the analyst/observers from the object of evaluation and temporarily placing some distance between the interpreter and the interpretation, given that parts of the analysis are carried out by a different entity from the eventual interpreter, that is, the 'machine', which has no vested interest in either disproving or corroborating the analyst's hypotheses. This process reduces analytical subjectivity:

> [O]nce the software is set in motion the researcher cannot interfere. There is therefore at least one phase of corpus-assisted research, the software analyses [...] which the researcher cannot either consciously or unconsciously manipulate. (Partington et al. 2013: 351)

All this is entirely congruous with scientific practice in general well beyond corpus linguistics. Scientific instruments are adopted precisely in order to 'see' physical phenomena in new ways in order to accumulate more precise insights into their nature. This breaking out of the closed hermeneutic circle greatly increases the risk of meeting unexpected serendipitous observations, and unexpected observations require explanation, given the challenge they often pose to the original hypothesis on which the research was predicated. New evidence can lead to new learning.

However, there are a number of potential flies in this research ointment. The first to consider is corroboration bias (also known as confirmation bias), in the worst cases of which a researcher actively seeks out examples to prove their case (sometimes called 'cherry-picking'). In its subtler form, confirmation *instinct*, researchers are tempted, indeed *primed*, to notice and remember data which confirm their original hypothesis and even personal biases (Marchi/Taylor 2009). Even what we *count* as evidence of a certain position when conducting socio-political CaDS can be affected by confirmation impulse. Perhaps the best way to guard against corroboration bias is to consciously seek out counterexamples to our hypothesis. For example, does a right-wing media source ever evaluate immigration positively and if so on what grounds?[2] However, even here we need to exercise care; how many

---

2 Partington et al. (2013: 335–9) report their surprise at how, in a case study of the UK's *Daily Telegraph*, they found that there were more positive than negative

counterexamples are needed in order to reject or refine a hypothesis? In the real world, one black swan is not enough, it may simply be a mutation. Indeed, researchers need to put up with a certain degree of cognitive dissonance, to allow for the fact that their hypotheses may not be entirely self-consistent.

There are two further problematic issues which at first sight seem to work against each other. The first is the well-known 'drama-impulse', the rush to publish striking findings, that is, ones which appear to either substantially add to existing knowledge or to challenge parts of it. Additional research is often needed to corroborate unexpected results. The second has been called the 'Semmelweis reflex', that is, either the hesitation to publish – or the difficulty in *getting published* – research that goes against the prevailing wisdom in the field or, indeed, its dominant ethical norms (see also note 4 on the related concept of the 'Overton window').[3] In its infancy, corpus linguistics itself had problems gaining legitimacy; basing language description on examples of authentic use rather than trained grammarians' introspection proved a paradigm shift too far for many linguists (Nelson Francis 1982).

One final issue has been named the 'not discovered here' syndrome, otherwise known as academic tribalism, in which one discipline either shuns or is simply unaware of research and discoveries made in others. This has been an issue for corpus linguistics, generally, especially well-put by Mautner 'the integration of CL is still not part of the mainstream methodological canon [in areas such as sociology or management studies]; their hero is Foucault, not Sinclair' (Mautner 2016).

---

opinions expressed on immigration. However, they also noted that these mainly regarded its positive contribution to the UK *economy*, rarely any *cultural* benefits.

3 The term derives from the name of the Jewish Hungarian physician, Ignaz Semmelweis who, while working and researching in the Vienna General Hospital in 1847, discovered that childbed fever mortality rates fell ten-fold when doctors washed their hands between patients, especially after conducting an autopsy. Semmelweis's suggestion of simple hand-washing was frequently met with derision by fellow doctors who, after all, were the medical experts, Austrian gentlemen and Gentiles to boot. Semmelweis was finally vindicated by the gradual acceptance of the pathogen or germ theory of disease transmission in the second half of the 19th century. He is rightly remembered as the Saviour of Mothers.

The data for the set of studies outlined in this chapter were collected in various ways. One frequent procedure was to search Lexis Nexis Academic for lexical items of interest (e.g. *post-truth*) and, if necessary, download the articles which contained them and use that set of articles as a corpus, examinable for frequency word listing, concordancing and collocate analysis. The first collection phase was the twelve months before a talk on this topic was delivered in April 2018 at the *Heidelberg Centre for American Studies*. The second collection phase was the six months prior to writing up the present paper in October of 2019. The interrogation and use of the specially-compiled Brexit news corpus is described in Section 6. Reference is also frequently made to the online, free-to-use Corpus of Contemporary American English (COCA; Davies 2009).

3 The age of the 'post-'

Turning to the title of this chapter, in this section we look at a number of items prefixed by *post-* which can be used to undermine a set of beliefs or a particular stance, and potentially delegitimise groups, entities and persons who are related in some way to that stance. Delegitimisation is here defined as 'the attempt to discredit the right or ability of an opponent to make a certain claim or argument or to hold a certain power' (Partington/Taylor 2018: 76). These items may well be related intertextually; *post-* in other words, may have become a productive item, one coinage spawning others, generally with negative evaluations.

The first term, 'post-history' was, famously, coined by Francis Fukuyama (1992) and has become one of the most misinterpreted notions of our day. Fukuyama was not predicting the end of historical events or even progress, but that the blood-soaked clash of ideologies which had distinguished 20thC history was at an end. His thesis was immediately countered by Samuel Huntington's far more pessimistic vision of the future, arguing that the temporary conflict between ideologies is being replaced by the ancient 'clash' between civilizations (Huntington 1996). COCA records only four uses of the item, none of which are related to Fukuyama's thesis, but two are from the field of geo-politics and express a decidedly negative evaluation, for example:

(1) Most Europeans don't acknowledge the great paradox: that their passage into **post-history** has depended on the United States not making the same passage. (COCA)

The term 'post-democracy', instead, was coined by Crouch in 2006:

> to describe a coming age where democratic institutions in Western countries seemed strong, but where power was subtly being transferred to an oligarchic politico-economic elite. According to Crouch's pessimistic model, elections gave the veneer of democratic control by changing governments, but did not actually change the fundamental substance of politics, which was shaped in private through exclusive dialogue between governments, and globalised business and corporate elites. For Crouch, political debate in a post democracy is a controlled spectacle, managed by communication experts and professional spin doctors, revolving around a prescribed set of issues debated within a narrow 'Overton window' by increasingly similar and ideology-free political parties. (Blaxill 2018: 57)[4]

Interestingly, although clearly intended as a critique of the debasement of democracy from a left-wing, anti-capitalist perspective, much of Crouch's analysis would chime with right-wing populist movements who decry the hegemonisation of western democracy by so-called liberal élites, who have taken control of decision-making away from ordinary people. COCA contains just two occurrences of the item, one of which makes mention of the European Union potentially being such a *liberal* post-democracy (see Section 6 on EU-scepticism):

(2) "Europe", points out National Review editor and syndicated columnist Rich Lowry, "is on the brink of a' liberal **post-democracy**,' a form of government that (usually) respects basic rights at the same time it lacks the mechanisms for ensuring the popular consent that characterizes traditional democracy? The unelected European Commission not the European Parliament initiates legislation and issues regulations." (*USA Today* 2012)

4 The 'Overton window' is the range of ideas tolerated in public discourse, also known as the window of discourse. The term is named after Joseph P. Overton (Wikipedia).

The next item, 'post-truth', was nominated by the *Oxford English Dictionary* in 2016 as its 'word of the year', a word which was felt to have played a prominent role in Anglophone discourse in that year. The item 'post-truth' was defined as 'relating to or denoting circumstances in which objective facts are less influential in shaping public opinion than appeals to emotion and personal belief'. While acknowledging it was not a new term, the dictionary nevertheless claimed it has gone from being 'a peripheral term to being a mainstay in political commentary' and is often used in the expression 'post-truth politics'. COCA records 25 uses of the term, all from 2015 and later. Many of these occurrences are present-time references:

(3) the **post-truth** climate of our 2017 (*A.V. Club* 2017)

(4) The nation's current **post-truth** moment (*The Atlantic* 2017)

including five which refer negatively to the current Trump presidency, for example:

(5) This Sunday, after a **post-truth** election, do the president-elect's words matter? (*NBC* 2016)

(6) The question is, after what many have dubbed the **post-truth** election, are we getting a look at a post-truth presidency? (*NBC* 2016)

while another three refer to supposed problems of current media communication, for example:

(7) In a "**post-truth**" era when journalism is under pressure [. . .] (*The Atlantic* 2017)

(8) And social media, which is becoming the primary news source for many people, amplifies it all. At its worst, it marinates people in conspiracy theories and helps to foster this "**post-truth**" era of politics. (*New York Times* 2016)

We return to 'post-truth' in section 3.

'Post-Trump', meanwhile, is a semi-sarcastic coinage meant to indicate the sentiment that the rise of Donald Trump to the US Presidency has drastically altered the political landscape, not only in the United States but around the world. For some of his denigrators, the advent of Trump was the Apocalypse (from Lexis Nexis):

(9) An environmentalist told journalist Alan Weisman before the 2016 elections that she was considering voting for Trump. "The way I see it," she said, "it's either four more years on life support with Hillary, or letting this maniac

> tear the house down. Maybe then we can pick up the pieces and finally start rebuilding."
> The philosophy of "things have to get worse before they get better" has sometimes worked out in the past. But that's the past.
> Unless we stop him, we'll be rooting around in the **post-Trump** ashes in vain for the pieces. The house will be gone. And there will be nothing we can salvage to rebuild it. (*Foreign Policy in Focus* 2019)

And even one of his Republican supporters describes him as 'an angel of destruction' (David Brooks, *New York Times* 2019). The term has certainly caught on. In the six months before beginning writing this chapter a Lexis Nexis Academic search of English-language news sources this article produced 92 instances of 'post-Trump era'.

Finally, the term 'post-trust' (see Singh/Luthra 2019) has become an object of media attention. A Lexis Nexis search of the term 'post-trust era' in English-language news sources in the six months previous to writing this article produced 40 results including the headline 'This is how to fight fake news at work in a post-trust era' (*Fast Company* 2019). The 40 articles were downloaded and concordanced for *post-trust*. The list of entities which people supposedly no longer trust include:

politicians, governments

banks, traditional economics

the media, press

the police

science, scientific organisations

charities

Most of these will not surprise the reader. As has often been noted, corpus techniques often produce results which, in hindsight at least, seem obvious (Louw 1993). Tongue-in-cheek, Partington (2017) has called this 'hindsight predictability' or 'postdictability'. However, again, the frequency of hindsight predictability should not surprise us. It would be a very strange set of tools and approaches which *always* came up with counter-intuitive results.

Most of these *post*-somethings, with perhaps the exception of Fukuyama's 'post-history', have a negative evaluation and can be seen, in the light of the next topic of this chapter, as strategies to delegitimise.

Calling a political system '*post-democratic*' – for example, the EU in example 1 above – undermines practically everything it does. Labelling the media (including social media) as *post-truth* may be a way of calling into question its abilities to be honest and fair; the phrase *post-truth election* of Trump delegitimises both the election and the winner. These *post*-prefixed items also appear to suggest that there was an earlier period in history in which politics and political discourse were, if not exactly in a Golden Age, in some way more open, more democratic and less debased.

4 The Golden Age?

The media and press figure prominently among the entities people no longer trust. However, any belief that there was once an era of political media 'truthfulness' and reliability meets immediate problems when one researches historical documents. Even someone as generally democratic and libertarian as Thomas Jefferson remarked that the temptation for even the most well-meaning of politicians to mistrust the press could be acute. Before achieving the Presidency he famously wrote:

> [...] were it left to me to decide whether we should have a government without newspapers or newspapers without a government, I should not hesitate a moment to prefer the latter. (Jefferson, letter, 1787)[5]

but after becoming President, he despaired of what today is often called 'fake news':

> Nothing can now be believed which is seen in a newspaper. Truth itself becomes suspicious by being put into that polluted vehicle (Jefferson, letter, 1807)

> I deplore with you the putrid state into which our newspapers have passed, and the malignity, the vulgarity, and mendacious spirit of those who write for them (Jefferson, letter, 1814)[6]

5 https://oll.libertyfund.org/quotes/302

6 *The Washington Post* online: https://www.washingtonpost.com/news/the-fix/wp/2017/02/17/trumps-war-with-the-media-isnt-new-thomas-jefferson-railed-about-newspaper-lies-too/

Nor was this disillusion with the press unknown in the UK, judging from the celebrated sardonic verse of the English poet Humbert Wolfe in 1930:[7]

> You cannot hope
> to bribe or twist,
> thank God! the
> British journalist.
> But, seeing what
> the man will do
> unbribed, there's
> no occasion to.

As for the alleged new aggressive divisiveness of modern democratic politics, there is little in contemporary political combat to match some of that seen in the past. As Partington and Taylor relate:

> In the 1800 campaign between John Adams and Thomas Jefferson, the former's campaign referred to Jefferson as 'the Anti-Christ', while the latter's campaign spoke of Adam's 'hideous hermaphroditical character which has neither the force and firmness of a man, nor the gentleness and sensibility of a woman'. In 1828, candidate Andrew Jackson's wife was repeatedly labelled a prostitute. More divisive still was the duel in 1804 between the Vice-President Aaron Burr and Andrew Hamilton, one of the Founding Fathers. Hamilton was shot dead. And finally the election of Abraham Lincoln in 1860 prompted seven southern states to form the Confederate States of America leading directly to the US Civil War, which surely qualifies it as the most divisive US election ever (2018: 207).

If we look back at the citation of Crouch's views on a supposed 'post-democracy age', where political antagonism is merely a sham and political élites are in collusion, it might appear that outside commentators are never happy. Contemporary politics is either overly aggressive or not nearly aggressive enough; in both cases, negatively evaluated.

To conclude, was there ever a Golden Age of Truth before this 'post-truth' era? The notion of 'post-truth' is certainly popular in the media. Lexis Nexis uncovered 1,111 occurrences of 'post-truth' in the 12 months prior to this start of this research. The articles in question were downloaded and using the WordSmith Tools (Version 5) collocates

---

7 Humbert Wolfe, 1930, in *The Uncelestial City*. London: Gollancz.

and clusters tools, the following sets of items were found to co-occur with *post-truth*:

> *world/era/age, politics, culture*
>
> *fake news, fiction, disinformation, alternative (facts/reality), bullshit, spin, information warfare, new lying*
>
> *suppression of freedoms*
>
> *Brexit, Trump's, populism*
>
> *peak, current*

The last group suggesting that political discourse has *recently* become dangerously debased. And yet, once again, past documents strongly suggest that political discourse in the past was far from pure:

> Political language... is [often] designed to make lies sound truthful and murder respectable, and to give an appearance of solidity to pure wind. (George Orwell 1946)
>
> Doublethink: To know and not to know, to be conscious of complete truthfulness while telling carefully constructed lies, to hold simultaneously two opinions knowing them to be contradictory and believing in both of them. (George Orwell 1949)

5 Delegitimising your opponents as a political strategy

Predating Orwell by a good period but sharing his suspicion of public discourse, or rhetoric, was Plato who in his 'Gorgias' (386 BC) viewed persuasion as manipulation and the professional orator as a *logodaidalos* or 'speech-rigger'(reminiscent of the modern accusation of 'dirty tricks'). Public decision-making should be left to philosophers not orators. More than ironically, both Orwell and Plato were, of course, supremely gifted in rhetoric. Persuading by adopting the stance or *ethos* (see below) of the non-persuader, or even the anti-persuader, is a rhetorical ploy in itself, used to great effect by Frederick Douglass in his 'This Fourth of July is Yours, Not Mine' (1852):

> Fellow citizens, pardon me, and allow me to ask, why am I called upon to speak here today? What have I or those I represent to do with your national independence? Are the great principles of political freedom and of natural justice, embodied in that Declaration of Independence, extended to us?'

by Mark Antony in his funeral oration for Julius Caesar:

> I am no orator, as Brutus is;
>
> But, as you know me, a plain blunt man
>
> That love my friend . . .

and by Nelson Mandela in 1990 after his release from prison:

> I stand here before you not as a Prophet, but as a humble servant of you, the people.

Plato's pupil, Aristotle, in 'The Art of Rhetoric' (368–322 B.C.) describes persuasion as opportunity and part of everyday life, and divides the skill of persuasion into three separate parts or structural principles, namely:

logos: persuasion by (apparent) appeal to reason, that what you are saying appears true, to make sense, seems relevant and logically coherent;
pathos: persuasion by appeal to emotion;
ethos: convincing an audience that you, the speaker, are worth listening to and have the right, the authority and the correct personality to speak on the matter in hand. This is clearly a rather different category of notion from the other two parts of rhetoric.

Although Aristotle's model has been extremely influential, in practice it is often difficult to disentangle persuasion by *logos* and *pathos*. In real life many arguments have both logical and emotional appeal. For example, most persuasion – including political argument – appeals to some degree to the self-interest of the audience, persuading them that a certain course of action is in their best interests. On the one hand, tax cuts will mean more money in your purse; on the other hand, higher taxes and increased government spending will improve your public services. Is this a logical or emotional means of persuasion? It clearly combines both inextricably.

Aristotle's model has been adopted and revised in modern linguistic theory. In Systemic Functional Grammar (SFG; Thompson 1996; Halliday/Matthiessen 2004), argument by *logos* and *pathos* are both subsumed under the *ideational* (sometimes also known as the *experiential*) function of language, which describes how speakers and writers represent the world through language, while *ethos* is studied as part of the *interpersonal* function of language, dealing with how speakers and audiences interact.

Aristotle's notion of *ethos* has also been adopted and updated in modern sociolinguistics as *face* and *facework* in politeness theory (Brown/Levinson 1987). According to Brown and Levinson's theory, all individuals possess face, that is, a 'public self-image' (1987: 61) which we all project of ourselves to the outside world. Facework is the behaviour we employ to project that image during social interactions. According to Brown and Levinson (1987), face consists of two complementary parts:

> negative face: the basic claim to territories, personal preserves, rights to non-distraction – i.e. to freedom of action and freedom from imposition
>
> positive face: the positive consistent self-image or 'personality' (crucially including the desire that this self-image be appreciated and approved of) claimed by interactants.
>
> (Brown/Levinson 1987: 61)

Negative face, or 'respect my space' face, the desire for freedom from imposition and freedom of action is recognizable as more or less the kind of phenomenon we mean when we normally refer to politeness ('first-order' perceptions, Watts et al. 1992), for instance, we pay attention to another's negative face when we knock on their door to request their permission to enter.

Positive face, instead, involves the desire to be respected, approved of, even liked and admired. Positive face, then, is a very similar notion to *ethos*, Aristotle's first – and, he says, most important – part of rhetoric (Aristotle 2012, Book 1:2), 'how the speaker/writer projects their personality and stance towards the audience/readership' (Taylor 2010: 222).

In politics, a persuader's positive face is divided into two types, namely, 'competence face', that is, one's image as well-informed, an expert, in control, authoritative and 'affective face', that is, one's image as likeable, good-humoured, normal, 'one of us', 'a regular guy' (Partington 2006). There is an inherent problem however, in that the two kinds of face are not always simultaneously compatible. It is not always possible to appear both an expert and 'one of us' at the same moment. It becomes a political skill when to privilege the one over the other.

In terms of interpersonal communication and facework, then, political persuaders need to project their own positive face and to attack their opponents' face, including, very commonly, via the process of delegitimisation, defined, we might recall, as attempting to discredit the right or ability of an opponent to make a certain claim or argument or to hold a certain power (Partington/Taylor 2018: 76). In other words, alongside attacking their arguments (their appeals to *logos*, reason, and *pathos*, emotions), an effective persuader can also undermine the *ethos*, that is the personal credibility, honesty, competence, even the likability of opponents. A key political delegitimising accusation, then, is that an opponent is *unfit* to perform a certain function. Lexis Nexis search for the term *unfit for + office* in English news sources in the first week in September 2019 revealed:

(10) Trump has proved again and again that he is **unfit for** the **office** he holds (CNN 03/09/2019)

(11) LABOUR MP: CORBYN **UNFIT FOR OFFICE** (Daily Mail, headline, 09/09/2019)

(12) Dominic Grieve, a former attorney general [. . .] said the British leader [Boris Johnson] was **unfit for office**. (Reuters 07/09/2019)

Others also potentially *unfit for office*, according to opponents, included US Senator Joe Biden, South Africa's Public Protector and Senator Hillary Clinton, as well as 'female leaders' in general (see Section 5). Demata (2018) in his corpus-assisted comparative analysis of tweets issued by the Clinton and Trump campaigns in the month before the Election, concordances the hashtags employed, and notes the instance '#CrookedHillary is unfit to serve'.

Bernie Sanders's campaign slogan during the 2016 US primary elections, 'Not For Sale' succeeded in projecting his own positive face/*ethos* as incorruptible and simultaneously delegitimising his principal opponent, Hillary Clinton, by implication of dubious campaign funding.

Senator Clinton herself ran the following campaign advert in 2007:

> It's 3 a.m. and your children are safe and asleep. But there's a phone in the White House and it's ringing.
>
> Something's happening in the world. Your vote will decide who answers the call, whether it's someone who already knows the world's leaders, knows the military, someone tried and tested and ready to lead in a dangerous world.
>
> It's 3 a.m. and your children are safe and asleep. Who do you want answering the phone?

The subtext clearly legitimises her as an experienced leader, while delegitimising her opponent, the neo-Senator Barack Obama, implying an *ethos* as inexperienced and therefore untrustworthy. At the same time she bolsters her own *ethos* as being as competent and tough as any man.

Other recent attempts at delegitimisation have been cruder, such as the 'lock her up' and 'crooked Hillary' slogans of Trump supporters, where the *ethos* of criminal is imposed on Clinton. And sometimes it is not just the politician who is the object of delegitimisation attempts, but their supporters, as in Clinton's characterisation of Trump supporters as 'a basket of deplorables'. Insulting a whole group can be a risky strategy however, not to mention unlikely to win any new friends from the other side, and Clinton later apologised. COCA lists 56 occurrences of *deplorables*, all related to Clinton's utterance, including examples where the description is eagerly re-appropriated – re-appropriation, of course involves principally reversing the evaluation – by Trump supporters:

> (13) Much of that money donated was given by Trump supporters, the **Deplorables** that have been demonized as racists by some on the hateful far left. (*Fox News* 2017)

Indeed, attempts at delegitimisation can be wholly counterproductive, as Trump himself describes:

> The cost of a full-page ad in the New York Times can be more than $100,000. But when they write a story about one of my deals, it doesn't cost me a cent, and I get more important publicity. I have a mutually profitable two-way relationship with the media – we give each other what we need [. . .] These media types sell

> more magazines when my face is on the cover, or when I bring a bigger audience to their television show than they normally attract, and by far. And what's funny is that it turns out the best way for them to get that attention is to criticize me. (Trump 2015: 11)

In other words, the more they attack me, the stronger my *ethos* becomes.

6 'All-purpose' delegitimisers

Aristotle writes that *ethos* is the most important of the three parts of rhetoric. If you can undermine the *ethos* of your opponent, then their *logos* and *pathos* arguments are consequently weakened too. Many of the examples of delegitimisation discussed so far have been of the *ad hominem* or *ad personam* kind, the undermining of an individual. It has been argued that there is also a form of *ad personam* which is gender-based, in other words, *ad feminam*. The argument runs that it is more difficult for women in politics to project an ethos of strength or toughness. It was put as follows:

> Women running for office [. . .] are subject to these two demands: Be a good leader! Be a good woman! While the qualities expected of a good leader (be forceful, confident and, at times, angry) are similar to those we expect of a good man, they are the opposite of what we expect of a good woman (be gentle, self-deprecating and emotional, but not angry). (*Washington Post* 2016)

In the terms used here, in other words, female candidates may find it more difficult to combine the projection of competence face as well as affective face. Partington / Taylor (2018: 214) collected the following negative media references to Clinton's gender during the 2016 campaign:

> Trump's claim that Clinton lacks the 'physical stamina' to be president (*Washington Post* 2016)
>
> Hillary Clinton's charisma deficit is a common problem for female leaders (*Quartz* 2016)
>
> Hillary Should Play Up Her Feminine Side (*Newsweek* 2015)

Hillary Clinton talks more like a man than she used to (*Washington Post* 2016)

Hillary Clinton tries warmth as US voters go cold (*Financial Times* 2016)

Donald Trump calls Hillary Clinton 'shrill' (*The Boston Globe* 2016)

This is a delegitimising argument to be extremely wary of and should not be used as a justification itself for not choosing women candidates.

The boot is on the other foot when the neologism *mansplaining* is used; COCA records 18 instances, all from 2014 and after. These examples show how the term can be used to delegitimise men's contribution to any verbal interaction:

(14) The other day, I was pointing out a new data set to a female student and asked if she wanted me to walk her through it. (It took me a couple of hours to get my head around it.) She told me I was **mansplaining** and that she knew what she was doing. This was brand new, very complex data that we just received. She (nor anyone else) knew we had the data yet or had ever worked with it. (USA, *Slate Magazine* 2016)

Five of the COCA entries are accusations against Trump and other Republicans in Democrat-leaning sources, for example:

(15) We've got to take a quick break. Just ahead, top Trump surrogate Newt Gingrich tangling with Megyn Kelly over Trump's female accusers? Was it an example of, some are saying, of **mansplaining** and misogyny? (*CNN (Anderson Cooper)* 2016)

(16) While we're discussing Trump's heretofore undisclosed health issues and his misogynistic **mansplaining** to a woman who's absolutely his superior in every way (*Salon Magazine* 2016 [the woman referred to is Hillary Clinton])

(17) "We so often have this position of Republican men **mansplaining** our lady parts and how they work, like we're too dumb to understand science and make our own decisions," she says. (*Mother Jones* 2015)

Napoletano / Aiezza (2018) analyse another recent attempt to delegitimise a whole category of supposed opponents. They compiled a corpus of Trump tweets in the six months after the election. They found a large number of items referring to the supposed unreliability and even downright mendacity of the news media, for example: *fake news* (48 occurrences), *dishonest* (13), *failing* (9), *wrong* (8), *biased* (5), *false* (4), *inaccurate* (5), *made up* (3), *crooked* (3), *lies* (3), *phoney* (3), *fabricated* (2), *unfair* (2), *unwatchable* (2).

Trump did not invent the term 'fake news'; COCA reveals instances of it appearing increasingly since 1992. But Trump uses the term and similar items repeatedly in an example of what Duguid (2009a) calls 'forced lexical priming' in order to attempt to take ownership of the 'fake news' narrative. 'Forced priming' describes a process whereby speakers or authors frequently repeat a certain form of words to deliberately 'flood' the discourse with messages for a particular strategic purpose. Trump's strategy in his 'fake news' narrative is to taint the *ethos* of the entire media as untrustworthy and possessing an inbuilt anti-Trump bias. It is an all-round, all-purpose delegitimisation that can be used on every and all occasions to dismiss any negative report or opinion appearing in the media. It also serves the purpose of projecting Trump's own *ethos* of 'authenticity', as the only font of truth, the only one telling the truth in plain language. Thompson calls this strategy 'authenticism' and argues that 'the authenticist prizes simplicity of language [. . .] because he associates simple expressions with honesty of emotion' (Thompson 2016: 155). Demata, after his corpus-assisted study of Trump's tweets (see above), adds 'authenticism is not a new tendency, but it surfaces every time that trust in politicians reaches a low' (2018: 75) and reminds us of the existence of #BigLeagueTruth, a self-organising internet community of Trump's 'fact-checker' supporters, also dedicated to delegitimising the media.

7 Competitive 'all-purpose' delegitimising: A case study. *Scaremongering* over Brexit

In order to study the reporting of the UK EU Referendum, Zuccato and Partington (2018) built two corpora of articles discussing Brexit from four UK newspapers downloaded via Lexis Nexis, using the search terms 'Brexit OR EU Referendum'. Two right-leaning and largely pro-Leave newspapers (a broadsheet, *The Telegraph* and a tabloid, *The Mail*) and two left-leaning and largely pro-Remain ones (again, a broadsheet *The Guardian* and a tabloid *The Mirror*) were chosen in order to encompass a cross-section of UK news reporting.

The first corpus contained all the articles in these papers which appeared in these papers the three months *before* the referendum (a total of 1,402 articles, 1,169,000 words). The second corpus consisted of all the articles published by them in the three months *after* the referendum (1,888 articles, 1,373,000 words).

Reading some of the articles in the pre-Brexit corpus, it became clear that *fear* was a common theme, and so a concordance was prepared of *fear** using WordSmith V5, which threw up the following items: *fear*, *feared*, *fearful*, *fearing*, *fearless*, *fears*, *fearsome* as well as *fear-mongering* and *fearmongering* (all but *fearless* express negative evaluations). The WordSmith frequency listing of the corpus also contained 122 occurrences of *scaremonger**; and by concordancing **monger**, another 15 occurrences of *doom-mongering* were uncovered.

The accusation of *scaremongering* was used amply by both the 'Remain' and 'Leave' sides:

	scaremonger*	**scare-monger***
The Mirror	12	2
The Daily Mail	21	1
The Guardian	64	-
The Telegraph	35	-

Tab. 1. *Occurrences of* scaremonger*/scare-monger*

The relatively large number of occurrences in the pro-Remain *Guardian* is largely a product of its much greater coverage of the Referendum in general. The vast majority of uses are in the form *scaremongering*, as either a noun indicating the practice of *scaremongering* or as an adjective modifying items such as *tactics*, *campaign*; *scaremonger* as a verb occurs just twice, as does *scaremonger* as a noun referring to an individual, e.g.

(18) He accused Mr Johnson of being a "scaremonger on wages". (*Telegraph* 15/06/16)0

The item *scaremongering* appears in four patterns. The first pattern supplies the fullest information on agency – *who* is accusing *whom* and of doing *what* – the fourth pattern supplies the least information, namely, just who is the supposed culprit of the act of 'scaremongering'. In the latter case, the delegitimising purpose of the accusation is clearest; all the audience needs to know is who is at fault. In the following annotation, (A) is the accuser (B) stands for the accused and (T) stands for the topic.

(i) (A) accuses (B) of scaremongering over/about (T), e.g.

(19) Dave Prentis, the head of public sector union Unison, reported the [Breaking Point, anti-immigration] poster to police, saying: 'This is scaremongering in its most extreme form.' (*Daily Mirror* 20/06/16).

Here (A) is Dave Prentis, (B) is the authors of the poster and (T) is immigration.

(ii) (B) is accused of scaremongering over/about (T). No (A), e.g.

(20) One of the big flaws of the Brexit campaign so far has been the failure of its leaders to give any detailed information about what the UK might look like if they are victorious. It's a serious weakness for the Out campaign, and explains why the Remain camp's Project Fear scaremongering over lost jobs and trade drying up appears so convincing. (*Daily Mail* 31/03/2016

Here (B) is 'Remain camp's Project Fear'; (T) is lost jobs and trade, but there is no explicit mention of (A), an accuser.

(iii) (B) is accused of scaremongering by (A). No (T), e.g.

(21) Several members of the studio audience directly accused the Prime Minister of "scaremongering" and failing to make a positive case for Britain to stay in the EU. (*Daily Telegraph* 03/06/2016)

Here (A) is members of a studio audience and (B) is the PM, but there is no explicit (T). A similar example:

(22) Boris Johnson, the former Mayor of London [. . .] accused Mr Osborne and the Remain campaign of "scaremongering" and "endlessly knocking our country". (*Daily Telegraph* 16/05/2016)

Here (A) is Boris Johnson (B) is Mr Osborne and the Remain campaign, but there is no (T).

(iv) (B) is accused of scaremongering. No (A) or (T), e.g.

(23) Scaremongering by pro-EU campaigners ahead of next month's referendum has triggered a surge in support for Brexit among businesses, a survey shows. (*Daily Telegraph* 10/05/2016)

where (B) is the Remain campaign. There is no (T). No (A) (except the writer).

There is a fifth sort, where *only* the topic of the *scaremongering* is mentioned, with no accuser (apart from the writer) and no overt accused:

> The referendum is over, the decision has been made, scaremongering about "bloody immigrants" for political purposes is no longer needed. (*Guardian* 05/09/2016)

However, the writer implies blame for a group who 'scaremonger' about immigration for political purposes. We can appreciate from all this Aristotle's point that what is an offensive delegitimisation strategy for one group is another group's self-evident truth.

In the majority of cases where Remain accuses Leave of *scaremongering*, it refers to the allegation of spreading false myths about immigration:

(24) The threats coming from the Brexiteers about Turkey joining the EU and millions of Turks coming here are scaremongering in the extreme (*Daily Mirror* 7/06/16)

The concordances of *scaremonger** in the pro-Leave texts, on the other hand, reveal that Remain's supposed *scaremongering* is constructed as continuous (with collocates like *constant* and *incessant*), but also as unreasonable, bordering on crazed (*baseless*, *demented*, *ludicrous*). In addition, it is perceived as deliberately shocking (*blatant*, *cynical*, *naked*, *outrageous*), all with negative evaluation. There is a larger array in the pro-Leave texts of specific indications of who is doing the 'scaremongering'. They include: the Prime Minister Cameron, pro-Remain Ministers (Osborne, Hammond), 'Downing St', the Establishment, the Bank of England, Goldman Sachs. Given the fact that, according to the data examined here, only the Remain side was successfully labelled by their opponents as launching *Project Fear* (there were 132 occurrences in this data, a further example of deliberate forced lexical priming; see Tab. 2 for a selection) it might be inferred that Leave was more successful than Remain in its attempts at delegitimising their opponents as *scaremongers*.

1	box on June 23. In particular the Leave campaign is very exercised by what they say is the **Project Fear** campaign, so-called, being run from 10 Downing Street. This nom-de-guerre was
2	nd co-founder of Brexit group Grassroots Out, said the Government's comments were "part of **Project Fear**". He told the PoliticsHome website: "Clearly any EU citizen that is legally
3	dramatic, in a long series of warnings issued by the Government as part of the so-called **"Project Fear"** agenda. Leave campaigners say that it is impossible to forecast economic ev
4	uperstate, the British voted for independence on June 23. To no one's very great surprise, **Project Fear** turned out to be a giant hoax. The markets were calm. The pound did not coll
5	cy, access to the single market is www.critical.No doubt I'll be accused of being part of "**Project Fear**" for raising these concerns, of lilylivered cowardice, of "talking the econo
6	od reason why Nicola Sturgeon, a faux supporter of the Remain campaign, has lambasted its "**Project Fear**" tactics. It's because Scotland's First Minister knows from experience that
7	nservative Party over Europe and lead to further allegations of scaremongering as part of "**Project Fear**" from those campaigning for a Leave vote. Speaking ahead of the report's pub
8	isolation runs deep. The Ottoman shadow is long. The Justice Secretary is right to dismiss **Project Fear** as craven and defeatist. A vote to leave the dysfunctional EU half-way house
9	ould not be worse off in the event of a Brexit vote, in a blow to the assembled forces of "**Project Fear**". The findings came despite warnings issued by the Treasury, the Bank of Eng
10	ields have fallen following the publication of pro-Brexit polls as evidence that so-called **Project Fear** is not working. Yesterday morning Douglas Carswell, the UK Independence Part
11	s but does not mention them. Why not? Ian Musgrave Laxey Isle of Man SIR - The latest from **Project Fear** is a possible £40 billion black hole, with which to threaten pensioners. Wh
12	r cent of companies traded with EU countries, yet they were all affected by EU regulation. **Project Fear** Mr Johnson said the difference between the Leave and the Remain campaigns wa
13	vice I can give is to relay what the Prime Minister himself said before the whole logic of **Project Fear** kicked in. He said there was no doubt Britain could thrive mightily and we c
14	ain can sink. It is another own-goal. Andrew Warbrick Market Bosworth, Leicestershire SIR - **Project Fear** is now targeting the elderly. Why doesn't Mr Cameron go the whole hog and su
15	the various camps. I had expected to come home to find Remain firmly in the driving seat, **Project Fear** having done its worst, but far from it. The most recent polls show a marked

Tab. 2. *A selection of concordance lines:* Project Fear

8 'Non-logical' delegitimising argument strategies

Partington / Taylor (2018) list a number of 'non-rational', 'non-logical' argument strategies which can be used to delegitimise an opponent, included the *ad hominen* (also known as *ad personam*), false parallel and false dichotomy. Non-rational they might be, but their frequent employment suggests they often have some psychological efficacy.

8.1 Ad hominem

Some of the examples included in the previous section could be counted as *ad personam* which consists of attacking the personality, ethos, motivation, and so on, of an opponent rather than dealing with their argument. Partington / Taylor (2018) invite us to consider whether an *ad hominem* argument, such as alluding to a person's private life, can be used to detract from their argument. The example they ask is whether Thomas Jefferson personal ownership of slaves undermined his message that 'all men are created equal'? Does it make the aspiration less real, or the notion less true?

8.2 False parallel

As an instance of a false parallel they cite the controversial headline 'global warming deniers are now on a par with Holocaust deniers' (*Boston Globe* 09/02/2006). The false parallel kind of delegitimisation has two elements, a questionable comparison accompanied by exaggeratedly negative evaluation. Somewhat similar false parallels were collected by searching Lexis Nexis for the expression *the New Nazis*, in the three years preceding the writing of this study. In the view of some argument-maker, all the following were accused of being today's 'Nazis':

> *progressives, liberals, the Democrats, ACLU (American Civil Liberties Union)*
>
> *the Republicans*
>
> *feminists (feminazis)*

Iran and the ayatollahs

Palestinians

Muslims

the (UK) government

Here are a few examples, collected from Lexis Nexis (my emphasis):

(25) A BBC News reporter is being investigated over a Facebook rant which branded **the Tories** the "new Nazis". (UK, *Daily Mirror* 2016)

(26) "**Liberals** are the new Nazis," someone scrawled this month in both of the restaurant's bathrooms. (US, *The New Yorker* 2018)

(27) the GOP is a fascist party and that **Christian conservatives** are the new Nazis (*Newstext blogs* 2017)

(28) **Feminazi**: the go-to term for trolls out to silence women; Last week, a young female barrister was called a 'feminazi' after complaining about a sexist message sent via LinkedIn. (Headline, UK, *Guardian* 2019)

Most frequent of all, however, was the following set:

Zionists, Israelis, Jews, 'Zionazis'

Of the 123 documents containing 'the new Nazis' recovered by Lexis Nexis, from newspapers and blogs, in this period, 61 related to this accusation – nearly always attributing it to some other source, rather than averring it, but its frequency suggests another example of forced priming (Duguid 2009a), of one or more parties flooding the public discourse with a particular set of lexical terms to construct a narrative, namely that Israelis and maybe Jews in general are 'the new Nazis'.

(29) In the new anti-Semitic circles and the BDS movement, the establishment of the State [of Israel] is called the Opposite Holocaust, in which the **Jewish Nazi victims** became the new Nazis (Israel, *Arutz Sheva* 22/04/2018)

(30) Mr Goldstein said there is 'no safe space' left for Jews inside Labour and wherever they go Jews are told 'Rothschilds run the world, ISIS is a fake front for **Israel and Zionists** are the new Nazis'. (UK, *Mail Online* 26/03/2018)

A UNESCO press release (also found on Lexis Nexis news) explains the pseudo-logical steps in this delegitimising antisemitic false parallel:

(31) In the view of all these anti-Jewish groups – recycling classical anti-Semitic themes – Jews control the press, own the banks, manipulate the markets, corrupt politics and politicians, and, via Israel, oppress other groups and peoples. More significantly, it is believed that the Jews conspire, à la the Protocols of Zion, to dominate the world for their own benefit. In particular, this self-interest is now understood to mean primarily the interests of the State of Israel [. . .] **The Jews** are the "new Nazis," and all the traditional anti-Jewish canards are recycled. (UNESCO Press Release, 23/01/2017).

Such a narrative combines exaggerated delegitimisation with the sheer racist hatefulness of identifying Jewish people with the ideology which tried to eliminate all Jews from Europe and beyond.

8.3 False dichotomy

The delegitimisation of people, whole groups and their arguments, can also be effected by using the argumentative strategy of false dichotomy, also known as the excluded middle, in which complex situations are depicted as a binary evaluative choice, in particular, between good (generally agreeing with the argument maker) and evil (disagreeing with them). Partington / Taylor (2018) note a case such as President George W. Bush's statement 'Every nation, in every region, now has a decision to make. Either you are with us, or you are with the terrorists' (20/09/2001), which was later echoed by President Erdogan of Turkey 'Pick a side. You are either on the side of the Turkish government, or you're on the side of the terrorists' (12/01/2016).

The term 'false dichotomy' was searched using Lexis Nexis and we found that the delegitimising function of this argument strategy was occasionally given explicit attention:

(32) We Turks are being asked to choose between "stability" and "democracy". But this is a **false dichotomy**. Those who believe in it have learned nothing from history. They have not understood that undemocratic nations are unhappy nations, and unhappy nations cannot possibly be stable. (UK *Guardian* 2017)

(33) **The Tyranny of False Dichotomies**

When, in the aftermath of the shooting incident in Mandaluyong City, Bato dela Rosa said he would rather have stupid people with good intentions instead of smart people with bad intentions, he was making use of a rhetorical device widely deployed in our political discourse: presenting **false**

> **dichotomies**, or making people pick between two things as if these were the only choices.
>
> A similar argument is presented in defense of Rodrigo Duterte's foul mouth: What would you rather have, a president who curses but cares for the country, or a president who speaks in flowery language but doesn't care for the people? Or: Which would you choose – a president who jokes about rape, or a president who is 'raping' the nation?
>
> [. . .] We see this as well when people's political stances are elicited: Are you 'pro' or 'anti'? There are so many issues facing the nation today, but because people simply assume that being 'Dilawan' or 'DDS' means opposing or supporting everything the government says or does, no middle ground, no nuance, is to be found. Here, the **false dichotomy** is between criticism and support.
>
> For politicians themselves, the use of **false dichotomies** is an effective tool to galvanize their base and defend their tenuous positions. But for the country, the result is further polarization – and the oversimplification of the debates that matter. (*Philippines Daily Inquirer* 2018)

9 Conclusions

The first part of this Chapter was dedicated to an overview of the state of the art of Corpus-assisted Discourse Studies, including a discussion of both the added values it brings and also the issues it can pose. The second part contained a discussion of the notion of delegitimisation in argumentation. We then moved on to examine some of the argument strategies and even structures used to attempt to effect delegitimisation, using as evidence data deriving from authentic sources, mostly viewed or downloaded from Lexis Nexis and COCA.

As mentioned above, the topic of the present research is somewhat unusual. CaDS excels in uncovering ways in which various sources represent and/or frame some group or issue e.g. how the media represent immigration (Taylor 2014) or Muslims living in the UK (Baker et al. 2013) or how right-wing groups construct a worldview in which minorities are negatively evaluated (Brindle 2016). Some work has been conducted on speech acts such as apologising (Duguid 2015), responsibility avoidance in answering question (Duguid 2009b) and interactive teasing in press briefings (Partington 2006: 144–181). In contrast, little work in CaDS has been dedicated to researching large scale 'macro' argument strategies such as delegitimisation, given corpus linguistics's historical tendency to look at large quantities of relatively 'micro'-contexts. As was seen here, in order to study language structures at a more macro level, corpus techniques are, of necessity, very much *assisted* by the researcher's intuitions, not to mention knowledge of the world.

References

Aristotle. 2012. *The Art of Rhetoric*. London: Collins.

Baker, Paul/Gabrielatos, Costas/McEnery, Tony. 2013. *Discourse Analysis and Media Attitudes: The Representation of Islam in the British Press*. Cambridge: Cambridge University Press.

Blaxill, Luke. 2018. Introduction. From 'Post-Democracy' to 'Post-Truth' in Political Language. *Textus* 31(1), 57–66.

Brindle, Andrew. 2016. *The Language of Hate: A Corpus Linguistics Analysis of White Supremacist Language*. New York: Routledge.

Brown, Penelope/Levinson, Steven. 1987. *Politeness: Some Universals in Language Usage*. Cambridge: Cambridge University Press.

Cockcroft, Robert/Cockcroft, Susan. 2005. *Persuading People: An Introduction to Rhetoric*. London: Palgrave Macmillan. 2nd ed.

Davies, Mark. 2009. The 385+ million word Corpus of Contemporary American English (1990–2008+). *International Journal of Corpus Linguistics* 14(2), 159–190.

Demata, Massimiliano. 2018. 'I think that maybe I wouldn't be here if it wasn't for Twitter'. Donald Trump's Populist Style on Twitter. *Textus* 31(1), 67–90.

Duguid, Alison. 2009a. Insistent voices, government messages. In Morley, J./Bayley, P. (eds.) *Corpus-Assisted Discourse Studies on the Iraq Conflict: Wording the War*. London: Routledge, 234–260.

Duguid, Alison. 2009b. Loud signatures: Comparing evaluative discourse styles-patterns in rants and riffs. In Romer, U./Schulze, R. (eds.) *Exploring the Lexis-Grammar Interface*. Amsterdam/Philadelphia: John Benjamins, 289–315.

Duguid, Alison. 2015. Public apologies and media evaluations. In Bondi, M./Cacchiani, S./Mazzi, D. (eds.) *Discourse In and Through the Media. Recontextualizing and Reconceptualizing Expert Discourse*. Newcastle: Cambridge Scholars Publishing, 146–169.

Fukuyama, Francis. 1992. *The End of History*. New York: Free Press.

Halliday, Michael/Matthiessen, Christian. 2004. *An Introduction to Functional Grammar*. London: Arnold. 3rd ed.

Hoey, Michael. 1983. *On the Surface of Discourse*. London: George Allen and Unwin.

Hoey, Michael. 1991. *Patterns of Lexis in Text*. Oxford: Oxford University Press.

Hoey, Michael. 2005. *Lexical Priming: A New Theory of Words and Language*. London: Routledge.

Hunston, Susan/Thompson, Geoff (eds.) 2000. *Evaluation in Text*. Oxford: Oxford University Press.

Huntington, Samuel. 1996. *The Clash of Civilisations*. New York: Simon & Shuster.

Louw, William. 1993. Irony in the text or insincerity in the writer? The diagnostic potential of semantic prosodies. In Baker, M./Francis, G./Tognini-Bonelli, E. (eds.) *Text and Technology. In honour of John Sinclair*. Amsterdam/Philadelphia: John Benjamins, 157–176.

Marchi, Anna 2018. Dividing up the data: epistemological, methodological and practical impact of diachronic segmentation. In Taylor, C./Marchi, A. (eds.) *Corpus Approaches to Discourse*. London: Routledge, 174–196.

Marchi, Anna/Taylor, Charlotte. 2009. If on a winter's night two researchers … a challenge to assumptions of soundness of interpretation. CADAAD 3(1), 1–20.

Mautner, Gerlinde. 2016. Mad about method. Challenges and opportunities at the CDA/CL interface. Plenary talk at the *3rd Corpora and Discourse International Conference*. Pontignano (Siena), Italy, 02.07.2016.

Napoletano, Antonella/Aiezza, Maria Cristina. 2018. The press war in the post-truth era: A corpus-assisted CDA of the discourse of US political analysts on Trump's figure and policy. *Textus* 31(1), 91–118.

Nelson Francis, William. 1982. Problems of assembling and computerising large corpora. In Johansson, S. (ed.) *Computer Corpora in*

English Language Research. Bergen: Norwegian Computing Centre for the Humanities, 7–24.

Orwell, George. 1946. Politics and the English Language. *Horizon* 13, 252–265.

Orwell, George. 1949. *Nineteen Eighty-Four: A Novel*. London: Secker & Warburg.

Partington, Alan. 2006. *The Linguistics of Laughter*. London: Routledge.

Partington, Alan. (ed.) 2010. Modern diachronic corpus-assisted discourse studies on UK newspapers. *Corpora* 5(2), 83–108.

Partington, Alan. 2017. Varieties of non-obvious meaning in CL and CADS: from 'hindsight post-dictability' to sweet serendipity. *Corpora* 12(3), 339–367.

Partington, Alan/Taylor, Charlotte. 2018. *The Language of Persuasion in Politics*. London: Routledge.

Partington, Alan/Duguid, Alison/Taylor, Charlotte. 2013. *Patterns and Meanings in Discourse: Theory and Practice in Corpus-assisted Discourse Studies*. Amsterdam/Philadelphia: John Benjamins.

Singh, Shiv/Lurthra, Rohini. 2019. *Savvy: Navigating Fake Companies, Fake Leaders and Fake News in the Post-Trust Era*. Kindle Edition.

Taylor, Charlotte. 2010. Science in the news: a diachronic perspective. *Corpora* 5(2), 221–250.

Taylor, Charlotte. 2014. Investigating the representation of migrants in the UK and Italian press: A cross-linguistic corpus-assisted discourse analysis. *International Journal of Corpus Linguistics*, 19(3), 368–400.

Taylor, Charlotte. 2018. Similarity. In Taylor, C./Marchi, A. (eds.) *Corpus Approaches to Discourse*. London: Routledge, 19–37.

Thompson, Geoff. 1996. *Introducing Functional Grammar*. London: Arnold.

Thompson, Mark. 2016. *Enough Said. What's Gone Wrong with the Language of Politics?* Bodley Head: London.

Trump, Donald. 2015. *Crippled America: How to Make America Great Again*. New York: Threshold.

Zuccato, Matilde/Partington, Alan. 2018. Brexit: before and after. A corpus-assisted study of the Referendum campaigns and the immediate aftermath. *Textus* 31(1), 119–140.

Tony McEnery, Helen Baker and Carmen Dayrell

Analysing the impacts of 19th-century drought: A corpus-based study

1 Introduction

In the 19th century, the United Kingdom had no equivalent institution to the Environment Agency and there was no national system which formally recorded occurrences of drought. Consequently, environmental scientists have much to learn about the nature, extent and representation of drought events in 19th-century Britain. In this study, we will explore whether it is possible to use corpus-based discourse analysis to reconstruct climate records and hence fill in some of these holes in our knowledge, specifically through the application of corpus methods to historical newspaper data. Using this approach we want to establish that corpora can help us to i) identify drought events; ii) construct a narrative of those events and iii) understand the impacts that drought had on society at the time.

The climate of the United Kingdom is often described as wet or rainy but, in reality, the country is vulnerable to water shortage.[1] Droughts are not necessarily caused by lack of rainfall alone and can be worsened by variables such as the rate of water consumption and the efficiency of the water-supply infrastructure. Expanding our knowledge of historical climate conditions will enable hydrologists to

1 See https://www.gov.uk/government/publications/water-abstraction-plan-2017/water-abstraction-plan-environment

uncover patterns in drought events of the past and to better understand public attitudes surrounding water scarcity, thus improving our resilience to drought as a society.

To achieve these goals we use close reading, via the scrutiny of concordances and scans of the original hard copies of the newspapers, both to establish data quality and to enable a qualitative analysis of the material. However, that close reading is guided by monthly and yearly frequency distributions to ascertain when references to drought peaked in the newspaper data. It is also supported by collocation analysis and an innovative technique named concordance geoparsing which enables us to focus on droughts which occurred in Britain.

2 The weather in the past

In 19th-century Britain, favourable weather was a crucial factor in securing the wellbeing of the population. In 1892, the *Glasgow Herald* emphasized the importance of a good growing season: "The difference between a good harvest and a bad one means the difference between comfort and misery for a very large proportion of our population, and it is felt more or less by all classes, although they may fail to understand the causes of the difference they feel."[2] A poor harvest would not cause Britons to starve, but it would impact their lives in a myriad of ways, starting with the small stock farmer and extending to regular householders and business owners. Communities in the past were more vulnerable to the effects of drought because they relied upon local sources of water and a scarcity of water entailed an increased risk of waterborne diseases.[3] Waddington (2016: 5) has explained how rural communities in particular relied on archaic water supplies even towards the end of the century, often obtaining water from natural sources such as

2 *Glasgow Herald* 26 August, 1892.
3 Cole/Marsh, (2006: 7).

wells, springs, or stored rainwater, rather than from commercial companies or the local authority.[4]

Despite droughts being a regular feature of the British climate, they have received little scholarly attention.[5] However, there have been attempts to supplement our knowledge of historical droughts. For instance, Todd et al. (2013) have reconstructed precipitation and temperature series in order to generate drought data from 1697, 1726 and 1767 to 2011 for three regions in south-east England. Todd et al. (2015) have constructed the rainfall record for the lowlands around Carlisle in north-west England in the period 1757–2012. Attempts to reconstruct drought records by researchers in disciplines outside of climatology are rarer. A notable exception is Stone (2014), who has studied account rolls of manors in 14th-century England to uncover how drought impacted communities in southern and eastern English counties.

3 Data used in this study

This study uses data from eight digitized newspapers taken from the British Library Newspapers collection, Part I: 1800–1900, which forms part of the British Library Newspapers series.[6] Tab. 1 details the newspapers which are included, the dates of publication for each title, including any missing years, and the number of words and texts in each title.[7]

4 Also see Pritchard (2002: 27).
5 See Cole/Marsh (2006: 4) and Taylor et al. (2009: 569).
6 https://www.britishnewspaperarchive.co.uk/
7 The British Library provides background information about each newspaper in its 19th-century database at https://www.bl.uk/reshelp/pdfs/headnotesconsolidatedlist.pdf

	Dates of publication in 19th century	**Extent**
The Era	1838–99 (1848, 1849, 1850 missing)	448,894,847 words in 3,096 texts
Glasgow Herald	1820–99 (1823–5, Feb 1827-Dec 1843, 1872–8, May-Dec 1879 missing)	1,780,103,461 words in 13,034 texts
Hampshire Telegraph and Sussex Chronicle[a]	1800–99 (1879 missing)	531,379,257 words in 6,197 texts
Ipswich Journal	1800–98 (1829, 1831–1832, 1897, 1899 missing)	424,191,798 words in 7,000 texts
Northern Echo	1870–99 (1871, 1872, Jan-Jun 1897, 1898 missing)	386,590,121 words in 8,543 texts
Pall Mall Gazette	1865–99 (1872, Jan-Mar 1873 missing)	468,324,154 words in 10,620 texts
Reynold's Daily	1850–99 (none missing)	289,617,880 words in 2,635 texts
Western Mail	1869–99 (1872, Jul 1875–Jun 1876, 1896, Jul 1897–Aug 1898 missing)	756,039,060 words in 8,718 texts
Total		5,085,140,578 words in 59,843 texts

Tab. 1: The dates and scale of 19th-century newspapers taken from the British Library newspaper archive

[a] The *Hampshire Telegraph and Sussex Chronicle* underwent several name changes. Between 1799 and 1802, it was known as the *Portsmouth Telegraph*; in 1802 it changed its title to *Mottley's Telegraph and Portsmouth Gazette* and then, in the same year, to the *Hampshire Telegraph and Portsmouth Gazette*. Between 1803 and 1899 it was known as the *Hampshire Telegraph and Sussex Chronicle*.

In order to optimize our access to over 5 billion words, we used the powerful corpus analysis system, CQPweb, to search and manipulate these newspaper corpora.[8] In the first instance, this enabled us to investigate a more complex search term: 'drought OR droughts OR droughty_JJ OR droughted OR drought-* OR drouth OR drouths'.[9] The

8 See CQPweb, see https://cqpweb.lancs.ac.uk/ and Hardie (2012).

9 Initial attempts to use a simpler search term, such as drought* generated too much irrelevant material, such as misspellings of *draughtsman* and surnames

British Library Newspapers website generates search results consisting of a list of article titles which must be perused in full in order to glean their content. CQPweb, on the other hand, provides concordances, lists of each occurrence of a search term presented with words to the left and right of it, which can be examined in brief much more quickly.

Fyfe (2016: 8) has argued that digitized collections should be approached as "distinct objects with histories of their own". The digitized British Library 19th-century newspapers tend to include omissions and errors. This is due to the way in which digital texts are generated from images of text using optical character recognition (OCR). Kettunen (2015: 95–96) has described why older newspapers pose challenges for OCR software due to the appearance of the typeface, the quality of the original source and microfilm, the layout of the page, the scanning resolution and file format and so on. The reproduction of newsprint in CQPweb is thus often littered with extra or incorrect letters and omitted letters or words, all of which can generate considerable noise for an analysis to overcome.

Accordingly, a significant drawback of OCRed material is that the errors it contains have an adverse effect upon the accuracy of searches: in other words, a search for DROUGHT will almost certainly fail to highlight every appearance of this term in the newspapers under investigation but will also include a number of articles in which words have been wrongly understood by OCR software as spelling DROUGHT.[10] The main way in which we overcame problems caused by

---

such as *Droughton*. The search term we eventually decided upon produced results which included the singular and plural of the term *drought*, the term *droughted*, hyphenated terms beginning with *drought*, (such as drought-stricken) alongside instances where *drought* was mistakenly hyphenated. We only included droughty when it was tagged as an adjective (JJ) which meant that references to the surname *Droughty* were excluded. Attempts to exclude the surname *Drought* using the tag NN1 were less successful due to tagging errors. We also considered both the singular and plural of *drouth*, an archaic word which was, admittedly, only occasionally used in the 19th century to mean drought. We will henceforth refer to our search term by the shortened form of *Drought*.

10 The terms *draught* and *brought* are sometimes mistaken for *drought* in 19th-century news corpora. For a discussion of false positives and false negatives see Baker et al. (2013: 237).

OCR errors was to undertake close reading which enabled us to apply qualitative assessments to the newspaper material at every stage of our analysis.[11]

4 Focusing on British droughts

The ways in which newspapers talk about drought can be divided into three broad categories: i) droughts which are reported as occurring in Britain; ii) droughts which are reported as occurring outside of Britain; and iii) references to drought which are mentioned in a more general context. We wished to focus upon droughts which occurred within Britain, so it was preferable to exclude those newspaper articles which referred to drought outside of Britain. Manually sorting the data to exclude foreign references to drought would have been a mammoth undertaking but the application of a technique named concordance geoparsing enabled us to improve this process substantially, both in terms of accuracy and speed.

Concordance geo-parsing is a methodological approach which combines corpus linguistics with GIS (Geographic Information Systems) methods.[12] The technique is achieved by means of a number of stages. Firstly, we used corpus linguistics software to extract each occurrence of a search term and a span of twenty words to the left and right of it. These concordances were then geo-parsed in order to identify instances of place-names which were annotated with geo-spatial co-ordinates. The results were manually analysed in order to reduce errors. By sorting results in terms of longitude and latitude, we were

11 Joulain-Jay (2017: 63–131) provides a very helpful discussion of quality assessments of the OCR in the 19th-century British newspaper collection and has analysed the effects of OCR errors on collocation statistics and frequency distribution.

12 See Gregory/Ell (2007); Gregory/Hardie (2011); Murrieta-Flores et al. (2015); Rupp et al. (2015); Donaldson et al. (2017).

then easily able to lift out drought concordances which included references to places outside the UK.

Using the categorized query function of CQPweb and our original search term, we created a query with two separate categories. The first category was composed of the drought concordances which included place-names belonging outside of the UK and the second one comprised of all other concordances generated by our search term, in other words, those which referred specifically to drought events within the UK and more general references to drought which were not connected to a specific place. For this study, we used data drawn from the second category thus effectively excluding references to drought which were mentioned in relation to places outside of the UK.

5 Searching for droughts in the past – frequencies of DROUGHT in 19th-century newspapers and what this can tell us

Figures 1a and 1b shows how many times DROUGHT was mentioned in six British newspapers over the course of the 19th century. The data was normalized in order to compare frequencies per million words. The graph provides an indication of peak periods where newspapers tended to be more interested in discussing drought.

For each newspaper, we collated the ten years which had the highest frequency of drought mentions per million words. We found that seven years – 1868, 1870, 1874, 1887, 1893, 1895 and 1896 – appeared as one of these top ten peak years in at least four newspapers. These years correspond with periods of probable drought which have been identified by researchers in hydrology (Cole/Marsh 2006) based on the incomplete records that exist. Our findings add credence to theirs by means of triangulation. Clearly, then, we have found evidence that newspapers talk of drought more frequently during periods of attested drought; this is a hypothesis which speaks to both the news values of the time (droughts were newsworthy) and the consequent benefit of the newspaper data for exploring such issues as extreme weather

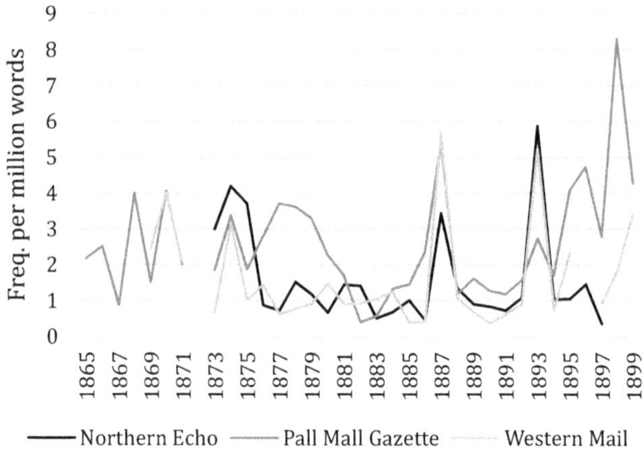

Fig. 1a: Mentions of DROUGHT in three UK newspapers, 1865–1899, excluding non-UK specific references. The start date shown on Figure 1a is 1865 because these three newspapers did not start publication until the second half of the 19th century

events. Although this is not an earth-shattering conclusion, it does provide reassurance of the utility of our method. However, we are able to go further than Cole/Marsh (2006) because, by digging into our news texts further, we can look for effect, which increases our understanding of the nature and impact of these droughts by recovering the media narrative of drought from the period.[13]

6 Recovering drought narratives

The newspapers we considered were published daily, biweekly or weekly and this means that we can access information regarding

13 Our analysis also produced a number of 19th-century drought years which have been previously undocumented, namely that of 1821–2; 1825; 1834; 1846; 1848; 1850–2 and 1880. See McEnery et al. (2019).

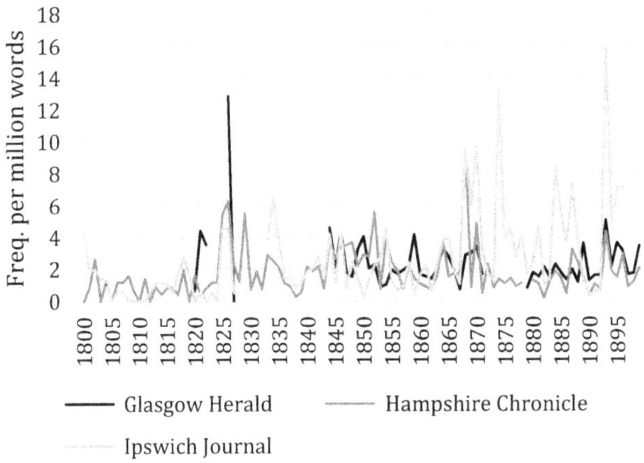

Fig. 1b: Mentions of DROUGHT in three UK newspapers, 1800–1899, excluding non-UK specific references

changing weather patterns in considerable detail.[14] For example, by studying monthly frequency data, we can trace the progress of one particular drought and identify the months of the year when UK newspapers discussed it the most. This information is particularly helpful for environmental scientists as the characteristics of a drought can partly be explained by what point during the year it was most intense – for instance, in recent times, a drought of 2010–12 peaked in early spring so had an intense impact on water resources.[15] Regional newspapers are of great use for this task as they can give us an indication of when the populations of certain areas of the country were particularly interested in drought. It is probably fair to assume, for instance, that the *Glasgow Herald* would include more references to drought in months when Scotland itself was experiencing a dry spell. A second approach we can take is entirely qualitative, reading articles which have been highlighted as

14 *Reynold's Newspaper*; *the Era*, *Ipswich Journal* and the *Hampshire Telegraph and Sussex Chronicle* were published weekly; the *Glasgow Herald* was initially available on a biweekly basis; and the *Western Mail*, *Northern Echo* and *Pall Mall Gazette* were published daily, except for Sundays.

15 See Kendon et al. (2013: 95).

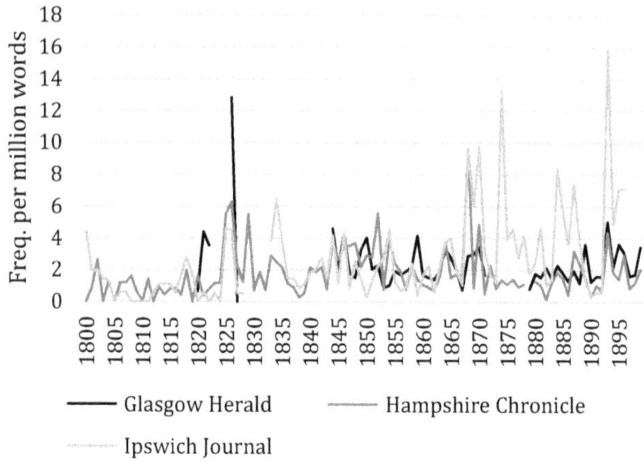

Fig. 2: Mentions of DROUGHT in 1893 by month

being concerned with drought, and constructing a narrative of a year of drought. We will demonstrate both of these approaches below.

7 The Great Drought of 1893 – by month

The drought of 1893 was the subject of a scholarly article by Brodie (1894) and was described in retrospect as the "great drought of 1893" by the *Northern Echo*.[16] Figure 2 shows the numbers of mentions of DROUGHT by month for 1893 in six newspapers using data which excludes non-UK references.

Figure 2 shows that the northern-based newspapers, the *Glasgow Herald* and the *Northern Echo*, mention drought more often in June, whereas the search terms peak slightly earlier, in May-June, for the Cardiff-based *Western Mail* and the *Ipswich Journal*. It appears that the drought of 1893 affected the south of England a few weeks before it hit the north. Interestingly, the newspapers seldom discuss the drought at the end

16 *Northern Echo* 5 February, 1895.

of the summer but mentions pick up a little in early autumn, perhaps as a result of increased interest due to harvesting.

By exploring the concordances of 1893 using close reading, we can illuminate which parts of the country exhibited anxieties concerning the dry weather first. The first hint of the approaching difficulties was provided by the *Ipswich Journal* in an article about a local cycling club on 22 April 1893. In the same issue, readers were informed that the weather had been "altogether delightful" but that the lack of rain was becoming increasingly serious.

The dry weather was being felt in Wales by late April. The *Western Mail* reported that scarcity of water was affecting several Welsh metal works and that work might be forced to stop if the drought continued.[17] Although Cardiff was said to still have a large storage of water in its reservoirs, the supply of water in Merthyr, further north, was under threat to the extent that it was going to be cut off to businesses that used it for machinery and motive power, including railway companies.[18] Meanwhile, the residents of Treboeth, to the north of Swansea, were very short of water and were concerned at the unsanitary state of their neighbourhood and the associated risk of cholera.[19] By 5 May, the *Western Mail* was reporting that Llanelli, to the east of Merthyr, was approaching a state of water famine and its residents were being visited by detectives organized by the borough supervisor intent on prosecuting those who were found to have wasted water. Here we have an early indication of who might be deemed responsible for the coming drought.

Lack of rain continued to affect the south of England. At the end of April, the *Hampshire Telegraph* reported that the drought had continued

---

17 *Western Mail* 26 April, 1893.

18 Pritchard (2002: 37, 41) has written of the difficulties faced by rapidly expanding urban centres such as Swansea, Merthyr Tydfil and Cardiff. Merthyr was an important centre for steel and iron and its local government was cowed by the demands of these industries, sometimes at the expense of local residents. The rights of the ironmasters were written into the Merthyr Water Works Act of 1858.

19 *Western Mail* 28 April, 1893. See Waddington (2016: 6–7) for a description of how rural water supplies were prone to pollution. Pritchard (2002: 25–6) has described how the link between polluted water and the spread of disease became accepted after the mid-19th century, partly due to the work of John Snow in London and to cholera epidemics of 1849–50, 1853–4, and 1866.

for sixty days, unparalleled in the records of modern meteorology, and was causing uneasiness.[20] The *Glasgow Herald* noted that while rainfall had been adequate in Scotland and Ireland, it continued to be lacking in England and Wales.[21] Our hypothesis – that the south and south-west of England were affected by the drought of 1893 before the north of England and Scotland – appears to be accurate. However, the drought in England did have a knock-on effect for Scotland. For instance, cattle breeders in the south of Scotland were reportedly finding it difficult to find buyers for their stock due to English farmers avoiding taking on more animals which would be difficult to maintain during drought.[22]

On 11 May, the *Western Mail* reported that tinplate manufacturers in South Wales were sinking wells of their own in order to access water. In the densely populated counties of Glamorgan and Monmouth, the watercourses were described as foul and a threat to public health. Medical experts feared outbreaks of cholera and fever, and it was reported that several people had suffered food poisoning in Cardiff due to eating pork pies. The reporter explained that this was caused by ptomaine poisoning attributable to the weather and urged food inspectors and tradesmen to observe greater vigilance. In the same issue, readers were told that the Bishop of St. David's had recommended the use in Divine Service of the prayer for rain.[23] Public prayers for rain were repeated in Wales on 15 May.[24] Readers were exhorted to ration their use of water; take care when choosing foodstuffs; and, as a last resort, appeal to a higher authority for rain. This emphasis on personal responsibility was not unusual: "Not to be as economical as possible of water where supplies seem likely to run short is a violation of social morality."[25]

---

20 *Hampshire Telegraph and Sussex Chronicle* 29 April, 1893.

21 *Glasgow Herald* 26 April, 1893.

22 *Glasgow Herald* 14 June, 1893.

23 On this day, the work at the Court Herbert Colliery at Neath had been suspended due to lack of water, which rendered around 200 men temporarily out of work.

24 *Western Mail* 15 May, 1893.

25 Prosecutions for water wastage did take place. On 13 July 1893, the *Western Mail* reported the case of Mr. Tabson from Cardiff who was fined the maximum penalty of 40 shillings for using a hose.

By May 1893, the drought was impacting on the lives of people residing in England to a considerable extent. A local intelligence column reported that remote districts of Hampshire were charging two-pence half-penny for a single pail of water and that between 5 and 6 millions of gallons were being imported into Portsmouth from the works at Farlington and Brockhampton. The directors of the water company were exhorting members of the public not to waste water. Another article in the same paper added that farmers in North Hampshire were being obliged to travel three or four miles to obtain water for their cattle.[26] The Agricultural Correspondent for the *Ipswich Journal* wrote that he had witnessed indications of drought in Suffolk with farmers unable to sow their fields with barley due to the dryness of the earth.[27]

References to drought sometimes increased when it had been broken and it appears that this dry spell was interrupted in some parts of the country during May.[28] For instance, on 23 May, the *Western Mail* told the story of a special meeting to pray for rain at a chapel in Barry being interrupted by a heavy shower. The shopkeepers present must not have had much faith in their prayers receiving an immediate response because they had hung perishable goods outside their businesses before attending the service: "...they dallied awhile, and then there was a stampede".[29]

These welcome showers did not mark an end of the drought. On 10 June, the *Ipswich Journal* noted that the drought had continued in Berkshire and Reading.[30] The hay crop in East Anglia was reported as being the poorest on record; crops were short in East Essex and there was a complete shortage of feed for cattle.[31] On 14 June, the *Western Mail*

---

26 *Hampshire Telegraph and Sussex Chronicle* 13 May 1893. See (Stone, 2014: 439) for an explanation of the impact of drought upon livestock.

27 *Ipswich Journal* May 13, 1893.

28 See *Northern Echo* 19 May, 1893 and *Hampshire Telegraph and Sussex Chronicle* 20 May, 1893.

29 *Western Mail* 23 May, 1893.

30 *Ipswich Journal* 10 June, 1893.

31 *Ipswich Journal* 17 June and 24 June, 1893.

reported many cases of diphtheria and scarlet fever in North Wales which were attributed to the drought. The Commercial Dry Dock at Cardiff had been utilized as a storage reservoir causing inconvenience at the port. The Thames, meanwhile, had become so low by Glover's Island, Richmond Bridge, and Brendford Eyot, that it was possible to cross the river by foot by jumping from one exposed strip of bed to another.

In Figure 2, the peak month of drought mentions for the *Glasgow Herald* is July and, accordingly, by 16 June, drought appeared to have reached Scotland. A report citing George Croucher, the observer at the Ochtertyre Station of the Scottish Meteorological Society, noted that there had not been such a deficiency of rainfall since 1855. The Kilbirnie Water Committee requested that the public did not waste water and that all pipes and fittings were in proper order.[32] In mid-July, the *Northern Echo* reported that the Mugdock Reservoir in Glasgow had fallen 4 foot in one day.[33] By June, the north and midlands of England were also taking their share in the suffering. A number of riveters employed in a local shipyard were compelled to stop working because of the intense heat.[34] The authorities in Birmingham, "usually one of the last places to feel the effects of drought upon the water supply", had decided to reduce the street water supply by half.[35]

As in May, showers in late June misleadingly suggested that the drought might be at an end.[36] On 3 July, the *Glasgow Herald* informed readers that the water supply in Kirnintilloch, north of Glasgow, was being cut off for 17 hours between 1pm and 6am. It insisted that the situation in Scotland was becoming increasingly serious for agriculture.[37] On 19 July, the *Glasgow Herald* included a lengthy report on the harvest prospects of Scotland. The corn crop was not expected to do well. Oats, the most important cereal crop in Scotland, had fared better in places where the crop had been sown earlier and in richly manured lands, but was predicted to have a deficiency of around 15 % throughout

32 *Glasgow Herald* 19 June, 1893.
33 *Northern Echo* 17 June 1893.
34 ibid.
35 *Northern Echo* 23 June, 1893.
36 *Glasgow Herald* 23 June, 1893 and *Northern Echo* 27 July, 1893.
37 *Glasgow Herald* 5 July, 1893.

the region. The reports of barley and wheat were more favourable and the root crops, potato and turnip, were thriving. The article noted that hay prices had risen due to the total destruction of crops by drought in parts of England and the Continent and were likely to be nearly twice the price of the previous year.

By mid-July it was reported that the midlands, southern and western counties of England were suffering a shortage of milk due to reductions in cattle numbers.[38] The *Western Mail* reported the sad story of a yeoman from the Mendip Hills district of Somerset who was forced to shoot his remaining cattle after two died from starvation.[39] In early August, the *Hampshire Telegraph* advised readers that the waterworks company was stopping the supply of water at 8pm every evening.[40] In the same month, a column on grouse shooting in the *Northern Echo* noted that fires had destroyed acres of land during the drought in Snilesworth, Wass and Kilburn.[41]

The impacts of the drought of 1893 continued into the autumn. On 1 September it was reported that the Hartlepool Gas and Water Company had struggled to provide water for its domestic and business companies and, for the first time, they had been obliged to ask their customers to economize their use of water.[42] The *Glasgow Herald* also noted the difficulties faced by the residents of Hartlepool, reporting that water for manufacturing purposes would be cut off, affecting employment.[43] On 24 November, it was reported that in some parts of Pembrokeshire drinking water was difficult to procure.[44] However, in general, mentions of drought in the newspapers noticeably reduce after the summer although the effects of the dry weather of 1893 continued to affect the water supply into the following year.

The analysis so far has clearly shown that corpus techniques can identify periods of drought in the past and, by moving between distant

38 *Glasgow Herald* 15 July, 1893.
39 *Western Mail* 11 July, 1893.
40 *Hampshire Telegraph and Sussex Chronicle* 5 August 1893.
41 *Northern Echo* 14 August, 1893.
42 *Northern Echo* 1 September, 1893.
43 *Glasgow Herald* 25 October, 1893.
44 *Western Mail* 24 November, 1893.

and close reading of the texts, we can reconstruct narratives of drought associated with a drought event in historical newspaper data. However, one thing that is clearly of importance in that narrative, as is apparent from the analysis so far, is the impact on the natural and social environment that the drought had. While close reading is an effective technique for reconstructing narrative, we explored the possibility that by focusing on collocation alone, we may be able to explore the impact of droughts in the newspaper corpus.

8 The impacts of 19th-century drought

Shifting our focus to impacts and collocation allows us to explore whether the issues linked to the drought of 1893 that we uncovered mark a change in the kinds of things the newspapers wrote about when they mentioned British drought. To explore this we had hoped only to use collocation, but the quality of the OCRed data made this difficult. Consequently, we worked in a mixed mode, beginning with collocation but then further investigating discourses surrounding drought in the seven years when the subject was shown to be particularly salient in newspapers. This was a lengthy process which demanded a great deal of close reading and often entailed consulting scans of original articles at the British Library website to overcome the issues with the OCR data. The approach was effective, however. The matrix below summarizes the impacts of each drought as they were reported in the newspapers in the 1800s.

To populate the matrix, if a newspaper mentioned a particular impact of drought in a particular year, then that box was ticked. In the public health category, we only checked a box if a particular illness had been specifically attributed to drought. In terms of reports of harvest failures, we only checked a box if a crop was reported as being deficient rather than likely to be deficient. This is important as the newspapers often carried reports of predicted failures of a particular plant which turned out to be nothing more than doom-mongering. Also, a checked box does not necessarily mean a crop was deficient throughout the

	Year →	**68**	**70**	**74**	**87**	**93**	**95**	**96**	
Impacts (grouped)	Impact group members								Total
cereal crops	wheat	✓					✓		2
	barley	✓	✓		✓	✓		✓	5
	oats	✓	✓		✓	✓	✓	✓	6
	corn	✓	✓	✓		✓		✓	5
legumes	peas	✓			✓				2
	beans	✓	✓	✓			✓		4
cruciferous veg.	cabbages						✓		1
	kohlrabi	✓							1
	rapeseed						✓	✓	2
root crops	turnips	✓	✓	✓	✓		✓	✓	6
	potatoes	✓	✓		✓	✓			4
	carrots	✓					✓		2
	mangolds	✓	✓				✓		3
	swedes	✓	✓		✓				3
	beetroot					✓			1
grasses	ryegrass							✓	1
	hay	✓			✓	✓	✓	✓	5
	lawns							✓	1
hops		✓		✓			✓		3
fruit	pears							✓	1
	plums			✓				✓	2
	strawberries				✓		✓	✓	3
	apples				✓			✓	2
	pears			✓					1
	cherries			✓	✓				2
	gooseberries			✓					1
flowers/garden produce		✓	✓		✓	✓	✓	✓	6
sheep and cattle farming	grazing shortages	✓	✓	✓	✓	✓			5
	water shortages for stock	✓			✓	✓			3
	low prices	✓	✓		✓			✓	4
	lack of sales	✓	✓		✓	✓	✓	✓	6
	milk shortages				✓	✓	✓		3
disease	in cattle		✓			✓			2

Tab. 2: Continued

Tab. 2: Continued

	Year →	**68**	**70**	**74**	**87**	**93**	**95**	**96**	
	in poultry			✓					1
price rises	hay	✓	✓			✓			3
	cereal crops	✓	✓			✓			3
	bread	✓							1
	milk				✓				1
	cheese				✓				1
water shortages	dried up ditches, streams, rivers, reservoirs, canals	✓	✓	✓	✓	✓	✓	✓	7
	water supply restricted (domestic)	✓	✓	✓	✓	✓	✓	✓	7
	water supply restricted (commercial)	✓		✓	✓	✓			4
	businesses closing or operating restricted hours		✓	✓	✓	✓	✓		5
	requests for public economy	✓		✓	✓	✓	✓		5
fires		✓			✓	✓			3
public health	diphtheria	✓				✓			2
	enteric fever (including typhoid)	✓			✓	✓			3
	cholera	✓							1
	scarlet fever	✓				✓			2
	food poisoning					✓			1
	diarrhoea	✓					✓		2
	lack of energy					✓			1
sport	grouse shooting	✓			✓	✓		✓	4
	otter hunting			✓					1
	angling		✓	✓	✓	✓	✓	✓	6

Tab. 2: Continued

	Year →	**68**	**70**	**74**	**87**	**93**	**95**	**96**	
	cricket					✓			1
	golf					✓	✓	✓	3
	horse racing	✓				✓	✓		3
roads		✓		✓		✓			3
area	Scotland	✓	✓	*	✓	✓	✓	✓	6
	Northern England	✓	✓	✓	✓	✓	✓	✓	7
	Southern England	✓	✓	✓	✓	✓	✓	✓	7
	Wales	✓	✓	✓	✓	✓	✓	✓	7
Total		39	23	21	31	35	26	24	

Tab. 2: Impacts of drought in seven major drought years of the 19th century
* Data from the *Glasgow Herald* is missing for 1874 but evidence for drought in Scotland in this year was not found in the other newspapers.

entire country. For instance, the *Glasgow Herald* reported on 20 September 1893 that the hay crop was plentiful in Ayrshire and Renfrewshire but deficient in Dumfries but, in this case, we still checked hay for that year. In most cases, however, failures of the same crop were reported in several newspapers and in more than one place in the country. Lastly, we only checked a box when a report was specific about the type of crop affected. Vague references to disasters regarding 'fruit' or 'cereal crops' were disregarded. By studying the totals in the column at the end of Tab. 2, we can surmise that turnips and oats, followed by barley and corn, were probably the most vulnerable crops during dry years. Of course, the checked boxes belonging to these crops may also be indicative of their popularity with farmers. It is doubtful, for instance, that kohlrabi was planted to the same extent as turnips.

The matrix not only tells us what kinds of things were affected by drought in 19th-century Britain, but gives us a good idea of what journalists of the time considered to be important to their readerships. For instance, while it is likely that the conditions of lawns were adversely affected by water shortage, there are only two mentions of this.[45]

45 *Ipswich Journal* 4 July and 12 September, 1896.

Although 19th-century Britons seemed to care about the produce from their garden, they appear to have been less concerned about its appearance, or at least found it less newsworthy. While golf and grouse shooting were often mentioned as being negatively impacted by dry spells, otter hunting was only mentioned in one article and football achieved no references at all.[46]

What stands out is the consistency of results. All the newspapers concentrated on the effects of drought in the same wide areas: the growth of crops; cattle farming; the supply of water; public health; and sporting events. The totals in the bottom row of the table suggest that the drought of 1868, closely followed by that of 1893, impacted the country in the greatest number of ways. In both of these years, public health suffered to the largest extent. Droughts in every year covered by Tab. 2 appear to have affected almost every area of the country. The exception is the drought of 1874 which does not appear to have affected Scotland. However, because we do not have access to the *Glasgow Herald* for this year, we cannot confidently conclude this was definitely the case.

9 Conclusion

This study demonstrates how corpus linguistics in combination with concordance geoparsing can be used in order to uncover how often, and in what ways, 19th-century newspapers discussed droughts within Britain. It can also help researchers to reconstruct media narratives surrounding drought events. The digitisation of newspaper text and development of advanced corpus analysis systems make such an endeavour possible. The data was approached in a number of ways: we compiled frequency distributions to reveal peak years when drought was prevalent in public discourse; we matched the monthly frequency distributions of drought in 1893 to the narrative of the drought's progress as

46 *Western Mail* 22 June, 1874.

told to us by 19th-century newspapers; and we compared the impacts of major 19th-century drought events by means of a qualitative analysis. Moreover, we were able to add a geographic dimension to our study. Not only were we able to exclude drought frequencies which related to countries outside of the UK by concordance geo-parsing, we used information from regional newspapers in order to chart the progress of major drought events as they moved through the country.

We found an overwhelming concordance among the newspapers we analysed in terms of when drought affected Britain and its impacts upon the British population. 19th-century Britons regarded drought with uneasiness and were preoccupied by its affects upon agriculture and cattle farming. The newspaper analysis suggests that the south of England and Wales suffered more at the hands of the 1893 drought than the north and Scotland.[47] However, the wellbeing of British and Scottish agriculturalists was linked. If English farmers were unable to provide grass to feed their cattle, they would be unwilling to purchase livestock from Scottish farmers.

Drought affected the livelihoods of working people. Newspapers carried accounts of various manufacturing businesses being forced to close due to lack of water and correspondents often noted how many men were out of employment as a result. Yet, newspapers also reported tensions between local residents and businesses over who had first claim to the water supply in times of scarcity. A discourse of blame is also present in the drought articles of 1893. In its simplest form, this was directed at domestic consumers who were deemed guilty of water wastage due to carelessness and extravagance. Such a narrative was often initiated by water companies who accused their customers of over-use as part of a defensive strategy to deflect blame which may have otherwise been directed at themselves.[48] Members of the public did not accept water shortage passively. The newspapers reported local

47 Fletcher (1961: 427) has cited residents of north Derbyshire who insisted that 1893 was the most productive year in living memory.

48 See Taylor et al. (2009: 571).

communities mobilising in order to exhort water companies to increase their supply and even organising meetings to pray for rain.

This study has demonstrated that newspapers are a reliable means of identifying dry weather events, attested by the fact that many of the droughts mentioned in newspapers also matched existing records. It has confirmed our hypothesis that newspapers discussed drought much more frequently during droughty periods. We have been able to take advantage of the daily renewal of news stories as presented by the newspapers to uncover how a dry spell progressed on a day-to-day basis. By discovering when drought was most discussed in contemporary newspapers, we have a starting-point from which we can delve further into the news texts to uncover the effects and scope of each drought, highlighting common or unusual discourses along the way. In this way, we can offer new information to environmental scientists in terms of the nature of historical drought.

References

Baker, Paul/McEnery, Tony/Gabrielatos, Costas. 2013. *Discourse Analysis and Media Attitudes: The Representation of Islam in the British Press.* Cambridge: Cambridge University Press.

Brodie, Frederick. 1894. The great drought of 1893, and its attendant meteorological phenomena. *Quarterly Journal of the Royal Meteorological Society* 20(89), 1–30.

Cole, Gwyneth/Marsh, Terry. 2006. *The impact of climate change on severe droughts: Major droughts in England and Wales from 1800 and evidence of impact.* Bristol, UK: The Environment Agency.

Donaldson, Christopher/Gregory, Ian/Taylor, Joanna. 2017. Locating the beautiful, picturesque, sublime and majestic: spatially analysing the application of aesthetic terminology in descriptions of the English Lake District. *Journal of Historical Geography* 56, 43–60.

Fletcher, T. W. 1961. The great depression of English agriculture, 1873–1896. *The Economic History Review* 13(3), 417–32.

Fyfe, Paul. 2016. An archaeology of Victorian Newspapers. *Victorian Periodicals Review* 49(4), 546–77.

Gregory, Ian/Ell, Paul. 2007. *Historical GIS: Technologies, Methodologies and Scholarship*. Cambridge: Cambridge University Press.

Gregory, Ian/Hardie, Andrew. 2011. Visual GISting: bringing together corpus linguistics and Geographical Information Systems. *Literary and Linguistic Computing* 26(3), 297–314.

Hardie, Andrew. 2012. CQPweb – combining power, flexibility and usability in a corpus analysis tool. *International Journal of Corpus Linguistics* 17(3), 380–409.

Joulain-Jay, Amelia. 2017. *Corpus Linguistics for History: The Methodology of Investigating Place-Name Discourses in Digitised Nineteenth-Century Newspapers*. PhD thesis, Lancaster University.

Kendon, Mike/Marsh, Terry/Parry, Simon. 2013. The 2010–2012 drought in England and Wales. *Weather* 68(4), 88–95.

Kettunen, Kimmo. 2015. Keep, change or delete? Setting up a low resource OCR post-correction framework for a digitized old Finnish newspaper collection. In Calvanese, D./De Nart, D./Tasso, C. (eds.) *Digital Libraries on the Move: 11th Italian Research Conference on Digital Libraries, Bolzano, Italy*. Bern: Springer, 95–103.

McEnery, Tony/Baker, Helen/Dayrell, Carmen. 2019. Working at the interface of hydrology and corpus linguistics: using corpora to identify unrecorded droughts in nineteenth-century Britain. In Baker, P./Egbert, J. (eds.) *Using Corpus Methods to Triangulate Linguistic Analysis*. New York: Routledge.

Murrieta-Flores, Patricia/Baron, Alastair/Gregory, Ian/Hardie, Andrew/Rayson, Paul. 2015. Automatically analysing large texts in a GIS environment: The Registrar General's reports and cholera in the nineteenth century. *Transactions in GIS* 19, 296–320.

Pritchard, John. 2002. Water supply in Welsh towns, 1840–1900: control, conflict and development. *The Welsh History Review* 21(1), 24–47.

Rupp, C. J./Rayson, Paul/Gregory, Ian/Hardie, Andrew/Joulain, Amelia/Hartmann, Daniel. 2015. Dealing with heterogeneous big data when geoparsing historical corpora. In *IEEE Conference on Big Data*, Bethesda, MD, 27 October 2014: 80–3.

Stone, David. 2014. The impact of drought in early fourteenth-century England. *Economic History Review* 67(2), 435–62.

Taylor, Vanessa/Chappells, Heather/Medd, Will/Trentmann, Frank. 2009. Drought is normal: the socio-technical evolution of drought and water demand in England and Wales, 1893–2006. *Journal of Historical Geography* 35, 568–91

Todd, B./Macdonald, Neil/Chiverrell, Richard/Caminade, Cyril/Hooke, Janet. 2013. Severity, duration and frequency of drought in SE England from 1697 to 2011. *Climatic Change* 121, 673–87.

Todd, B./Macdonald, Neil/Chiverrell, Richard. 2015. Revision and extension of the composite Carlisle rainfall record, northwest England: 1757–2012. *International Journal of Climatology* 35, 593–607.

Waddington, Keir. 2016. 'I should have thought that Wales was a wet part of the world': Drought, rural communities and public health, 1870–1914. *Social History of Medicine* 30(3), 590–611.

Salvador Enguix-Oliver and Beatriz Gallardo-Paúls

Coverage of the far-right in the Spanish written press: The case of Vox[1]

1 Introduction and objectives

On 7 October 2018 the Spanish far-right party Vox held a rally at the Palacio de Vistalegre Arena in Madrid that marked a milestone as regards the media attention given to this party, which then had no representation in parliament. On the chronological axis of that 7 October, this chapter presents the results of a corpus analysis on the treatment of Vox in the Spanish written press. The analysis seeks to contribute some specific evidence to the often-debated hypothesis that the media attention received by far-right European parties favours their access to democratic institutions, as was precisely the case of Vox in the Andalusian parliament in the regional elections of 2 December 2018. The analysis we conduct takes the political nature of journalistic discourse as its premise (Borrat 1989; Charron 2000; Mc Nair 2000; Enguix 2015), and its role in the rise of extremism, for which we rely on the idea of "media populism" put forward by Mazzoleni (2008):

1 The present work is included in the research project *PRODISNET-02: Procesos discursivos en internet: desplazamientos enunciativos y efectos hiperbólicos en el discurso político*. Ref. RTI2018-093523-B-I00, funded by the Spanish Ministry of Science, Innovation and Universities.

> The example of social and political malaise– a common precondition for the growth of anti-political sentiments – shows that both political and media factors form a unique alliance, whose catalyst may be found in the country's political culture at a given time. This malaise is certainly not pro-voked by the media, but the media do play a role in disseminating it (Mazzoleni 2008: 50).

Against this backdrop, we examine the journalistic pieces that most widely read Spanish newspapers published about Vox on the days before and after the rally held in Madrid on 7 October 2018.

2 Theoretical and methodological aspects

2.1 The corpus

The data that used in this work are part of the corpus on political discourse PRODISNET (Discursive Process on the Internet) which our research group started compiling in 2016. The general corpus contains different sub-corpora that have been the basis for several publications, including data for social media sites and the press. The corpus for the present work (sub-corpus PRODINET-201) covers the treatment of the Spanish ultra-right in the written press. In order to delimit the corpus of texts, we took as time signpost the rally held by Vox at the Palacio de Vistalegre in Madrid on 7 October 2018; we then gathered data from this day until 2 December 2018 (the date of the Andalusian elections), and went back the same number of days (56) until 12 August 2018. Using the database *Factiva*, we entered the search word VOX to download all the documents in this time span in eight national newspapers: four of them online-born and four in print.

For the selection of printed sources, we used the third wave of the General Survey of Media (EGM 2018), and we relied on the *ojdinteractiva* platform for the digital media. In the former case, excluding sports agencies and dailies, the most relevant media for our purposes were *El País* (EP), *El Mundo* (EM), *La Vanguardia* (LV) and *ABC*; and, in the latter, *El Español* (EE), *eldiario.es* (ED), *Público* and *Infolibre* (INF). However, there were no data available from *Público* either on *Factiva* or on *Nexis*. For this reason, we chose *El confidencial.com* (CONF) as an alternative, as was highly ranked in *ComScore* metrics (June 2018).

2.2 Strategic framing theory

For data analysis we use a broad approach to the notion of framing, which distinguishes three pragmatic levels of discourse production (sender, text, receiver) with three basic strategies for each of them (Gallardo 2019a). We assume that framing is a strategic activity because it intends to direct the receiver's interpretation (in this case, the reader of each newspaper):

- Enunciative framing strategies: intentional strategy (the communicative action of the subject of enunciation, that is, predominant illocutionary acts); lexical strategy (designation and inference, that is, propositional speech acts); and predicative strategy (subject of enunciation, actantiality; that is, the allocation of roles in political action).
- Textual framing strategies: thematic strategy (topicalization and focalization); structural strategy (structure of the argumentative or narrative text); and paratextual strategy (text material nature, introduction of images, typography or prosody).
- Interactive framing strategies: dialogic strategy (other texts in the text, citation mechanisms and quoted discourse); alignment strategy (predictability, reactivity of texts to other previous political messages); and affiliation strategy (ideology expressed in the texts).

3 Far-right discourse and discourse on the far-right

Prior to the analysis of the discourse of mainstream written media on the coverage of Vox, we will briefly consider first some similarly discursive traits of the populist phenomenon they are covering. This

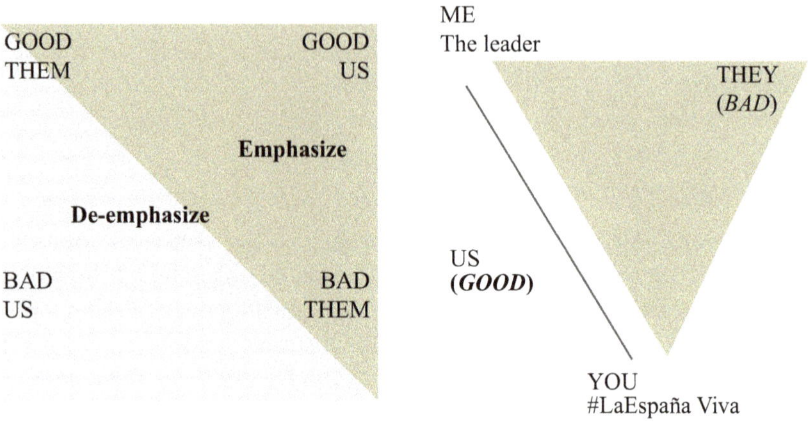

Fig. 1. On the left, the structure of the ideological square that characterises political discourse, according to Van Dijk; on the right, the schism of "we" that distinguishes populist rhetoric (Gallardo 2018b: 31)

is a major issue because political journalism can be conceived as a secondary discourse insofar as its main source is the primary political discourse generated by political leaders and institutions. Besides, contrary to other political tendencies, ultra-right parties like Spanish Vox, the French Front National, the US Tea Party or the Italian Lega Nord are distinguished by a specific *discursive hallmark*, a discourse normally associated with populist rhetoric. Such rhetoric radicalises some discursive features that are typical of all political discourses, while retaining others. For instance, they maintain the discursive construction of "we vs. them" – as proposed by Van Dijk in his analysis of ideology and power (1998: 267). However, one can notice a clear schism in the "we" that increases the significance of the "I" vs "you, the people".

The following tweet by Vox's leader Santiago Abascal illustrates this populist triangle:

(1) «A los insensatos, progres y separatistas les digo que España unida no será vencida». (Santiago Abascal in a rally at the closing of the 28 April voting campaign).
[ENG. "I say to the foolish, lefties and separatists that a united Spain shall never be defeated."]

A second trait generally ascribed to such populist rhetoric is the axiological radicalisation around "theirs bad" and "ours good", since the leader gains power as he emerges as the solution (and as the one that holds the balance of power) to the opposition us vs them. This moralising quality confers on the discourse the sentimental, emotional and expressive hues that all literature on populism has noted, regardless of their ideology. This sentimentality translates into a discursive position which can be bound to two prevailing frames (Entman 1991; Semetko & Valkenburg 2000: 96): the attribution of responsibility and morality, which in turn trigger a predominant expressive illocution (Gallardo 2018a).

Hochschild (2016: 37) analyses the positions of the supporters of the US Tea Party and links the significance of emotions with different sentimental system apparatuses for the leftists and for the rightists. This scholar assumes that those discourses widely regarded (and distinguished) as left or right bear different belief systems as underlying structures (as *frame*, ultimately). In the same vein as George Lakoff, Hochschild couples this underlying principle with a metaphorical structure that she calls "deep story", which refers to the experience of "what I should or should not feel" that each individual goes through.

While the Tea Party builds a negative discourse on "them" that comprises the Federal Government, in Spain the ultra-right conceptualisation of "them" shows diverse lexicalisations: *the lefties dictatorship*, *the enemies of Spain*, *the separatists*, *feminism*, *gender totalitarians*, *communists*, *media*, etc. These groups are invariably portrayed by means of extremely negative expressions, often abounding in insults and discredit, as well as typically resorting to sarcasm and falsehood. Given this preponderance of negativity, De Santiago Guervós (2016/2017: 115–116), along the lines of Charaudeau (2008, 2009), explicitly defines populism as a "discursive technique" with clearly negative connotations:

> Populism sits next to demagogy, improvisation, irresponsibility, empty statements, extremes, revolution, anti-democracy, manipulation, complacency towards the people, xenophobia, fascism, etc. [Original in Spanish].

There is also, however, a fervent positive expressiveness that is addressed to the creation of the "us" that in the case of Vox is manifested in the idea of *la España viva* ("Living Spain"):

(2) «Los cobardes siempre pierden, por eso España ha sido una nación tan grande a lo largo de su historia, porque ha estado llena de valientes. El 28 de abril todos tenemos que serlo, no podemos sucumbir al miedo, que nadie os quite la ilusión de votar en lo que creéis #EspañaViva» (Tuit de @voxnoticias_es, 29/03/2019, 10:34 h.).
[ENG. "Cowards always lose. That's why Spain has been such a great nation through history, because it has been full of courageous people. On 28 April we all have to be brave, and not to succumb to fear. Don't let anyone deprive you of your hopes to vote what you believe in #EspañaViva" (Tweet by @voxnoticias_es, 29.03.2019, 10:34am)]

These features give some insight into the kind of reported discourse that features in the texts of the corpus. However, we might expect the journalistic discourse of mainstream media to be alien to this emotionality of the texts, which is more typical of sensationalist press, or of what Mazzoleni (2008) calls "populist journalism": «One could hypothesize that tabloid media tend to favor populism while up-market media tend to oppose it» (Wirth et al. 2016: 29).

The analysis of the corpus shows the extent to which mainstream media coverage of Vox accommodates these features or maintains the referential distance that is inherent to political journalism.

4 Analysis and discussion

4.1 A disproportionate coverage

A first issue that arises in the compilation of the corpus is the increase in media attention that Vox attracts after the Vistalegre rally. With the aforementioned selection criteria, the initial corpus was made up of 1491 documents, which shows an undoubted difference in attention in the two mentioned periods. Once cleaned up of duplicates, false positives, etc., the final sample was reduced to 1186 news pieces, distributed between the two periods as shown in Fig. 2. As can be observed, all newspapers dramatically increase the coverage of a non-parliamentary party: from 109 texts in the 56 days prior to 7 October to the 1077 texts in the 56 days after (an increase of 888.07 %):

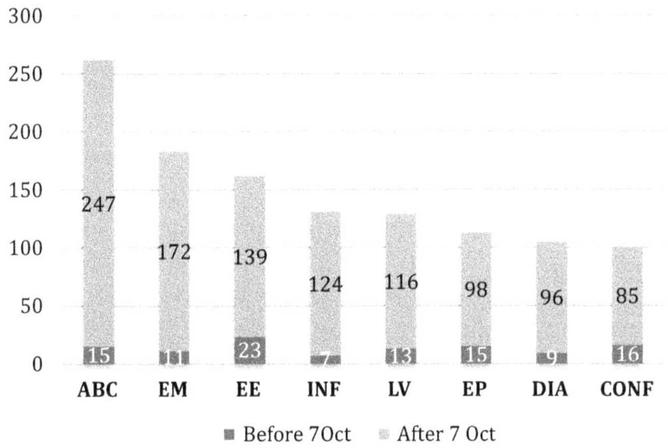

Fig. 2. Distribution of the corpus in the two periods: before and after the rally of 7 October

Although we have highlighted the vast difference in media interest between Vox and other non-parliamentary parties (specifically, the animalist party PACMA), it is true that, from the point of view of newsworthiness, the political/media interest about the far-right could be considered more urgent than in other non-parliamentary parties. However, the Vistalegre rally gave rise to an upsurge in media coverage that is strikingly surprising when compared to the situation of other emergent parties. For instance, in a previous study (Gallardo/Enguix 2015) on the media reporting of the 2014 European elections by the written press, we found that *El País*, *El Mundo*, *La Vanguardia* and *ABC* had hardly paid attention to Podemos, which nevertheless obtained 5 MEPs (Members of the European Parliament). The analysis of the voting coverage of these four quality dailies between 24 April and 27 May 2014 (the elections were held on 25 May) was carried out on a corpus of 1698 texts and 2996 relevant topicalizations, only 72 of which focused on Podemos. Besides, most of them were dated on 26–27 May, after the elections.

Of course, it is essential in this contrast that the study deals only with written press, while most media attention to Podemos in 2013 and 2014 occurred on TV. In the present study, we can also say that general-interest TV broadcasters like *La Sexta* and *TV3* have also notably contributed to the visibility of Vox, although we do not have quantitative data. Another relevant factor (Krämer 2017) worthy of research attention is the visibility that these minority parties are given in off-mainstream written and audio-visual media, which would fit into the definition of populist/sensationalist formats: *casoaislado.com, okdiario.com, libertaddigital.com, periodistadigital.com, gaceta.es, aplausos.es, lajunglaradio.com, eltorotv.com*, etc.

The question that arises is whether such an emphatic reporting plays a part in the rise of extremist parties, and whether there is a causal or deterministic relationship between the advent of a party in the media and their success in the polls; a recurrent issue in the recent surge of the European far-right. Indeed, previous research notes that the media coverage given to small or non-parliamentary parties – especially in the case of European far-right parties – can contribute decisively to the increase in the number of followers and voters. For instance, Esser et al. (2016: 369) identify three patterns commonly used by European press in the coverage of the far-right:

1. In the first pattern (Belgium, The Netherlands), media give low-intensity coverage and scarce visibility when the voting relevance of these parties and their position in the polls are both low. This is also the case when other parties set a cordon sanitaire to separate them from power. Nevertheless, media attention shifts when these situations change.
2. In the second pattern (Sweden, Switzerland), negative coverage is not entirely objectionable for the sake of information; it is shown that, even in the case of adverse reporting, this pattern ultimately leads to an increase in votes for these parties.
3. In the pattern of treatment for populisms (Germany, Portugal), there is a critical coverage that stresses their threat to democracy.

These authors point out that the rise in media coverage of the Sweden Democrats or the Swiss People's Party, despite being negative (second pattern), resulted in more electoral success for the party: «The positive effect of increased visibility appeared to have trumped the negative effect of the tone of the coverage».

Murphy/Devine (2018) analyse the coverage given to the British UKIP (United Kingdom Independence Party) from January 2014 to April 2017. They conclude that a causal relation can be established "in a substantially non-trivial fashion") between the media attention afforded to far-right parties and the public support they gain; to the extent that a decline in media attention does not tie in a downturn in public support to previous levels.

> The extraordinary media coverage that has been given to UKIP cannot be explained or defended on grounds of public opinion dynamics as measured by polls. We find that media coverage has no reliable relationship to public opinion polls in the one month, two months or three months before a particular month of coverage. Indeed, we find that coverage may have independently and uniquely driven some of the very public support that media regulators would later point to as their justification for the extraordinary coverage given to UKIP (Murphy/Devine 2018: 14).

In any case, we may wonder whether patterns 2 and 3 identified by Esser et al. (2016) can be of use to explain the rise in the coverage of Vox since 7 October. According to these, this coverage would soar, either to underscore their negative elements or to adopt a critical stance and defend democracy. To answer this question, it is necessary to examine the different strategic levels of the framing of texts.

4.2 Intentionality and structure: A strongly opinionated press

As said above, our focus is the informative framing of Vox through enunciative strategies. However, we note that a fairly consistent correlation between intentional and structural strategies emerges from the analysis of the texts, which is primarily due to the conventions of the press. Thus, the *intentional strategy* of representative predominance mainly tallies with the *structural strategy* of information genres (news, reportages, chronicles), while the strategy of expressive predominance correlates more frequently with opinion genres (columns and editorials).

The basic distribution of the texts is based on this approach, whether they are news, on the one hand, or opinion columns and editorials, on

Intentional strategy	Representative illocutionary force	Expressive illocutionary force
Structural strategy	News Reportage Chronicle	Opinion column Editorial

Fig. 3. Stable association between the two basic framing strategies: intentionality (illocutionary force) and text packaging (superstructure)

the other. Thus, they are conventionally separated according to genre, representative illocutionary force and expressive/evaluative illocutionary force. However, it should be noted that this allocation is particularly complex in some texts with a news format but clearly affiliated to the so-called *infopinión* (Tranche 2019: 112):

> The overabundance of opinion, the premise that no important or falsely shocking news can spare being rendered contentious – that is, reasoned and countered in dual and antagonistic terms – both weakens and contaminates the preconceived notion of truthful information (...) It is the realm of what we might call *infopinión*. To treat as controversial some facts that, by their very nature, should be incontrovertible and general principles of an apodictic kind, indicates the extent to which reality is subdued to a varying relativism [original in Spanish].

The group of editorials (clearly identifiable as the *voice* of the newspaper) and columns is also open to debate, since journalistic practice dictates that the opinions of columnists do not need to coincide with the editorial line of the newspaper. In this regard, the corpus includes a text by David Lema in *El Mundo* (09.11.2018) entitled: *La dulce cultura del desacuerdo* ['The gentle culture of disagreement'], in which he justifies publication of critical and pro-Vox columns in this newspaper. However, readers are thought to perceive opinions as part of the daily's editorial line and, therefore, this association was maintained. The global results are shown below:

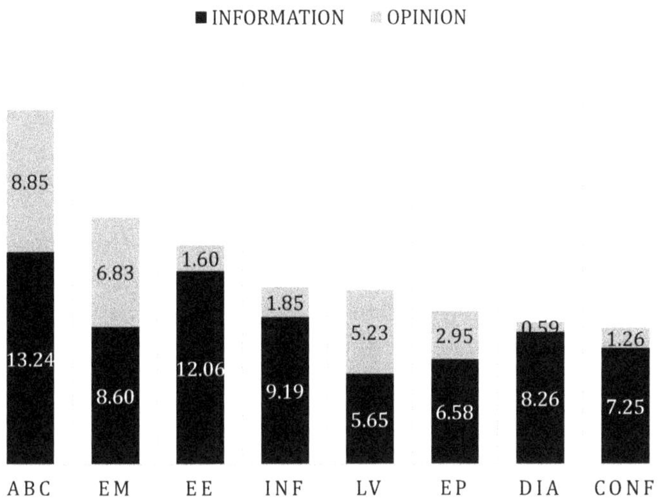

Fig. 4. Percentages of distribution of texts with predominance of informative (news) or evaluative illocutionary force (columns and editorials)

As can be seen, it is columnists and editorialists of *ABC*, *El Mundo* and *La Vanguardia* who speak more profusely of the fair-right during the sample period, yet a comparative analysis of each newspaper shows that they use different frames in such discourse.

4.3 Naming and suggesting: Inferential density

As mentioned, the criterion for corpus gathering is any reference to Vox in the newspaper texts. In a first stage of data processing, three ways of referring are distinguished, which involve different degrees of thematisation (thematic strategy):

1. Cases in which Vox is simply named (for instance, the often-cited triad "PP, Cs and Vox"; or nominalisations such as "the emergence of Vox"). This reference is often coupled with an evaluative neutrality, but it naturalises this ultra-right party as one more faction in the spectrum of the right. Thus, their textual function is not entirely neutral.

2. Cases where the text includes only one or two contextual predications ("Vox has burst into the voting scene among a very young right-wing voter who has hitherto nurtured a sceptical abstention", ABC 26.11.2018 [original in Spanish]), at times appearing in some paragraph as sub-topic.
3. Cases of specific thematisation of the party.

We use the sentiment analysis software *Lingmotif* (Moreno & Pérez 2018) in order to refine the analysis of expressiveness, which allows us to examine lexical uses related to expressive illocutivity on the basis of two measures: on the one hand, the sentiment intensity of the corpus (TSI Average) and, on the other, the predominance of negative or positive sentiment (TSS Average). In this way, the analysis attends to the *lexical strategy* by studying the way propositional speech acts control denotation and connotation.

As shown in Fig. 5, our corpus is markedly evaluative (a score of 68 for predominantly informative texts and of 79 for opinion texts). This fact would initially seem contradictory for a news corpus, whose standards aim at referential neutrality. Regarding the differences among the eight newspapers, we also note that:

- In informative texts, all newspapers show a significant sentiment intensity with two polarities embodied by *El Español* (73) and *La Vanguardia* (65); expressiveness is slightly negative in all newspapers, without considerable differences among them.
- In opinion texts, the tool assigns a maximum of sentiment intensity to the columns and editorials in *Infolibre* (91) and *ABC* (88).

These results, which the software retrieves via the literal parsing of texts, led to a review of the lexis used by news writers to convey

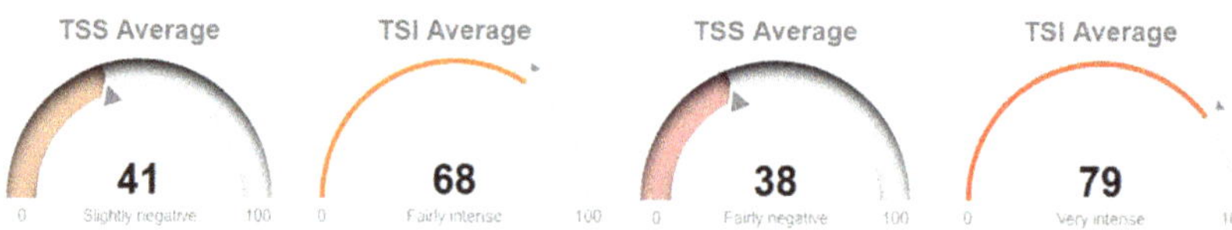

Fig. 5. Outcome of the Lingmotif global corpus analysis, dividing informative texts (left) and opinion texts (right)

negative expressiveness, which had already been revealed in the reading of the 1186 texts. The most relevant feature of this analysis was the relatively high frequency of *inference-activating speech acts* in these texts, that is those acts that convey some kind of meaning over the propositional speech act: connotations, presuppositions, implicatures and implicit meanings that are projected onto the texts, thereby shaping the *model reader* for each newspaper and, hence, providing a view of the far-right party. It was therefore essential to complement *Lingmotif*'s literal analysis with additional observations.

We thus found that much of the evaluation in the texts was conveyed implicitly, not literally. In the first place, we observed how presuppositional triggers were used to insert political judgements; existential presuppositions prompted by definite articles allow for the introduction of implicit meanings in the texts:

(3) «Poco más que la foto del "contamos contigo" ofreció el domingo presidencial, ni una palabra sobre *el golpe* en Cataluña o *el aluvión de inmigrantes* irregulares llegados este fin de semana» (ABC, 08/10/2018).
[ENG. "The presidential Sunday offered little but the "we count on you" photo, not a single word on *the coup* in Catalonia or *the flood of illegal immigrants* who arrived this weekend"]

(4) «Fundamentalmente, Abascal se propone liberar a los ciudadanos descontentos de la vergüenza y de toda responsabilidad. No son culpables de nada, son víctimas. Y su defensa consiste en pasar al ataque contra los partidos traidores y los trabajadores extranjeros. Es ahí donde el líder de Vox coloca toda *la bazofia xenófoba*» (EM, 25/11/2018, F. Pascual).
[ENG. "Ultimately, Abascal seeks to free discontented citizens from shame and from all liability. They are not guilty at all, they are victims. And their defence entails to attack disloyal parties and foreign workers. This is where Vox leader places all *xenophobic hogwash*"]

Implicit political evaluations are also inserted by means of factive verbs and change of state verbs:

(5) «El expresidente también *reconoció* que la fuerza electoral que los últimos sondeos le otorgan a Vox "ha salido del propio PP"» (INF 07/10/2018).
[ENG. "The former president also admitted that the electoral power that the latest polls grant to Vox 'has emanated from the PP' "]

(6) «Sánchez *volvió a* generar ayer confusión e incertidumbre en España» (ABC 20/11/2018).
[ENG. "Sánchez *once again* caused confusion and uncertainty in Spain yesterday"]

(7) «El Gobierno *celebra que* su estrategia rompe la unidad independentista» (LV 10/10/2018).
[ENG. "The Government *is pleased* that their strategy is breaking the separatist unity"]

(8) «Casado *admite* por primera vez que Vox puede hacer daño al PP» (EE, 20/11/2018).
[ENG. "Casado *recognises* for the first time that Vox may harm the PP"]

In addition to presuppositional triggers, we also registered two basic lexical uses that enabled the embedding of (especially negative) inferences through anomalous implicatures of manner and quality:

- Along with the use of explicit insults (of reiterated appeal in *ABC*, *EM* and *EE*), news reporters use some lexis that is inherent to semantic fields related to the offensive, catastrophic, etc., thus activating inferences of contempt or aggression for being an unsuitable vocabulary for the formal register of newspapers:

(9) «El vergonzoso cambio de postura de la Abogacía que *mangonea* el Ministerio de Justicia en la causa del Supremo contra el golpe en Cataluña supera todo lo visto hasta ahora» (ABC, 05/11/18, I. San Sebastián).
[ENG. "The disgraceful change of position of the State's Attorney, who *bully* the Ministry of Justice on the case of the Supreme Court against the coup d'état in Catalonia, exceeds all we have seen so far"]

(10) «. . .los votantes del PP, defraudados por la *blandenguería* de Rajoy y por la *dictadura del perfil plano* dictada al partido por el *malhadado* marido de Celia Villalobos, por Arriola» (ABC, 07/11/18, A. Burgos).
[ENG. ". . .PP voters, disappointed by Rajoy's *weakness* and by the *low-key tyranny* dictated by Celia Villalobos's *ill-fated* husband, by Arriola"]

- Lexis of non-negative semantic fields that activate negative inferences due to their figurative use; we include here tropical stylistic resources, such as irony, sarcasm, hyperbole and metonymy, which are often used to convey argumentative fallacies:

(11) «Yo, naturalmente, después de leer el correspondiente *artículo menstrual* de alguna de *las chicas de El País* la mandaría a fregar; pero me aguanto. Hay que aguantarse. Virilmente» (EM, 02/12/2018, A. Espada).
[ENG. "Of course, after reading the corresponding *menstrual article* of one of *the girls* from *El País*, I would send her to scrub; but I hold back. I have to hold back, like a man"]

(12) «Ahora, sin embargo, muchos miran *hacia el extremo del escenario* y sienten la tentación del *voto duro, cimarrón, pedregoso, arriscado*, un voto *visceral* al margen de un liberalismo que consideran timorato, plegado a la hegemonía de un régimen casi hereditario» (ABC, 29/11/2018, I. Camacho). [ENG. "Now, however, many people are looking *towards the edge of the stage* and feel tempted by the *hard, wild, rocky, rough vote*, a *hot-blooded* vote away from what they consider timorous liberalism, subdued to the hegemony of a quasi-hereditary regime"]

(13) «Bonilla sigue sin ver *la viga en el ojo propio. Saca la cruz y la ristra de ajos ante la posible llegada del vampiro rojo*, pero se niega a repudiar a Vox. A estas alturas de la campaña, los miembros de este partido xenófobo ya no les parecen *hijos de* la extrema derecha» (EP, 29/11/2018, A. Soler). [ENG. "Bonilla can't still see *the rafter in his own eye. He takes out the crucifix and the string of garlic against the arrival of the red vampire*, but he refuses to repudiate Vox. At this point in the campaign, the members of this xenophobic party are no longer *the offspring* of the far-right"]

To carry out this analysis, we used QDA Miner (Provalis) and manually tagged all inferences. For this purpose, we reduced the corpus to 50 % (593 texts) and created a code logbook in order to annotate presuppositions, anomalous (positive and negative) implicatures, and specific euphemisms of this "neo-language", also distinguishing journalistic from referred discourse.

The result of this tagging gave rise to the concept of *inferential density* (Gallardo 2019b), which refers to the number of inferences in a text per 1000 words. The computation excludes those words that pertain to discourse in direct speech. From the overall analysis of the 593 texts, we highlight two aspects:

- A very disparate use of inference depending on the illocutivity of text, with mean scores of 5.4 inferences in informative texts, as compared to 22.3 in opinion ones.
- The particular overuse of this type of negative inferences in the opinion texts in *ABC*, *El Español* and *El Mundo*, specifically when discourse is aimed at the construction of "them".

This analysis provides more accurate information than *Lingmotif*'s literal parsing to describe the expressiveness of texts, and relates lexical and intentional methods to an *affiliative strategy*, which aims to show the political position of the writer, given that a substantial number of the inferences identified in the text contribute to determining ideological standpoints. Thus, to the extent that newspapers are political agents (Borrat 1989) and, hence, subjects of enunciation, we can reasonably conclude that opinion genres are the most suitable for the expression of newspapers' affiliation or – using the common concept in journalistic theory – their *political parallelism* (Hallin/Mancini 2004). Here the analysis is not limited to the predominant expressiveness of texts (*intentional strategy*) but it also examines their political position with respect to Vox. Texts are coded according to whether they convey a critical view of Vox (framing 2 and 3), a neutral vision that helps to naturalise their presence in the political landscape, or a positive outlook:

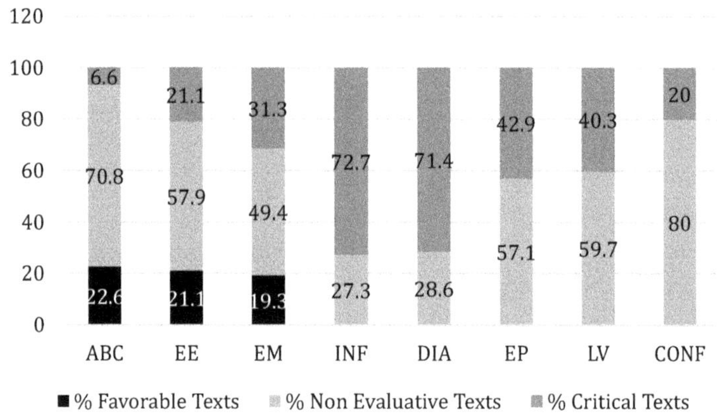

Fig. 6. Percentage of opinion texts per newspaper devoted to an affiliative framing with respect to Vox. Neutral texts can implicitly mediate their affiliation

All newspapers show negative texts and critical/analytical texts regarding Vox that conform to coverage patterns 2 and 3 pointed out by Esser at al., although with some variations. In some texts, the critique of *ABC*, *El Mundo* and *El Español* does not address Vox's ideology but their threat to the electoral weight of the PP, the party with which these dailies show greater political affiliation.

Non-evaluative, apparently neutral, texts draw attention to Vox without expressly judging their proposals, which enables to implicitly communicate affiliation, either positive or negative (for instance, *eldiario.es* inserts the presupposition that Vox is an ultra-right party in virtually all their texts). These references, with their varying degree of thematisation, play a part in naturalising their political importance. Notably, *ABC*, *El Mundo* and *El Español* describe Vox as a member of "the three rights" (quoting Aznar's appreciation on the way Rajoy's government had divided the electorate of the PP), or of "the constitutionalist parties":

(14) «Creo que la situación es tan grave y complicada que los líderes constitucionalistas, PP, Ciudadanos y Vox tendrán que guardar sus diferencias y plantearse una candidatura común de la característica que sean capaces de negociar, pero no pueden arriesgar el bien común por su propio bien» (EE, 26/10/2018, M. L. Simón).
[ENG. "I think that the situation is so serious and complicated that the constitutionalist leaders, PP, Ciudadanos and Vox will have to set aside their differences and consider a joint candidature of the kind they may be able to agree on, but they can't risk our welfare for their own good"]

However, along with these positions, data show in opinion texts a fourth framing option that aligns with Vox's stance both explicitly and implicitly. The most implicit form opts for a negative expressiveness in the construction of "them" (the independentists, Sánchez's government, PSOE, Podemos, etc.):

(15) «El socialismo en general y su desarrollo natural, el comunismo, se basan en la negación del derecho de propiedad y en el afán de quitársela a los que la tienen para administrarla según les parezca. Como a la gente no suele gustarle que le quiten lo que le ha costado mucho conseguir y se resiste, hay que matarla. (...) Así que lo que ha hecho Sánchez es robar, como sus compañeros de partido Negrín, Prieto y otros criminales de guerra, que, tras provocarla, asaltaron las propiedades particulares y el patrimonio del Estado desde el primer día» (EM, 24/09/2018, F. Jiménez).
[ENG. "Socialism in general and its natural development, Communism, are based on the denial of the right to property and on the zeal to take it away from their owners in order to govern it as they please. Since people do not usually like to be deprived of that which they struggled to achieve and they resist, they have to be killed. (...) Thus, what Sánchez did is steal, like his fellow party members Negrín, Prieto and other war criminals, who, after causing the war, assaulted private properties and the state heritage from day one"]

(16) «El Gobierno se atrinchera contra el acto de Alsasua y se alinea con los radicales. Miembros del Ejecutivo cuestionan la convocatoria y acusan a

Rivera, Casado y Abascal de estar "trabajando en generar imagen de tensión"» (ABC, 06/11/2018, V. Ruíz).
[ENG. "The Government is entrenched in opposing the Alsasua action and aligns itself with the radicals. Some members of the Government raise objections to the protest and accuse Rivera, Casado and Abascal of 'causing a climate of tension' "]

The pro-Vox explicit manner relies on positive expressiveness to speak about this far-right party. These newspapers devote various texts to ascertain that Vox is not an ultra-right party, to victimise them when their provocations spark reactions, or to praise their proposals. This explicitly positive opinion of the far-right party corresponds to texts in *ABC* (22.6 % of their opinion texts), *El Mundo* (19.3 %) and *El Español* (21.1 %).

(17) «Además de una profunda injusticia, empeñarse en hacer un "cordón sanitario", de momento mediático, a Vox, como partido "inconstitucional" o "anticonstitucional" me parece un gravísimo error. (. . .) Vox está ahí porque el Gobierno del PP traicionó a España antes, durante y después del golpe en Cataluña. Con un 155 de verdad, hoy los golpistas no estarían en el poder» (EM, 07/11/2018, F. Jiménez).
[ENG. "Besides a profound injustice, to insist on building a 'cordon sanitaire' around Vox, so far only in the media, as an 'unconstitutional' or 'anti-constitutional' party, is a very serious error. (. . .) Vox is here because the Government of the PP betrayed Spain during and after the coup d'état in Catalonia. With a genuine application of art. 155, the perpetrators would not be in power today."]

Example 18 is abundant in what we have called 'bleaching euphemism':

(18) «Porque me pregunto si pedir una inmigración regulada ¿es racismo?; si mostrar oposición a la Ley de Memoria Histórica del PSOE ¿es ser extremista?; si defender la unidad de España ¿es ser facha?; si pedir la ilegalización de los partidos secesionistas ¿es ser antiespañol?; si criticar el monumental gasto que supone mantener las autonomías ¿es ser inconstitucional?; si defender a nuestros policías y miembros de la Guardia Civil ¿es ser franquista?; si querer mantener nuestras tradiciones ¿es ser retrogrado?; si apoyar los contratos laborales que premien el esfuerzo y el mérito ¿es ir contra los trabajadores?; si facilitar la fiscalidad de los emprendedores y de la clase media ¿es no progresar?; y por último, si pedir el respeto a la propiedad privada ¿es ser capitalista?. Para mí y para muchos todas estas preguntas que forman parte del contenido del discurso tienen la misma respuesta «No». Y saludemos a este nuevo partido que viene a ocupar el espacio político de una verdadera derecha.» (ABC, 11/10/2018, Javier Pérez Quesada).

[ENG. "Because I wonder if it is racist to ask for controlled immigration; if it is extremist to oppose PSOE's Historical Memory Act; if it is fascist to defend the unity of Spain; if it is anti-Spanish to demand the illegalisation of secessionist parties; if it is unconstitutional to criticise the massive cost of maintaining autonomous regions; if it is francoist to defend our police forces and our Guardia Civil; if it is backward-looking to wish to uphold our traditions; if it is against workers to give support to labour contracts that reward effort and merit; if it is not progress to make taxation easier for entrepreneurs and the middle class; and last, if it is capitalist to demand respect for private property. For me and for many others, all these questions that are part of the content of their discourse have the same answer: 'No'. Let us salute this new party that comes to regain the political space of a genuine right"]

(19) «Vox –ése es mi vaticinio– va a conseguir muchos más votos de los que las encuestas, los politólogos y el *wishful thinking* de sus casi correligionarios, mal que les pese, les auguran. Su arreón en las elecciones andaluzas y, sobre todo, en las del mes de mayo va a ser arrollador. Ya iba siendo hora» (EM, 25/11/2018, F. Sánchez).
[ENG. "Vox – this is my prediction – will obtain many more votes than those estimated by the polls, political experts, and the wishful thinking of their quasi co-religionaries, whether they like it or not. Their rise in the Andalusian elections and, especially, the ones in May will be overwhelming. It was about time"]

These are insights that exhibit typical features of fascist discourse, such as the rhetoric, solemnity, "idiomatic grandiloquence" or pseudo-lyrism (Pérez Bowie 1988):

(20) «Vistalegre ha sido el rugido enorme del humillado león de España, presto a sacar sus zarpas para luchar por el país que ama. Compatriotas que jamás volverán a sobornar su conciencia por la supuesta utilidad de otorgar su voto a aquellos que no hablaban claro en cuestiones esenciales, y que, a la postre, ha evidenciado su inutilidad. ¿Extrema derecha? No. Extrema necesidad» (ABC, 11/10/2018, J. Rodríguez).
[ENG. "Vistalegre has been the mighty roar of the humiliated lion of Spain, ready to pull out their claws to fight for the country they love. Compatriots that will never again suborn their conscience for the alleged convenience of giving their vote to those who did not speak clearly on essential issues, which, after all, has evidenced its futility. Extreme right? No. Extreme necessity"]

5 Conclusions

The arrival of the far-right party Vox to the Andalusian Parliament after the vote on 2 December was preceded by unprecedented media attention after the rally held at Vistalegre on 7 October. The analysis of the different framing strategies in the coverage of the leading newspapers corroborates, firstly, that this party had an excessive media coverage for a party without institutional presence; this coverage was manifest in both informative and opinion texts.

While the lexical parsing by means of the sentiment analysis software *Lingmotif* reveals a prevalence of negative appraisal, the close reading of the 1186 texts also highlights the need to scrutinise the use of evaluative inferences. In this respect, our findings point to a remarkably higher inferential density in opinion texts as compared to informative texts. Thus, a large part of negative political evaluations is conveyed through presuppositions and, mostly, anomalous implicatures of manner (changes of register, colloquialisms and insults) and quality (irony, hyperbole, sarcasm and argumentative fallacies).

As regards the political parallelism of the newspapers, which correlates with the affiliative strategy of framing, the analysis shows that all dailies – with no exception – contain opinion and informative texts that conform to patterns 2 and 3 of far-right coverage identified by Esser et al. (2016). That is to say, a negative coverage and one that warns of the risks of these political options for democracy. However, what is particularly noteworthy in the corpus is the presence in *ABC*, *El Español* and *El Mundo* of (especially opinion) texts that do not fit into any of the three patterns. Instead, they publish texts that praise and defend Vox. These texts adopt a discourse that Vox itself may undertake, using a marked rhetoric in the construction of "them" that occasionally discloses features of hate speech, in spite of their status of mainstream media.

References

Borrat, Héctor. 1989. *El periódico, actor político.* Barcelona: Gustavo Gili.

Charaudeau, Patrick. 2008. Pathos et discours politique. In Rinn, M. (coord.) *Émotions et discours. L'usage des passions dans la langue.* Rennes: Presses Universitaires de Rennes, 49–58.

Charaudeau, Patrick. 2009. Réflexions pour l'analyse du discourse populiste. In *Les discours politiques en Amérique latine: filiations, polyphonies, théâtralités.* Colloque international, Université Paris-Est, 12–14 February 2009.

Charron, Jean Marie. 2000. *La nature politique du journalisme politique.* Québec: Université Laval.

De Santiago Guervós, Javier. 2016–2017. Análisis del discurso populista en la España actual. *Analecta Malacitana* 39, 115–141.

Enguix Oliver, Salvador. 2015. *Periodismo político: fundamentos, práctica, perspectivas.* Bellaterra/Barcelona/Castelló/València: UAB, UJI, UPF, UV.

Enguix Oliver. Salvador 2017. Impacto político e informativo de las redes sociales: esferas de actuación y comparación con los medios. *Anàlisi. Quaderns de Comunicació i Cultura,* 56: 71–85.

Entman, Robert M. 1991. Framing US coverage of international news: contrast in narratives of the KAL and Iran air incidents. *Journal of Communication* 41, 6–27.

Esser, Frank/Stępińska, Agnieszka/Hopmann, David Nicolas. 2016. Populism and the Media. Cross-National Findings and Perspectives. In Aalberg, T. *et al.* (eds.) *Populist Political Communication in Europe.* New York: Routledge, 365–380.

Gallardo Paúls, Beatriz. 2014. *Usos políticos del lenguaje.* Barcelona: Anthropos/Siglo XXI.

Gallardo Paúls, Beatriz. 2018a. *Tiempos de hipérbole. Inestabilidad e interferencias en el discurso político.* València: Tirant Lo Blanch.

Gallardo Paúls, Beatriz. 2018b. Discurso político y desplazamientos discursivos. In Llamas, C. (ed.) *El análisis del discurso político: géneros y metodologías.* Pamplona: EUNSA, 13–41.

Gallardo Paúls, Beatriz. 2019a. Texto y comunicación: el encuadre y la eficacia textual. In Loureda, Ó./Schrott, A. (eds.) *Manual de lingüística del texto.* Berlin: De Gruyter, in press.

Gallardo Paúls, Beatriz. 2019b. El recurso a la inferencia en la cobertura mediática de la ultraderecha. *Seminar: ¿El dinosaurio todavía estaba allí o acababa de llegar? El nuevo espacio político: discursos, medios e imágenes,* Universidad Complutense de Madrid, May 2019.

Gallardo Paúls, Beatriz/Enguix Oliver, S. 2015. Opciones discursivas en la cobertura electoral: los temas de la campaña europea de 2014. In Hernández, E./López, M. I. (eds.) *Sodalicia Dona. Homenaje a Ricardo Escavy Zamora*. Universidad de Murcia, 231–252.

Hallin, Daniel C./Mancini, Paolo. 2004. *Comparing Media Systems: Three Models of Media and Politics*. Cambridge: Cambridge University Press.

Hochschild, Arlie R. 2016. *Extraños en su propia tierra*. Madrid: Capitán Swing, 2018. Transl. Amelia Pérez de Villar.

Krämer, Benjamin. 2017. Populist online practices: the function of the Internet in right-wing populism. *Information, Communication & Society* 20(9), 1293–1309.

Mazzoleni, Gianpietro. 2008. Populism and the Media. In Albertazzi, D./McDonnell, D. (eds.) *Twenty-First Century Populism: The Spectre of Western European Democracy.* Basingstoke/New York: Palgrave Macmillan, 49–64.

McNair, Brian. 2000. *Journalism and Democracy. Evaluation of Political Public Sphere.* New York: Routledge.

Moreno-Ortiz, Antonio/Pérez-Hernández, Chantal. 2018. Lingmotif-lex: A Wide-coverage, State-of-the-art Lexicon for Sentiment Analysis. *Proceedings of the Eleventh International Conference on Language Resources and Evaluation (LREC-2018),* 2653–2659.

Murphy, J./Devine, Daniel. 2018. Does media coverage drive public support for UKIP or does public support for UKIP drive media coverage? *British Journal of Political Science,* 50(3), 1–18.

Pérez-Bowie, José Antonio. 1988. Retoricismo y estereotipación, rasgos definidores de un discurso ideologizado. El discurso de la derecha durante la Guerra civil. In Aróstegui, J. (ed.) *Historia y Memoria de la Guerra Civil. Encuentro en Castilla y León (Septiembre, 1986).* Valladolid: Junta de Castilla y León, Vol. I, 353–373.

Semetko, Holli A./Valkenburg, Patti M. 2000. Framing European politics: A content analysis of press and television news. *Journal of Communication* 50(2), 93–109.

Tranche, Rafael R. 2019. *La máscara sobre la realidad. La información en la era digital.* Madrid: Alianza.

Van Dijk, Teun A. 1998. *Ideology: A Multidisciplinary Approach.* London: Sage.

Wirth, Werner et al. 2016. The appeal of populist ideas, strategies and styles: A theoretical model and research design for analyzing populist political communication. *Zurich: NCCR Working Paper*, 88.

Ana Belén Cabrejas-Peñuelas and Rosana Dolón

Evaluation in Theresa May's political discourse: A study of the PM's seminal Brexit speeches

1 Introduction

That language is rife with linguistic mechanisms to express the speaker's or writer's personal attitudes and assessments has been demonstrated by many researchers (Hunston/Thompson 2000, Martin/White 2005, Simon-Vandenbergen 2008, Cabrejas-Peñuelas/Díez-Prados 2014, Díez-Prados/Cabrejas-Peñuelas 2018). Several labels have been used to refer to language expressing opinion, including *evidentiality* (Chafe 1986), *hedging* (Hyland 1996), *evaluation* (Thompson/Hunston 2000), *appraisal* (Martin/White 2005) and *stance* (Conrad/Biber 2000). The difference between them lies in the perspective taken and methodology used. Despite the differences, all of them focus on the meaning of the speaker's assessments, the linguistic realizations of stance and the functions of evaluation in expressing the speaker's opinion, in building and maintaining relations between speaker/writer and listener/reader and in organizing discourse (Thompson/Hunston 2000: 6).

Political discourse in general, and political speeches in particular, is a type of persuasive discourse that serves politicians to show their attitudes when evaluating, opposing and supporting an idea or event. They do so by presenting their personal, but also that of the party, point of view on certain issues and, thus, distinguishing themselves from other opinions. This is why there is a good reason to express stance, i.e. criticizing contrary opinions and praising one's own. There are indeed texts that show faceless stance – defined as "relative absence of all affective and evidential stance features" (Biber/Finegan 1989: 108) –; however, in cases in which politicians need to convince and appeal to the public, faceless stance seems unlikely to happen.

Ample research has been done on the evaluative uses of academic writing (Jiang 2017), political debates (Simon-Vandenbergen 2008, Cabrejas-Peñuelas/Díez-Prados 2014, Díez-Prados/Cabrejas-Peñuelas 2018), product reviews (Fuoli 2012) and public discourse (Paterson et al. 2015). It is our purpose in the present study to test Hunston's (2000) evaluation of status in a political discourse type, which, to our knowledge, has not been studied before: political speeches. According to Finlayson/Martin (2008: 450) a political speech is "an argument of some kind; an attempt to provide others with reasons for thinking, feeling or acting in a particular way". While evaluation has been found to play an important role in persuasion in pre-election debates (Simon-Vandenbergen 2008, Cabrejas-Peñuelas/Díez-Prados 2014, Díez-Prados/Cabrejas-Peñuelas 2018), it is less clear how evaluation and persuasion are related in political speeches, such as Theresa May's Brexit speeches. In these, the PM does not present a distinct profile for herself to win votes, while painting the opposing candidate in a negative light. Instead, she attempts to convince the overall public of the kind of deal she is seeking in the EU-UK Brexit negotiations, while at the same time she tries to persuade people that she is a competent leader in the challenging times ahead. We analyse three of May's seminal Brexit speeches: The Lancaster House speech, the Florence speech and the London Mansion House speech. These are of interest because they attracted much attention worldwide and sparked a heated debate in the UK and the EU. In order to gain insight into May's political speeches, we attempt to answer the following research questions:

1. RQ1. Are there any similarities and differences between PM May's political speeches in terms of the expression of evaluation of status (i.e. degree of alignment between a proposition and the world, Hunston 2008: 65)?
2. RQ2. Does PM May's evaluative language contribute to the persuasive power of her political speeches? If so, to what extent?

Section 2 deals with evaluation as used in political discourse, while section 3 offers some background information of the three speeches Theresa May gave and of their importance for the Brexit negotiations.

Section 4 introduces the framework we are going to use to analyse evaluation. Section 5 discusses the methodology employed and the methodological decisions made. Section 6 offers the results of the analysis of evaluation and of the role of evaluation for persuasion in political speeches. Finally, section 7 provides the conclusions to the present study.

2 Evaluation in political discourse

A wealth of literature (Simon-Vandenbergen 1996, 1997, 2008; Ponton 2011, 2020; Cabrejas-Peñuelas/Díez-Prados 2014; Aloy Mayo/Taboada 2017; Díez-Prados/Cabrejas-Peñuelas 2018) addressing the language of evaluation in political discourse has concluded that politicians attempt to create a distinct profile for themselves and evaluate themselves and their opponents either positively or negatively. Also, they evaluate issues, such as the healthcare system, unemployment benefits and social benefits to show how they would handle them differently. The final aim is to convince the electorate to vote for them. In more concrete terms, politicians use explicit realizations of attitude that are inscribed in the text "through the use of attitudinal lexis" (Martin/White 2005: 61). These include three semantic categories in Martin/White's (2005) Appraisal framework: affect, to evaluate people's emotions (e.g. *happy*, *unhappy*); judgement, to praise a person's capacity and propriety (e.g. *capable*, *fair*) and to criticize a person's incapacity and impropriety (e.g. *incapable*, *unfair*); and appreciation, to evaluate issues positively or negatively (e.g. *boring*, *harmonious*). Evaluation of people's emotions is not common in political debates (Cabrejas-Peñuelas/Díez-Prados 2014: 14), which instead show high rates of appreciation and judgement and these are "related to the topic and the content of the speeches" (Simon-Vandenbergen 2008: 58; Cabrejas-Peñuelas/Díez-Prados 2014: 171). Politicians also use positive judgement to stress their own positive qualities (i.e. their capacity, tenacity or propriety), while they address negative judgement to their opponents' qualities. In a similar vein, they use positive appreciation markers to refer to their own plans or ideological preferences and negative ones to those of their adversaries'. For example, in the 2011 Spanish debate, the Socialist politician Rubalcaba, who defended the public system, accuses his right-wing opponent, Rajoy, of defending private institutions (private health and education) instead of public ones. "It is obvious that *private* hospitals [Appreciation: Social Valuation: Negative] will keep on making money, but the *public* system [Appreciation: Social Valuation: Positive] will then go bankrupt" (Cabrejas-Peñuelas/Díez-Prados 2014: 180).

Politicians' use of evaluative markers further comprises lexical and grammatical expressions showing their attitudes towards the content of their propositions (Simon-Vandenbergen 1996, 1997; Simon-Vandenbergen et al. 2007). These include "evidentials, hedges, concession, negation and others" (2007: 34) that are used as a rhetorical strategy for persuading the audience by creating an image of cognitive certainty that is complementary with the picture of a non-committal, hesitating and evasive politician presented by Harris (1991). Expressions such as "it is our firm conclusion", "we had very little evidence", "we have no evidence at all", "I certainly think" (Simon-Vandenbergen 1996: 392–396) assert the truth of the politicians' statements by presenting them as deriving from rationality and factual evidence. This contributes to their image of "a knowledgeable person who 'knows what he or she is talking about' and who therefore deserves public trust and political power" (1996: 408). Politicians also use modality to build an image of a "confident politician" (Simon-Vandenbergen 1997: 344) through certainty adverbs (e.g. "doubtless", "obviously", "certainly", "of course" and their related formulations "as you know", "needless to say/it goes without saying", "as everyone knows") that have an obvious ideological potential and are, thus, a tool for manipulation. Indeed, "they construe [a] value position as universally shared, thus positioning any who might dissent from the viewpoint as at odds with what is common knowledge or common sense" (Simon-Vandenbergen et al. 2007: 40).

Evaluation has been further studied (Díez-Prados/Cabrejas-Peñuelas 2018) to find out how the world is depicted by politicians in their claims and, thus, the focus is on the source of evaluation (i.e. engagement in Martin/White's (2005) Appraisal model). The results indicate that politicians resort to World-reflecting statements – Fact/event, Interpretation and Assessment – rather than World-creating ones – Assumption, Hypothesis and Recommendation – in Hunston's (2000, 2008, 2011) model of evaluation. This is not but an attempt to be seen by the audience as "taking an objective and down-to-earth position, even when it is not backed up with evidence" (Díez-Prados/Cabrejas-Peñuelas 2018: 191). Individual politicians may also show different tendencies depending on their particular interests. Thus, they may adopt a more direct and practical stance to convince the audience (Facts/events and Recommendations) or a more interpretative and theoretical one (Hypotheses and Assessments) (2018: 191).

3 Theresa May's Brexit speeches

Following the UK's vote to leave the European Union on 24 June 2016 and the resignation of David Cameron, PM Theresa May is appointed the new Prime Minister. Although she had supported the Remain campaign, she takes on the challenge of respecting the results of the referendum and of convincing Tory Brexiters that she really wants to leave the EU. After months of speculation about her intentions, May delivers a speech to an audience of diplomats at London's Lancaster House on 17 January 2017, in which she sets out her plans for Britain and her key priorities in the upcoming Brexit negotiations. In the Lancaster House speech, May's speech rules out membership of the EU single market and custom union, although a customs agreement with the EU would be necessary. The speech further sets out the priority of controlling immigration after Brexit and the need for an implementation period to avoid an economic disaster after a cliff-edge. However, the PM warns that Britain would not accept a punitive deal on the part of the EU27. The Lancaster House speech triggers different reactions on the part of British politicians: while some Remain supporters claim to be prepared to vote down the deal in Parliament, Labour politicians criticize May's approach to Brexit, one that would end up harming British workers' rights and turn the UK into a tax haven. In contrast, Senior Conservatives praise her speech and European leaders give a cautious welcome to it (Dominiczak, January 2017, online).

On 29 March 2017 Theresa May signs the letter that officially confirms the UK's exit from the EU and is then handed out to European Council President Donald Tusk. After several rounds of EU-UK talks dealing with the Irish border and a financial settlement, it is clear that the divorce talks are not progressing quickly enough. Theresa May gives a speech in Florence on 22 September 2017 in an attempt to restart stalled talks and to try to convince the European Commission that progress had been made in the first phase of negotiations and, thus, they could move on to the second phase. PM May wants a transition period between leaving the EU and beginning the new trading relationship, offers to pay enough to honour the commitments made, suggests legal protections for EU citizens living in the UK, but gives no indication as to what kind of future relationship she wants (Henley, September 2017, online). Reactions to the PM's speech follow, which acknowledge May's willingness to move forward, but also indicate that the concrete implications of her words remain unexplained.

In November 2017, May and EU leaders agree a deal, but it was rejected in Parliament by an ample majority. Despite the rejection, the EU is unwilling to reopen negotiations, but consider delaying the UK's departure if a deal is not agreed before 29 March 2019. On 2 March 2018 Theresa May gives a speech at the London Mansion House, in which she concedes that after Brexit UK will have less access to the single market and EU legal decisions will continue to affect the UK, but she is still committed to having no hard border in Ireland (Asthana, March 2018, online). On 19 March 2018 UK and EU agree on Brexit transition terms, later modified by Boris Johnson, who negotiated some changes mostly related to the status of the Irish border after Brexit.

4 Theoretical framework: Hunston's (2000, 2008, 2011) evaluation of status

The present study looks into political speeches – three of the most important Brexit speeches of Theresa May's – to find out how evaluation is used in this type of persuasive discourse. We opt for Hunston's model in the belief that "evaluation of status may be the most important type of evaluation in an apparently 'objective' text" (2011: 29), where the reader/listener's role as interpreter of information is key.

Hunston's (2000, 2008, 2011) evaluation of status is based on the concepts of "status" and "value". She defines "status" as "the degree of alignment, or correspondence, between a proposition and the world", which is averred by the speaker/writer in every single act of communication (2008: 65). For example, a book may be assigned a status of fiction or non-fiction or a proposition, a status of hypothesis, possibility or fact. Thus, "all propositions in texts are evaluated in terms of how they are aligned with the world" (2011: 27) (e.g. as a fact, as an opinion, as fictional and so on). In other words, "evaluation of status is an obligatory element throughout all texts" (2011: 27).

While most propositions are unmodified, as in "Doctors have began analyzing the results of the experiment" and, thus, they "express 'what is', others are modified by adverbs, modal verbs or clauses governing that-clauses" (2011: 28). E.g. "There is no evidence that the drug can prevent or treat the virus", in which the fact that the drug can prevent or treat the virus is represented as 'what is unlikely to be'. This suggests that even apparently objective texts perform an act of evaluation. However, this may be even more so in political texts, since "indicating an attitude towards something is important in socially significant speech acts such as persuasion and argumentation" (2011: 3).

In order to analyse status, Hunston (2000) suggests some categories (see Fig. 1) for the classification of statements:

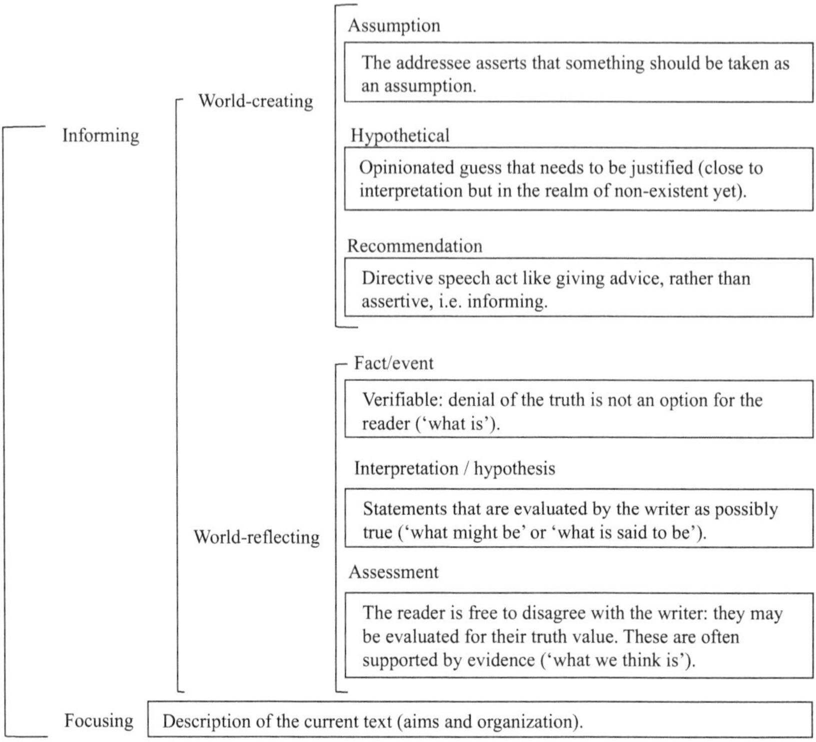

Fig. 1. Classification of statements (Hunston 2000: 187–189)

Hunston also distinguishes two different sources for any given averral[1] (see Fig. 2):

1 The distinction between *attribution* and *averral* goes back to Sinclair (1987). Averral refers to statements originating in the writer and attribution refers to statements originating in someone else.

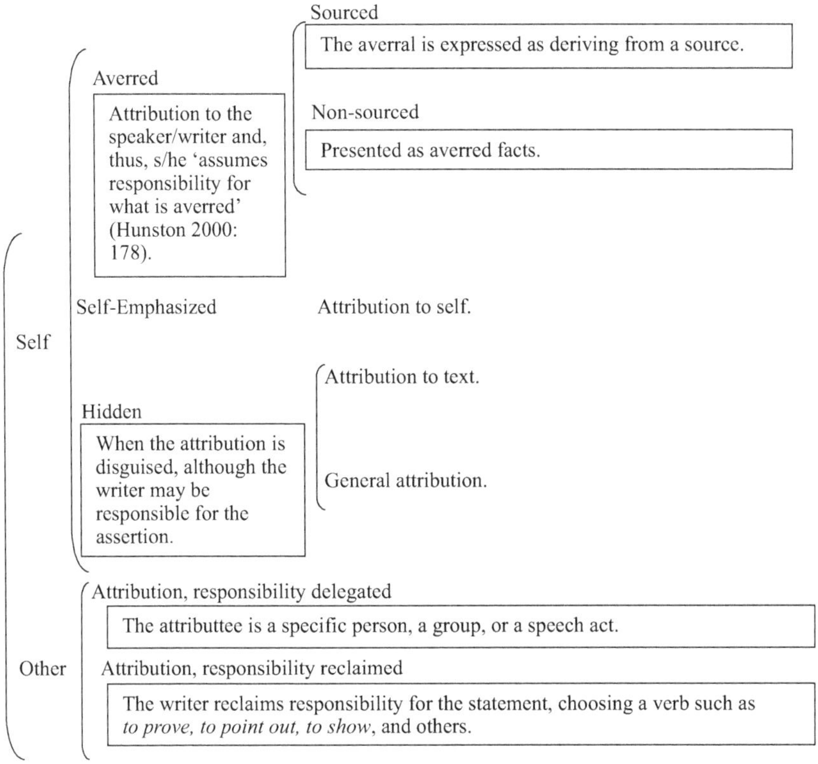

Fig. 2. Types of averral and attribution

This model has been used to categorize the propositions in Theresa May's Brexit speeches. It is our belief that status helps reveal the persuasive strategies used by the PM, with the time difference intervening in the expression of evaluation of status. Indeed, in her speeches she presents the world in an attempt to influence the audience's beliefs regarding the EU-UK present and future relations by using "the rhetorical devices of 'suggestion' against 'proof' [among others], and of maintaining an apparently objective stance" (Hunston 2011: 27). These are key in the persuasive strategy followed by Theresa May.

5 Methodology

For the present study, we selected three of the most important Brexit speeches delivered by the PM: the Lancaster House speech (17 January 2017, 6,444 words), the Florence speech (22 September 2017, 5,379 words) and the London Mansion House speech (2 March 2018, 6,709 words)[2]. There were several reasons behind the choice: (1) all three of them were regarded as seminal speeches, because they deal with key moments along the Brexit negotiations[3]; (2) there is a short time span between them; (3) they could be considered of equivalent size and, thus, comparable; and (4) they all deal with the new post-Brexit UK-EU relationship.

The study focuses on the verbal content of the data, based on transcriptions, as if they had been produced as written text. No indication of oral features or other multimodal features were included, since what was at stake here is the propositional content of the speeches and not their actual performance on the stage. All three speeches were uploaded in text format into a freeware program called UAM Corpus Tool developed by Mick O'Donnell (2012). This software is, in fact, a set of tools to annotate text and to run descriptive and inferential statistics. For the present study, we inserted Hunston's coding scheme in the program before carrying out the analysis. The unit of analysis for status was the statement, which would generally coincide with the orthographical sentence unit.

---

2 The transcripts of all three debates can be consulted on 'Theresa May's Brexit speech in full: Prime Minister outlines her objectives for 12 negotiations' *The Independent*, 17 January 2017, 'Theresa May Florence speech in full: Read UK Prime Minister's Brexit strategy' *The Independent*, 22 September 2017 and 'In full: Theresa May's speech on future UK-EU relations' *BBC*, 2 March 2018.

3 Cardiff University states about all three speeches: 'The speech given on the 2 March 2018 was seen as the third key speech by Mrs. May on Brexit. The other two were at Lancaster Gate, London in January 2017 and in Florence September 2017' (University Library Service, Cardiff University, *European Sources Online*).

The procedure was as follows: first, each of the speeches was divided into its constituent propositional statements. This process was carried out manually. Then, one researcher analysed all the statements individually. To guarantee interrater reliability, the second researcher subjected 30 % of the samples to a second analysis to find out the rate of interrater reliability. The rate of coincidence was 85.65 % for the segment of samples that was analysed by both. In the following section the results obtained are presented and discussed.

6 Results and discussion

This section has been divided into two parts. The first one offers a description and interpretation of the quantitative results derived from the contrastive study of the three seminal speeches delivered by PM Theresa May; in the second part we reflect on the persuasive power her use of statements entails. Both subsections will eventually lead to an answer for RQ1 and RQ2 respectively, which will be laid out in the Conclusions section.

6.1 Results from the contrastive analysis of evaluation

The three speeches delivered by May are related inasmuch as they represent reference points in a timeline that was to eventually lead to the so-called Brexit, and subsequently to a new EU-UK relationship. Tables 1–3 below summarize the corresponding comparative results and highlight the statistical significance of the findings, generated by UAM Corpus Tool.

As can be seen in Tab. 1, when comparing the first and the second speech, Theresa May's choice of both World-creating and World-reflecting types of statements proved statistically highly significant ($p<0.02$), although only in the categories of Assumption and Recommendation, Fact/event and Assessment. Along the eight-month time

	Speech 1		Speech 2		Statistics	
Feature	N	Percent	N	Percent	Chi Squ.	Signif.
INFORMING ST.	N = 271		N = 210			
W-creating	108	39.85	101	48.10	3.27	+
W-reflecting	163	60.15	109	51.90	3.27	+
W-CREATING TYPE	N = 108		N = 101			
Assumption	79	73.15	36	35.64	29.66	+++
Hypothetical	22	20.37	28	27.72	1.55	
Recommendation	7	6.48	37	36.63	28.55	+++
W-REFLECTING TYPE	N = 163		N = 109			
Fact/event	81	49.69	81	74.31	16.44	+++
Interpretation/hypothesis	19	11.66	9	8.26	0.82	
Assessment	63	38.65	19	17.43	13.97	+++

Tab. 1. Cross-tabulation speech 1 (January 2017) and speech 2 (September 2017)
+ Weak significance (90 %); ++ Medium significance (95 %); +++ High significance (98 %)

	Speech 1		Speech 3		Statistics	
Feature	N	Percent	N	Percent	Chi Squ.	Signif.
INFORMING ST. TYPE	N = 271		N = 294			
W-creating	108	39.85	144	48.98	4.75	++
W-reflecting	163	60.15	150	51.02	4.75	++
W-CREATING TYPE	N = 108		N = 144			
Assumption	79	73.15	58	40.28	26.88	+++
Hypothetical	22	20.37	45	31.25	3.74	+
Recommendation	7	6.48	41	28.47	19.36	+++
W-REFLECTING TYPE	N = 163		N = 150			
Fact/event	81	49.69	112	74.67	20.61	+++
Interpretation/hypothesis	19	11.66	27	18.00	2.51	
Assessment	63	38.65	11	7.33	42.44	+++
SOURCE	N = 271		N = 294			
Self	265	97.79	284	96.60	0.72	
Other	6	2.21	10	3.40	0.72	
SELF-TYPE	N = 265		N = 284			
Averred	223	84.15	250	88.03	1.73	
Emphasized	33	12.45	18	6.34	6.08	+++
Hidden	9	3.40	16	5.63	1.58	

Tab. 2. Cross-tabulation speech 1 (January 2017) and speech 3 (March 2018)
+ Weak significance (90 %); ++ Medium significance (95 %); +++ High significance (98 %)

	Speech 2		Speech 3		Statistics	
Feature	N	Percent	N	Percent	Chi Squ.	Sign.
INFORMING ST. TYPE	N = 210		N = 294			
W-creating	101	48.10	144	48.98	0.04	
W-reflecting	109	51.90	150	51.02	0.04	
W-REFLECTING TYPE	N = 109		N = 150			
Fact/event	81	74.31	112	74.67	0.00	
Interpretation/hypothesis	9	8.26	27	18.00	5.01	++
Assessment	19	17.43	11	7.33	6.29	+++
SOURCE	N = 211		N = 294			
Self	209	99.05	284	96.60	3.19	+
Other	2	0.95	10	3.40	3.19	+
SELF-TYPE	N = 209		N = 284			
Averred	175	83.73	250	88.03	1.87	
Emphasized	28	13.40	18	6.34	7.09	+++
Hidden	6	2.87	16	5.63	2.16	
AVERRED-TYPE	N = 175		N = 250			
Sourced	21	12.00	15	6.00	4.78	++
Non-sourced	154	88.00	235	94.00	4.78	++

Tab. 3. Cross-tabulation speech 2 (September 2017) and speech 3 (March 2018)
+ Weak significance (90 %); ++ Medium significance (95 %); +++ High significance (98 %)

difference that holds between the two, no variable affecting the source of statements, however, was found to be of any statistical significance.

When comparing the full time span, which covers thirteen months, between the first and the third speech, we find the same high statistical significance ($p<0.02$) as before, holding for her use of Assumptions and Recommendations (both World-creating types of statements) and Fact/event and Assessment (both World-reflecting types of statements) (see Tab. 2 below). The source of her statements, specifically the category of Emphasized self-type also proved statistically highly significant here ($p<0.02$), as opposed to the previous table.

The shorter time span of six months holding between speech 2 and 3 brings about important changes: World-creating statements no longer are of any statistical value, which is only restricted to the World-reflecting statement category of Assessment, with Interpretation/Hypothesis taking on a medium statistical significance (see Tab. 3). The emphasized expression of source is here as well of high statistical significance (p<0.02), and as to the averred type of statements, the subcategories of Sourced vs. Non-sourced also proved to be of medium significance (p<0.05).

A closer analysis of the results yielded by UAM corpus tool allows for more specific insights and interpretations of the statistical values (see Figures 3 and 4 below).

Along the eight-month time distance that separates speech 1 from speech 2, Theresa May does importantly restrict her uses of Assumptions (from 73 %to 36 %), favouring instead a much more frequent choice of Recommendations (from 7 % to 36 %). This statistically highly significant shift in her use of World-creating statements (p<0.02) means that she changes from making assumptions about the new EU-UK partnership to employing directive speech acts (suggestions, pieces of advice, recommendations) in an attempt to have her interactants take a course of action for what would mean a successful Brexit delivery according to her. See (1) and (2) below:

(1) The same rules and laws will apply on the day after Brexit as they did before (speech 1) [Informing: W-creating: Assumption].

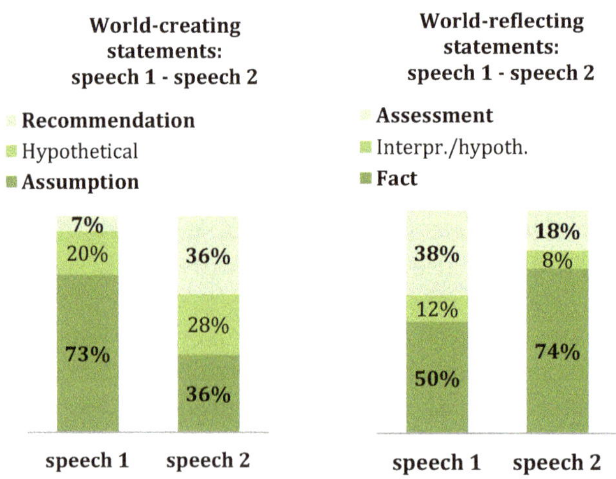

Figs. 3 and 4. Significant differences sp.1–sp.2 (types of statements) in bold

(2) And this [special partnership with the European Union] should span both a new economic relationship and a new relationship on security (speech 2) [Informing: W-creating: Recommendation].

As to the World-reflecting statements, May's use of Assessments in speech 1 (shifting from 38 % to 18 %) is outweighed by the use of factual information in the speech 2 (from 50 % to 74 %), thus proving a preference for undeniable information rather than informing via representing reality through some qualifications. See (5) and (6):

(3) And it is an exciting time for many in Europe too (speech 2) [Informing: W-reflecting: Assessment].

(4) Unlike other European countries, we have no written constitution, but the principle of Parliamentary Sovereignty is the basis of our unwritten constitution settlement (speech 1) [Informing: W-reflecting: Fact].

The combination of the two bar charts implies an overall shift from aligning with the world in terms of Assumptions and Assessments to a more down-to-earth stance, which relies more importantly on Facts and Recommendations. The same tendency can be observed when we consider the thirteen-month time difference between speech 1 and 3. Again it is the categories of Assumption and Recommendation for World-creating statements and Assessment and Fact for World-reflecting statements which bear a statistically high significance. And as we observed in the previous, eight-month time span, here as well Recommendations and factual information supersede Assumptions and Assessments, confirming the PM's tendency to align with a more down-to-earth realistic stance as time unfolds (see Figures 5 and 6). Interestingly, Emphasis as an information source variable proved to be statistically highly significant ($p<0.02$). Theresa May's strong expression of opinion becoming significantly reduced with an ever more directive and factual speech behaviour: The more factual and directive she becomes, the less emphatic is the expression of her opinions (see Fig. 7). See (5) to (9):

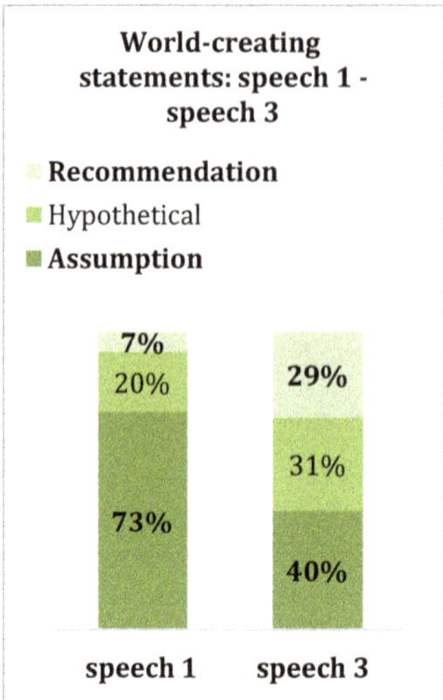

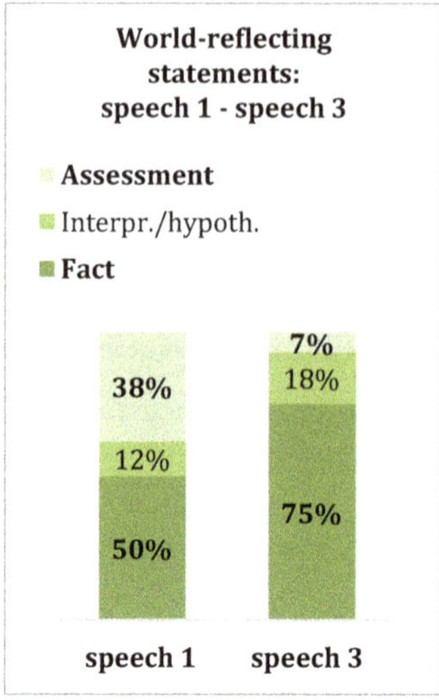

Figs. 5 and 6. Significant differences sp.1–sp. 3 (types of statements) in bold

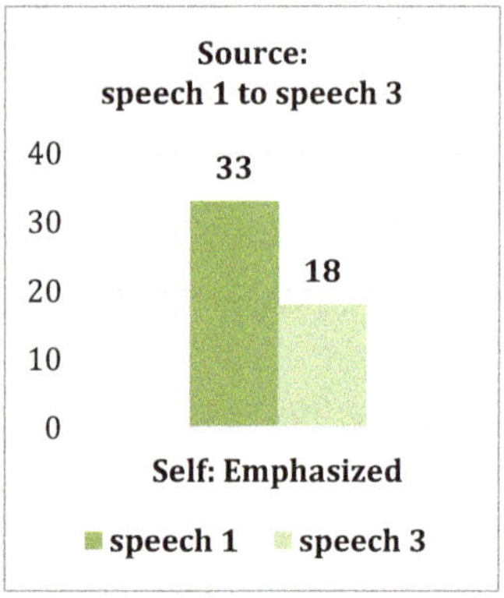

Fig. 7. Significance of source

(5) And not everybody will be able to know everything at every stage (speech 1) [Informing: W-creating: Assumption].

(6) We must also build a new and lasting relationship while, given the uncertainty inherent in this negotiation, preparing for every scenario (speech 3) [Informing: W-creating: Recommendation].

(7) It was a vote to take control of our borders, laws and money, and a vote for wider change, so that no community in Britain would ever be left behind (speech 3) [Informing: W-reflecting: Assessment].

(8) A little over six months ago, the British voted for change (speech 1) [Informing: W-reflecting: Fact].

(9) And I know that this – and the other reasons Britain took such a decision – is not always well understood among our Friends and allies in Europe (speech 1) [Source: Self: Emphasized].

When comparing speech 2 and speech 3, which covers a six-month time difference, what can be observed is that World-creating statements no longer bear any statistical significance, which does now solely rely on World-reflecting statements. This significant reliance on statements which attempt to refer to the world as it is rather than as it could or should be, along with the outstanding resource to factual information, which represents around 75 % of all the statement types in both speeches, reinforces Theresa May's strong tendency to adopt a more rational, factual stance (see Fig. 8). The objective was to persuade the European Commission of her down-to-earth position for Britain and the EU-UK relations. This coincides again with her discourse becoming more de-emphasized as time unfolds (see Fig. 9). It is considering this time span when the type of averral proved to be significant: Theresa May showed a significant statistical preference for non-sourced over sourced contributions of information (see Fig. 10), the important difference in number depicting a speaker who does importantly avoid presenting what she contributes as being derived from a specific source, which in turn leads to a self-representation as a knower and almost exclusive originator of her statements. See (10) to (12):

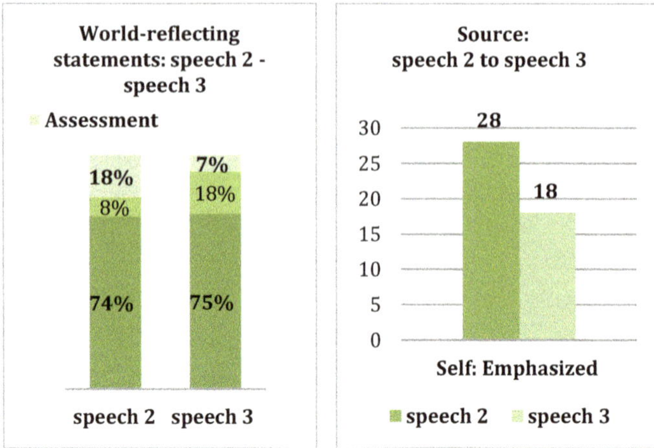

Figs. 8 and 9. Significant differences in bold sp.2–sp.3 (types of statements)

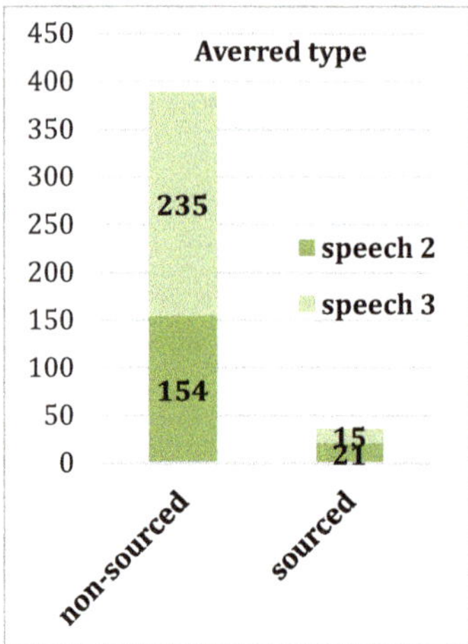

Fig. 10. Source: significant changes sp.2–sp.3

(10) And perhaps because of our history and geography, the European Union never felt to us like an integral part of our national story in the way it does to so many elsewhere in Europe (speech 2) [Informing: W-reflecting: Interpretation/hypothesis].

(11) It is not surprising that our decision to leave has caused anxiety and a desire for concrete solutions (speech 3) [Informing: W-reflecting: Assessment].

(12) So I believe we share a profound sense of responsibility to make this change work smoothly and sensibly, not just for people today but for the next generation who will inherit the world we leave them (speech 2) [Source: Self: Emphasized].

6.2 Theresa May's use of statements and its persuasive power

In order to interpret the use of Theresa May's statements as a persuasive device, the analyst is to trace how the PM was found to express status, that is how her choice of acts of communication was found to align with a specific representation of the world. It is important to consider the three seminal speeches as specific reference points within a timeline that covered thirteen months, with May's clear endeavour to persuade her audience (British and European citizens) of a specific course of action to be taken for a "successful" Brexit, hence a new EU-UK post-Brexit relationship.

Looking into the choice of statements, a stable statistically significant tendency was highlighted, with Theresa May progressively shifting from expressing herself in terms of Assumptions (73 % decreasing to 36 %) to a meaningful increase in the use of Recommendations (7 % changing to 36 %) when comparing speech 1 with speech 2. The same progression was observed when considering the 13-month time difference holding between speech 1 and 3 (with slightly different percentages: Assumptions shifting from 73 % to 40 % and Recommendations increasing from 7 % to 29 %). In the context of World-reflecting statements, factual statements increased from 50 % to 75 %and Assessments as a counterpart decreased from 38 % to 7 %).

PM May's persuasive behaviour translates into the ever more frequent use of factual information, which is by definition unquestionable and does therefore not invite to inquiries about its truth value. This use, in combination with the employment of Recommendations, to some extent allows the possibility of disguising the directive speech act as a logical deduction derived from the factual information. From speech 2 to 3 World-creating statements were found to no longer be of statistically significant value, but only the World-reflecting ones. This contributes to a strategic understanding of May's persuasive behaviour, relying as time unfolds most importantly on information that aims to depict the world as it is rather than as what it could be.

As to the source of her statements, PM May showed a clear preference for Non-sourced averrals, thus overwhelmingly attributing the source of all information to herself and giving the impression of a strong self-assurance. This tendency can also be understood as an overt way of claiming authorship and responsibility for herself. As was observed above, the category that proved to be statistically meaningful was that of Emphasis, with Theresa May progressively becoming less emphatic as she would take on a more factual and directive speech attitude. This is a way of "erasing" from her representational choices any trace of emotional contribution that might interfere with her intended factual behaviour.

7 Conclusion

The present study aims to answer two research questions regarding the evaluation of status, a concept which according to Hunston (2008: 65) refers to the degree of alignment between a proposition and a representation of the world. Both research questions revolve around the political figure of PM Theresa May and her use of statements in her three seminal speeches she delivered to talk both UK and EU citizens into a desirable Brexit, which was initially scheduled for 29 March 2019, as well as into a new EU-UK partnership. The research questions are as follows:

> *RQ1: Are there any similarities and differences between her political speeches in terms of the expression of evaluation of status?*

> The similarities and differences which could be highlighted regarding Theresa May's choice of statements in her speech point to a statistically highly significant tendency in her discourse behaviour ($p<0.02$). As we get closer to the last speech, and thus further away from the initial one, we witness a PM whose use of World-reflecting statements progressively outnumbers and outweighs World-creating statements, showing a preference for undeniable information (i.e. factual information), at the expense of Assessments.

On the other hand, in the context of World-creating statements, Recommendations are found to supersede Assumptions. As we approach the third speech, and along with it the initially scheduled date for Brexit delivery, May's statements rely most importantly on Facts and Recommendations. It is interesting to note the effect of directive acts (Recommendation statements) mapped onto undeniable information (factual statements), allowing for an understanding of the propositional content of the first as being logically derived from the latter. Her reluctance to draw on others or, in general, other sources of information, turns the claims she makes as deriving from her own voice. This is a way of reclaiming responsibility and authorship, which does also project an image of self-assured identity.

RQ2: Does PM Theresa May's evaluative language contribute to the persuasive power of her political speeches? If so, to what extent?

While the persuasive potential behind speeches seems to be a defining characteristic, it is also true that the present study provides sufficient statistical proof that the choice of statements, the evaluative criteria, the source of information, are by no means random, but seem subjected to a specific persuasive intention.

What the research proves is that there is a statistically significant purpose behind the progressive shift from resorting to statement types such as Assessments and Assumptions to a consolidated preferred choice of Recommendations and Facts. The persuasive component of May's speeches suggests a rhetorical strategy that relies on an interesting interplay: contributing undeniable information (Facts) and suggested courses of action (Recommendations) at the expense of personal assumptions and assessments. If we map Recommendations onto factual information, a sense of objective necessity is created as to what the right course of action is for post-Brexit UK and a new EU-UK partnership. This turns the statistically meaningful change in May's choice of statements into a strategic behaviour, where the audience is led to understand that nothing requires further inquiry, as nothing is presented as questionable. Theresa May thus seems to have sought to recreate some kind of incontestable political speech. This meaningful change is combined with a progressively less emphasized expression of opinion on the part of Theresa May, all of which can be interpreted as an attempt at sounding down-to-earth and objective.

These findings unveil a strategic behaviour behind evaluation in political speeches as understood by Hunston (2000, 2008, 2011), in the context of Political Studies. The study offers an insight into how the use of statement types may bring about a specific persuasive effect. It would be interesting to extend this study to the speech behaviour of other political actors, especially in the Brexit context.

References

Aloy Mayo, María/Taboada, Maite. 2017. Evaluation in Political Discourse Addressed to Women: Appraisal Analysis of *Cosmopolitan's* Online Coverage of the 2014 US Midterm Elections. *Discourse, Context & Media* 18, 40–48.

Asthana, Anushka/Boffey, Daniel/Anne Perkins, Anne. 2018. Theresa May Says Brexit will Reduce UK Access to Single Market. *The Guardian* 2-03-2018, <https://www.theguardian.com/politics/2018/mar/02/theresa-may-says-brexit-will-reduce-uk-access-to-single-market>, accessed 10 July 2019.

Biber, Douglas/Finegan, Edward. 1989. Styles of Stance in English: Lexical and Grammatical Marking of Evidentiality and Affect. *Text* 9/1, 93–124.

Cabrejas-Peñuelas, Ana Belén/Díez-Prados, Mercedes. 2014. Positive Self-Evaluation versus Negative Other-Evaluation in the Political Genre of Pre-Election Debates. *Discourse and Society* 25/2, 159–85.

Chafe, Wallace. 1986. Evidentiality in English Conversation and Academic Writing. In Chafe, Wallace/Nichols, Johanna (eds.) *Evidentiality: The Linguistic Coding of Epistemology*. Norwood, NJ: Ablex, 261–72.

Conrad, Susan/Biber, Douglas. 2000. Adverbial Marking of Stance in Speech and Writing. In Hunston, Susan/Thompson, Geoff (eds.) *Evaluation in Text: Authorial Status and the Construction of Discourse*. Oxford: Oxford University Press, 56–73.

Díez-Prados, Mercedes/Cabrejas-Peñuelas, Ana Belén. 2018. Evaluation of "Status" as a Persuasive Tool in Spanish and American Pre-Electoral Debates in Times of Crisis. *Atlantis: Journal of the Spanish Association of Anglo-American Studies* 40/2, 169–95.

Dominiczak, Peter. 2017. Brexit: Theresa May Tells EU that "No Deal is Better than a Bad Deal for Britain". *The Telegraph* 17-01-2017. <https://www.telegraph.co.uk/news/2017/01/17/brexit-theresa-may-tells-eu-no-deal-better-bad-deal-britain/>, accessed 10 July 2019.

Finlayson, Alan/James, Martin. 2008. "It Ain't What you Say . . .": British Political Studies and the Analysis of Speech and Rhetoric. *Journal of British Politics* 3, 445–64.

Fuoli, Matteo. 2012. Assessing Social Responsibility: A Quantitative Analysis of Appraisal in BP's and IKEA's Social Reports. *Discourse and Communication* 6/1, 55–81.

Harris, Sandra. 1991. Evasive Action: How Politicians Respond to Questions in Political Interviews. In Scannell, Paddy (ed.) *Broadcast Talk*. London: Sage, 76–99.

Henley, Jon. 2017. Theresa May's Florence Speech: Key Points'. *The Guardian* 22-09-2017. <https://www.theguardian.com/politics/2017/sep/22/theresa-mays-florence-speech-key-points>, accessed 10 July 2019.

Hunston, Susan. 2000. Evaluation and the Planes of Discourse: Status and Value in Persuasive Texts. In Hunston, Susan/Thompson, Geoff (eds.) *Evaluation in Text: Authorial Status and the Construction of Discourse*. Oxford: Oxford University Press, 176–207.

Hunston, Susan. 2008. The Evaluation of Status in Multi-Modal Texts. *Functions of Language* 15/1, 64–83.

Hunston, Susan. 2011. *Corpus Approaches to Evaluation: Phraseology and Evaluative Language*. London/New York: Routledge.

Hunston, Susan/Thompson, Geoff (eds.) 2000. *Evaluation in Text: Authorial Stance and the Construction of Discourse*. Oxford: Oxford University Press.

Hyland, Ken. 1996. Writing without Conviction: Hedging in Science Research Articles. *Applied Linguistics* 17/4, 433–45.

Jiang, Kevin Feng. 2017. Stance and Voice in Academic Writing: the "Noun + that" Construction and Disciplinary Variation. *International Journal of Corpus Linguistics* 22/1, 86–107.

Martin, James R./White, Peter R. R. 2005. *The Language of Evaluation: Appraisal in English*. Houndmills, Basingstoke: Palgrave Macmillan.

O'Donnell, Mick. 2019. *UAM Corpus Tool: Annotation for the 21st Century*, <http://www.corpustool.com/index.html>, accessed 12 June 2019.

Paterson, Laura L./Coffey-Glover, Laura/Peplow, David. 2015. Negotiating Stance within Discourses of Class: Reactions to *Benefits Street*. *Discourse and Society* 27/2, 195–214.

Ponton, Douglas Mark. 2011. *For Argument's Sake: Speaker Evaluation in Modern Political Discourse*. Newcastle: Cambridge Scholars Publishing.

Ponton, Douglas Mark. 2020. *Understanding Political Persuasion: Linguistic and Rhetorical Analysis*. Delaware: Vernon Press.

Simon-Vandenbergen, Ann-Marie. 1996. Image-building through Modality: The Case of Political Interviews. *Discourse and Society* 7, 389–415.

Simon-Vandenbergen, Ann-Marie. 1997. Modal (Un)certainty in Political Discourse: A Functional Account. *Language Sciences* 19/4, 341–56.

Simon-Vandenbergen, Ann-Marie. 2008. *Hillary Clinton vs. Barack Obama: A Linguistic Study of Appraisal in Political Speeches.* Master's thesis, University of Ghent.

Simon-Vandenbergen, Ann-Marie/White, Peter R. R./Aijmer, Karin. 2007. Presupposition and "Taken-for-Granted" in Mass Communicated Political Argument: An Illustration from British, Flemish and Swedish Political Colloquy. In Fetzer, Anita/Lauerbach, Gerda A. (eds.) *Political Discourse in the Media: Cross-Cultural Perspectives.* Amsterdam/Philadelphia: John Benjamins, 31–74.

Sinclair, John. 1987. *Mirror for a Text.* Unpublished ms. University of Birmingham.

Thompson, Geoff/Hunston, Susan. 2000. Evaluation: An Introduction. In Hunston, Susan/Thompson, Geoff (eds.) *Evaluation in Text: Authorial Stance and the Construction of Discourse.* Oxford: Oxford University Press, 1–27.

University Library Service (Cardiff University). 2019. European Sources Online <https://www.europeansources.info/record/pm-speech-on-our-future-economic-partnership-with-the-european-union/> accessed 10 July 2019.

White, Peter R. R. 2002. Appraisal: The Language of Attitudinal Evaluation and Intersubjective Stance. In Verschueren, Jef/Östman, Jan-Ola/Blommaert, Jan/Bulcaen, Chris (eds.) *Handbook of Pragmatics.* Amsterdam/Philadelphia: John Benjamins, 1–27.

Leanne Victoria Bartley

'Nobody is guilty in football. That's the first thing to understand': A corpus-assisted critical discourse analysis of the UK press coverage of the Ched Evans case[1]

1 Introduction

In recent years a number of celebrities have found themselves at the centre of sexual abuse scandals, including actor Kevin Spacey, singer Michael Jackson, film producer Harvey Weinstein and media personality Jimmy Savile, to cite but a few examples. That said, a number of these cases did not result in a conviction, unlike the high-profile and striking case at the heart of this paper, which involved British footballers Ched Evans and Clayton McDonald.

In 2012, Ched Evans was at the forefront of, potentially, one of the most controversial rape cases in recent decades. Nine years after the start of his football career, having played for Manchester City, Sheffield United as well as represent his country, Ched Evans was accused, alongside his former teammate, Clayton MacDonald, of raping a 19-year-old woman in a hotel room in Rhyl, North Wales, after a night out together. This case is particularly remarkable given that, whilst Clayton MacDonald was found innocent of raping the alleged victim at his 2012

1 I would like to thank John Bartley and Nuria Lorenzo-Dus for their insights and advice on previous versions of this paper. As always, they are much appreciated and, without a doubt, invaluable.

trial, Ched Evans was found guilty of the same crime against the same complainant on the same night. Consequently, as Clayton McDonald walked out of court a free man, Ched Evans received a 5-year prison sentence, of which he served just 2 years, before being released in 2014. Nonetheless, his release by no means brought this case to a close; rather, having maintained his innocence since day one, Evans petitioned for his conviction to be reviewed and, in 2016, he was successful and not only had his conviction overturned by a Court of Appeal, but also received £800,000 in compensation from the legal firm that had represented him in his original 2012 trial.

When this case was presented in court in 2012 and subsequently reported in the British press, the prosecution argued that what occurred that night was rape and not consensual sex on the grounds that the alleged victim was too intoxicated to knowingly consent; the defence team, in contrast, argued that the victim had willingly taken part in the events that took place that night, thereby serving to show how the same events may be linguistically represented in different ways, to meet each side's objective. What proves particularly interesting about this case is the fact that, in the case of Ched Evans, the former version of events was deemed most credible, whilst in the case of Clayton McDonald, it was the latter version that the jury accepted as true. The aim here is not to determine how this difference of opinion came about because to do so would require access to court records.[2] However, given that Evans' original guilty verdict in 2012 was later overturned in 2016, using a corpus-assisted critical discourse analysis (CADS henceforth) approach, this paper investigates how both the alleged perpetrator (i.e. Ched Evans) and victim were represented in the British press at different stages of the case: (i) prior to and immediately after the original trial in 2012; (ii) following Evans' release in 2014; and (iii) during and post Evans' 2016 retrial and overturned conviction. In order to examine how each party is portrayed in the UK press at these different periods of time, Martin / White's (2005) Appraisal theory, together with subsequent amendments

2 Access to court records in the UK is only permitted if the individual who requests these is in some way involved in the case (e.g. lawyer, family member of the defendant or victim, etc.)

made to the framework by Bednarek (2008), is applied to the dataset. Specifically, attention is paid to the core system of Attitude[3] for the purposes of drawing out whose feelings (AFFECT) and behaviours (JUDGEMENT) are brought to the forefront, whether positive or negative and in relation to whom or what. In addition, evaluation, as Macken-Horarik / Isaac (2014: 67) argue, "is both everywhere and – at its most powerful – invisible", which means that as well as more explicit appraisals (i.e. inscribed), it is necessary to also account for more implicit (i.e. invoked) (Martin/White 2005: 67) ones in the analysis, as we do here. Thus, all in all, this study sets out to address the following research questions:

(1) Are there changes over time in how Ched Evans and his victim are represented across British newspapers?

(2) Whose feelings (AFFECT) or behaviours (JUDGEMENT) come to the forefront across newspapers and are these, in general, more positive or negative?

(3) Is there a tendency for more inscribed or invoked evaluations across newspapers and, if more often invoked, are readers primed to perceive Ched Evans and his victim in a particular light through consistent positive or negative exposure over time?

2 Theoretical background

There are a number of studies across disciplines such as criminology, psychology or sociology that examine sexual crimes and sex offenders and, recently, this area appears to be gaining popularity in the field of applied linguistics (cf. Cotterill 2007; Meyer 2010; Bartley 2016; Lorenzo-Dus/Izura 2017). That said, as Estrich (1987: 6) rightfully remarked some 30 years ago, a lot remains to be done in order to address the laws surrounding rape and, more specifically, just what constitutes sexual assault. According to Estrich (1987) in her book entitled "Real Rape", a series of factors are necessary for

3 *Appraisal* theory comprises 3 systems, namely *Attitude*, *Engagement* and *Graduation* (see Martin/White 2005 for details).

rape to be considered actual rape, to include: (i) the fact that the rapist is a stranger; (ii) the fact that the rapist is armed; and (iii) the fact that the rapist approaches his victim uninvited. Should this not be the case, taking an alleged rapist to trial far from ensures a clear-cut conviction; by the same token, depending on the circumstances of the sexual assault, it is important to acknowledge the power of media coverage (Fowler 1991: 92) and how linguistic portrayals of certain people (i.e. alleged rapists or alleged victims) is likely to serve to perpetuate certain ideas and myths surrounding rape and rapists or victims in society more generally. It is this latter idea that we explore in the current paper using a CADS approach to do so.

CADS consists of employing a combination of corpus linguistics and (critical) discourse analysis (CDA henceforth) (cf. Baker et al. 2008), although this is by no means a novel approach to examining representation in newspaper discourse (cf. Coffin/O'Halloran 2004; Baker et al. 2008; Gabrielatos/Baker 2008; Bartley/Hidalgo-Tenorio 2016; Gómez-Jiménez 2018). Whilst corpus linguistics facilitates a quantitative analysis of the dataset (O'Halloran/Coffin 2004: 294), CDA invites a qualitative analysis, with a focus on the notions of representation and ideology. That is, CDA seeks to expose underlying ideologies in language use and, in turn, show how power and dominance penetrate discourse (Fowler 1986; Wodak/Chilton 2005), which soon becomes apparent if we consider, as van Dijk (2001) argues, the various ways in which we can represent the same social reality linguistically.

Although a growing area of research, as acknowledged by Blauenfeldt (2014), there is a dearth of studies surrounding the linguistic representation of sexual predators and their alleged victims in newspaper discourse. That said, there are a few studies that merit mention in this paper, starting with a study by Clark (1992), who analysed a corpus of newspaper articles from *The Sun*, a well-known UK tabloid. Clark (1992) examined the transitivity patterns as well as naming devices employed in the press to refer to both alleged rapists and their victims and reached the conclusion that through regular use of the passive voice, the person responsible for the sexual crime was often obscured in the newspaper data under analysis. Moreover, she noted that this same linguistic strategy often invited readers to blame the victim, as opposed to the perpetrator, for the rape having occurred at all.[4]

Another relevant study to the current paper was carried out by O'Hara (2012), who conducted a lexical analysis in order to see how perpetrators and their victims were portrayed across newspapers. To do this, O'Hara considered three separate rape cases: (i) a case of stranger rape; (ii) a case of gang rape; and (iii) a case of date rape. In all three cases, O'Hara (2012) notes that, as with the study by Clark (1992), the victim is often backgrounded or, on many occasions, even blamed for the rape, which would, thus, seem to be nothing short of a common occurrence.

A final piece of research worth citing was carried out by Statham (2016) and closely aligns with the aforementioned studies discussed. However, unlike Clark (1992), who examined the transitivity patterns and employed a naming analysis, Statham (2016) employed, as we do here in this chapter, APPRAISAL theory. In any case, one may consider a naming analysis and APPRAISAL as sharing similarities given that the labels we assign to individuals, whether positive or negative, may simultaneously reflect examples of JUDGEMENT (e.g. *X is a sicko*, *X is a monster*). Among the main findings reported by Statham (2016) are the fact that the press reinforce the idea that "[...] only extra-societal monsters attack 'respectable' women and when 'unrespectable women' are attacked their sexual availability is to blame" (Statham 2016: 205). Furthermore, Statham (2016) remarks on how, both in the press and beyond, at trial, the alleged rape victim is often branded as, for instance, a party girl, or someone who goes willingly with their attacker, and at no stage shows signs of resistance. Thus, "[W]hen cast as 'sexually available' and 'unrespectable', women can be portrayed as responsible or at least complicit in crimes committed against them" (Statham 2016: 206). These observations are particularly interesting given that (i) they seem to coincide more generally across studies and (ii) they, thus, serve as a valid point of comparison against my own findings regarding how an alleged rape victim and her attacker are portrayed in the British press, as outlined in Section 4 below.

4 Similar findings are also reported by Adampa (1999), who looked at the linguistic representation of a man and a woman in a corpus of newspaper articles of a case of (non-sexual) physical violence.

Year	*Phase of case*	*N° articles*	*Word count*	*Newspapers*
2011–2012	Arrest and lead up to first trial	93	31,812	All available
October 2014	Release from prison	240	170,096	*The Daily Mail*
October 2016	Retrial and conviction overturned	146	122,195	*The Guardian* *The Mirror* *The Sun*

Tab. 1. Distribution of newspaper corpus.[5]

3 Materials and data

The corpus used in this paper comprises a selection of newspapers that were retrieved from LexisNexis (https://www.lexisnexis.com/uk), an online database that enables free access for academic scholars to a wide range of news, business and legal documents. The search terms used were *Ched Evans and *Evans, which led to a dataset of 479 texts and a total corpus size of 324,103 words. The distribution of texts analysed thus far is detailed in Tab. 1.[6]

During the initial data collection process, all of the newspaper articles listed above were downloaded from LexisNexis as word documents and subsequently filtered to ensure that any duplicate articles were removed as well as check that all articles dealt only with the Ched Evans rape case. Once verified, all articles were then converted into .txt files. In order to distinguish between time period, newspaper origin, as well as instances where more than one article was published in the

5 Due to the high volume of newspaper articles published on the Ched Evans case in 2014 and 2016, and space constraints in this paper, only four newspapers are considered during these two time periods.

6 The corpus of newspapers collected for 2011–2012 is smaller because the total number of available articles for this time period is 93. Nonetheless, the UAM corpus tool (O'Donnell 2016) enables a quantitative analysis to test for statistical significance and account for effect size when making comparisons across time periods.

same newspaper on the same day in relation to the Ched Evans case, each individual .txt file was assigned a code that would facilitate comparative analyses at a later stage.

To carry out a quantitative and manual qualitative analysis of the dataset, the UAM Corpus Tool (O'Donnell 2016), an invaluable piece of software that is readily available online, was employed. The UAM Corpus Tool (O'Donnell 2016) comprises schemes for different SFL frameworks, including APPRAISAL, which can be used by analysts to carry out manual as well as automated annotations of language data in .txt format. When conducting a manual annotation of linguistic data, as is the case in this paper, it is possible to create a personalised annotation scheme with the UAM Corpus Tool and, thus, implement the relevant categories and subcategories of, for instance, the APPRAISAL system ATTITUDE (Martin/White 2005; Bednarek 2008). That is, this paper adheres to the changes proposed by Bednarek (2008) regarding the subsystem AFFECT (see 3.1) and, as such, benefited from the possibility to make manual amendments to the scheme and, in turn, carry out a more reliable analysis of the newspaper corpus in question. The UAM Corpus Tool also comprises in-built statistical tests in order to determine whether or not one's findings are statistically significant and, thus, provide quantitative results that can be used as a point of departure for subsequently providing more qualitative interpretations of the data.

3.1 Procedure

As indicated above, a CADS approach (Baker et al. 2008) is adopted here for the purposes of exploring the appraisal patterns employed in a corpus comprising newspaper articles that date from May 2011 (when the alleged rape was first reported) until October 2016 (when Evans was found not guilty at a retrial). As part of the CADS methodology, one if not the most influential CDA approaches is employed, namely Norman Fairclough's dialectal-relational approach (Fairclough 1989, 1992, 1995). Fairclough's approach stems from an already existing approach, formerly known as Critical Linguistics (Fowler et al. 1979), in which systemic functional grammar (SFG) is a central component.

SFG maintains that language serves "to make sense of our experience, and to carry out our interactions with other people" (Halliday/Matthiessen 2014: 25) and proposes that there are three language metafunctions, namely (i) the ideational metafunction (concerned with how we use language to construe our inner and outer experiences), (ii) the interpersonal metafunction (concerned with how we use language to interact with others as well as express our standpoint) and (iii) the textual metafunction (concerned with how we organise our messages through language) (Halliday/Matthiessen 2014: 30). Each of these metafunctions are thought to work with the other two simultaneously. That said, the focus in this paper is on the interpersonal metafunction and, more specifically, APPRAISAL theory (Martin/White 2005; Bednarek 2008).

Appraisal theory (Martin/White 2005; Bednarek 2008) pertains to the interpersonal metafunction on the basis that it is concerned with the linguistic choices made by speakers that serve as an indication of his/her position towards a proposition and, equally, reveal the relationship between the interlocutors (Martin/White 2005: 7). The framework comprises 3 systems, namely (i) ATTITUDE (defined as the system of meanings that represents feelings and emotions, ethics and aesthetics) (Martin/White 2005: 42), (ii) ENGAGEMENT (defined as the resources for positioning the author's voice with respect to the propositions and proposals conveyed by a text) (Rentel 2012: 342) and (iii) GRADUATION (concerned with the value of attitudes that may be raised or lowered in discourse) (Oteiza 2017: 463); in light of space constraints, this paper focuses on ATTITUDE.

As outlined above, the ATTITUDE system concerns our feelings (AFFECT), our evaluations of our own and others' behaviours (JUDGEMENT) and our evaluations of things, processes or states of affairs (APPRECIATION). Since Martin / White's (2005) original proposal, Bednarek (2008) has suggested slight changes to the system of AFFECT in order to more closely align the subcategories to reflect polar opposites (i.e. positive vs negative) and these changes are implemented[7] in this paper. Thus, the

7 The revised terms employed by Bednarek (2008) for AFFECT are indicated in italics.

categories and subcategories used for each domain (i.e. AFFECT, JUDGEMENT and APPRECIATION) are listed in Tables 2–4 below.

Happiness/Unhappiness		**Satisfaction/Dissatisfaction**	
cheer	misery	pleasure	displeasure
affection	antipathy	interest	ennui
Security/Insecurity		**Inclination/Disinclination**	
quiet	disquiet	desire	*non-desire*
trust	*distrust*	***Surprise***	

Tab. 2. Affect (Bednarek 2008)

Social Esteem	**Social Sanction**
normality (how normal is X?)	propriety (how ethical is X?)
capacity (how able is X?)	veracity (how honest is X?)
tenacity (how resolute is X?)	

Tab. 3. Judgement (Martin/White 2005)

Reaction	**Composition**	**Valuation**
impact	balance	
quality	complexity	

Tab. 4. Appreciation (Martin/White 2005)

Examples of APPRECIATION were encountered to a minor degree in the corpus; as such, section 4 will focus primarily on AFFECT and JUDGEMENT.

4 Results and discussion

4.1 Are there changes over time in how Ched Evans and his alleged victim are represented across British newspapers?

The question of whether there are changes over time in how Ched Evans and his alleged victim are portrayed in the British press may be considered from two angles: firstly, by looking at whether the distribution of positive or negative appraisals concerning each party is higher or lower over time and, secondly, by observing whether each of the ATTITUDE domains (i.e. AFFECT, JUDGEMENT and APPRECIATION) reveal a change in frequency between 2012 and 2016 for either side. Using the UAM Corpus Tool, which employs the Chi-squared test, two time periods (2012 surrounding the original trial and 2016 surrounding the retrial and overturned conviction) are compared in order to determine whether the difference over time is significant. These findings are presented in Tables 5 and 6 below.

On closer inspection of the abovementioned tables, there are a number of findings that stand out. Starting with Tab. 5, we observe how the number of positive appraisals of Ched Evans rises from 2012 to 2016; nonetheless, this increase, as evidenced in the table, reveals a weak

Participant	***First_trial_2012***		***Conviction_ overturned_2016***		***Significance***	
Ched	188	49.09 %	226	55.80 %	3.561	Weak (90 %)
Victim	36	9.40 %	42	10.37 %	0.208	No

Tab. 5. Positive appraisals of both participants 2012–2016

Participant	***First_trial_2012***		***Conviction_ overturned_2016***		***Significance***	
Ched	229	30.37 %	215	35.25 %	3.649	Weak (90 %)
Victim	173	22.94 %	168	27.54 %	3.800	Weak (90 %)

Tab. 6. Negative appraisals of both participants 2012–2016

level of statistical significance. Simultaneously, in Tab. 6, we encounter a slight decrease in the number of negative appraisals concerning Ched Evans, but this again is revealed as an example of weak statistical significance. Thus, it is possible to already observe a more general trend of how the events in this rape case seemed to have impacted on how the press report on, at least, the party originally alleged to be at fault. To consider the alleged victim, the number of positive and negative appraisals more or less remains steady, with the difference over time proving either weakly (for negative appraisals) or not statistically significant at all (for positive appraisals).

To now turn to the different APPRAISAL domains, as evidenced in Fig. 1 below, it is also clear that there are shifts in the rate of occurrence of, more notably, JUDGEMENT followed by AFFECT. The minimal difference over time of examples of APPRECIATION may be explained by the fact that the focus in this case is on the representation of people, as opposed to things, processes or states of affairs.

As Fig. 1 demonstrates, there is an inverse tendency for AFFECT and JUDGEMENT, with the former showing a marked increase between 2012 and 2014 and later declining between 2014 and 2016. Thus, one may infer from this that the feelings of certain individuals come to the forefront on and around Ched Evans' release; when looking more closely at the dataset, this finding is, in large part, explained by the fact that numerous references are made to whether or not people wanted

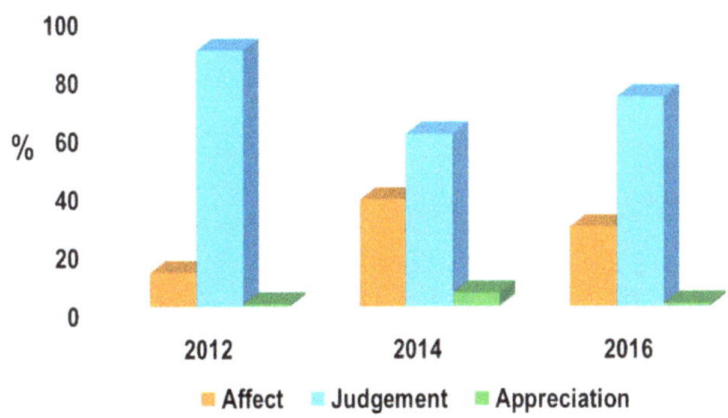

Fig. 1. Distribution of APPRAISAL domains over time

Ched Evans to return to a football career, having served his sentence as a convicted rapist, as in (1) below.

(1) [. . .] 90,000 fans signed a petition saying they *did not want* him back. [. . .] (*The Daily Mail* 14/10/14)

In contrast to AFFECT, the number of JUDGEMENT examples decreases between 2012 and 2014 and later rises again in 2016. The high number of cases in 2012 is the result of recurrent references to the fact that Ched Evans and his former teammate, Clayton MacDonald, are believed to have raped a girl, who was in no fit state to have consensual sex, as in (2) below.

(2) Two footballers *"procured" a drunk teenage girl* and *raped her* as two of their friends watched and filmed, a court has heard. (*South Wales Echo* 12/04/12)

One may argue, in fact, that here we witness two examples of JUDGEMENT; that is, on the one hand, a teenager is drunk (inscribed JUDGEMENT: capacity) and, on the other hand, two footballers procured and raped her (invoked JUDGEMENT: propriety). Meanwhile, in 2016, a large number of JUDGEMENT examples appear to question the honourability of the victim, as in (3).

(3) [. . .] He [a witness] thought it inconsistent that she had slept with him a fortnight after she was attacked [. . .] he came to the conclusion she was *motivated by greed* when she went to the police. (*The Guardian* 14/10/16)

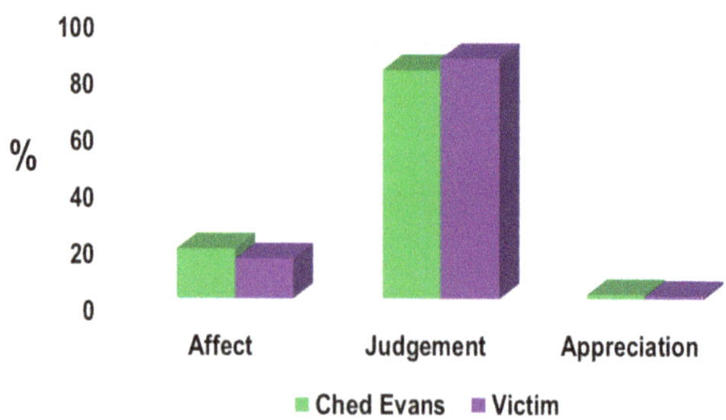

Fig. 2. Distribution of APPRAISAL domains for both parties

The latter is perhaps unsurprising, given that Ched Evans is, at this stage, fighting to have his conviction overturned.

4.2 Whose feelings (Affect) or behaviours (Judgement) come to the forefront across newspapers and are these, in general, more positive or negative?

To address the second research question in this paper, the findings retrieved from the UAM Corpus Tool reveal that the most frequent Attitude domain in the dataset is Judgement, as exemplified above in Fig. 1; moreover, this finding is not participant dependent; that is, it proves just as apparent for the alleged perpetrator as for the victim, as exemplified below in Fig. 2.

To explore this finding in more detail, the specific subcategories of Judgement were examined in order to determine the types of behaviours and/or character traits associated with each side of the case. These findings are illustrated in Fig. 3 below.

As Fig. 3 shows, there is clear focus on references to Judgement: Propriety in the case of Ched Evans, followed by references to Judgement: Capacity, whilst at the heart of the discourse relating to the alleged victim, we encounter the opposite tendency. On closer inspection, examples of Judgement: Capacity for Evans predominantly concern his abilities as a professional footballer and, thus, this subsection will deal solely with instances of Judgement: Propriety

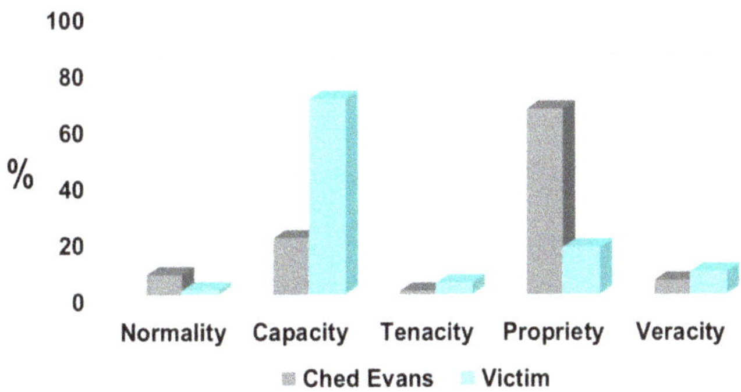

Fig. 3. Distribution of Judgement Subcategories for both parties

for Evans. It is worth remarking that the examples analysed tend to take on a more positive or negative spin according to the time period in question; that is, in 2011–2012, the vast majority of examples of JUDGEMENT: PROPRIETY relating to Ched Evans are negative and, more specifically, this negative interpretation is often achieved through using a combination of language items in close proximity that together portray an overall negative image of the accused. An example is provided in (4) below, which suggests that Ched Evans is somewhat devious in nature.

(4) 'Ched Evans had booked that room *with the main or sole purpose of procuring a girl or girls* that night.' (*Bristol Post* 12/04/12)

By the time Ched Evans is due to be released from prison in 2014, negative examples of JUDGEMENT: PROPRIETY continue to surface in the dataset, as in (5) below, but their occurrence is notably less and less; simultaneously, we witness increasingly more optimistic references to Ched Evans' behaviour start to emerge, with people coming to his defence by insinuating that although a rapist, he is not a violent one, as seen in (6).

(5) 'Unfortunately, he still hasn't acknowledged he is *a rapist* [. . .]' (*Daily Mail*, 10/10/14)

(6) 'He has served his time. [. . .] *He didn't cause any bodily harm to the person.*' (*Daily Mail* 13/10/14)

In line with the latter, by 2016 and Ched Evans' overturned conviction, negative examples are still apparent, as in (7); nonetheless, most notably is the fact that positive JUDGEMENT: PROPRIETY examples continue to mount, with references provided by others recounting his good nature, as in (8), and instances in which Evans himself is given a voice to assert his positive traits, as in (9).

(7) [. . .] 'Medland told the jury: "Evans said he would never hurt a girl." But he added: "*He treated her with a callous, self-centred indifference essentially indistinguishable from utter contempt.*"' (*The Guardian* 13/10/16)

(8) 'Khan, for the defence, said *Evans was a man of good character*, practically a household name.' (*The Guardian* 13/10/16)

(9) "*Whilst my innocence has now been established*, I wish to make it clear that I wholeheartedly apologise to anyone who might have been affected by the events of the night in question." (*The Sun* 15/10/16)

To consider the instances of JUDGEMENT: CAPACITY central to the discourse surrounding the alleged victim, we note that across all newspapers and primarily in 2012 and 2014, the press report on how she could not possibly have consented to sex on the night in question, due to her intoxicated state, as shown in examples (10) and (11).

(10) '[. . .] prosecutor John Philpotts told Caernarfon crown court *the girl, who had downed wine, vodka and sambuca on a night out in Rhyl, "was in not fit state to consent"*', (*The Mirror* 12/04/12)

(11) '[. . .] Evans victim "deserved no credit" because *she was so drunk, she could barely stand*.' (*The Sun* 23/10/2014)

Although notably less frequent, the second most common subcategory for the victim is JUDGEMENT: PROPRIETY, which seems to come to the forefront in 2016; what we witness is a shift from focusing on her inability to consent to sex to remarking on her socially inappropriate sexual behaviour, as in (12).

(12) 'The witness [. . .] told jurors the 19-year-old's confidence in bed 'shocked' him, adding that *she 'dictated' unprotected sex*.' (*Daily Mail* 13/10/16)

Thus, during the retrial phase and Evans' overturned conviction, implicit references start to emerge regarding the victim's promiscuous behaviour (i.e. having multiple sexual partners over a short period of time) as well as what generally may be considered by society as acting inappropriately and, consequently, her character is undermined. This latter finding coincides closely with what Statham maintains regarding unrespectable women who are considered, at least, partly to blame for being prey to a sexual attacker (Statham 2016: 206).

Attitude Domain	***Inscribed appraisals***		***Invoked appraisals***		***Significance***	
AFFECT	387	31.88 %	982	25.56 %	18.652	High (98 %)
JUDGEMENT	723	59.56 %	2794	72.72 %	75.539	High (98 %)
APPRECIATION	104	8.57 %	66	1.72 %	133.174	High (98 %)

Tab. 7. Distribution of inscribed vs invoked appraisals across newspapers

4.3 Is there a tendency for more inscribed or invoked evaluations across newspapers and, if more often invoked, are readers primed to perceive Ched Evans and his victim in a particular light through consistent positive or negative exposure over time?

Based on the findings retrieved from UAM Corpus Tool, there is a significantly higher number of invoked examples used across all three ATTITUDE domains, as summarised in Tab. 7. Furthermore, this is also apparent when observing inscribed vs invoked appraisals at each period in time.

Whilst invoked examples of evaluation are clearly a common occurrence in the dataset, with an example cited in (4) above, inscribed examples, such as (13) were encountered, although predominantly in tabloid newspapers.

(13) 'He's cleared of rape *but as a "slimeball who treats women like meat", Evans is guilty*' (*The Sun* 15/10/16)

One could argue that the type of newspaper will have likely contributed to the frequency of explicit and implicit appraisals in the present study and this may well be true; that is, examples such as (13) may indeed be more customary in newspapers such as *The Sun* in light of the fact that tabloids are considered far more subjective and somewhat direct; broadsheets, on the other hand, are instead deemed to adopt a more objective and serious style of journalism.

In view of the fact that there is always a higher number of invoked examples of Attitude across the dataset, it is difficult to reach a firm conclusion regarding whether or not readers have been primed to view the perpetrator in this case and the victim in a particular light. That said, it is worthwhile pointing out that the number of invoked examples is most dominant in the initial stages of this case (i.e. 2012), which may lead one to argue that there is no evidence of priming occurring on this occasion.

5 Conclusion

This chapter provides a quantitative, as well as in-depth qualitative analysis of the linguistic representation of Ched Evans and his alleged victim in the British press at three different periods of time. A CADS approach was used and, more specifically, APPRAISAL theory was employed as the analytical framework, given that the aim here was to identify the evaluative nature of the discourse concerning the two aforementioned participants. Although this article is certainly not the first to report on representation of sexual assault criminals and their victims in the press (cf. Clark 1992; Adampa 1999; Statham 2016), there is nonetheless a dearth of research in this area and, specifically, using APPRAISAL theory; in this way, the current paper is thought to serve as a valid contribution to the field.

To turn to the main findings in this paper, a number of things come to light. To begin with, we witness clear changes in how Ched Evans and his alleged victim are represented over the 4-year period (2012–2016) examined. Whilst across all three stages of the case there are recurring negative appraisals of Evans, these become gradually less frequent with the passing of time. This may be explained by the fact that, when Evans is found guilty of rape in 2012, a high percentage of negative attitude towards him in the press is arguably foreseeable. By the same token, after serving time for his alleged crime, many now come to his defence arguing that he has been punished and, thus, deserves to return to society and to his football career in the same way that any other criminal would be able to do in these circumstances; subsequently, having his conviction overturned at a retrial in 2016 makes it inevitable for the image of Ched Evans in the news to take on a more positive spin. The portrayal of Evans' alleged victim also revolutionises over time, with the focus in 2012 and 2014 on how the victim was incapable of consenting to sex on the night the alleged rape took place as a result of being extremely intoxicated; by contrast, in 2016, the emphasis shifts from the latter to the notion that the alleged victim is someone who appears to engage in inappropriate sexual activities with, for instance, multiple partners. As such, what is inferred at this point is that the alleged victim is among those *unrespectable women* (Statham 2016: 206), who are far from innocent if they act irresponsibly and expose themselves to precarious situations of sexual violence.

Finally, and worthwhile remarking upon, is the notably higher incidence rate of invoked by comparison to inscribed appraisals found in the dataset, which as perceived in other similar studies (cf. White 2004; Coffin/O'Halloran 2006), is far from a rare occurrence. That said, it is likely that the type of newspaper had an impact on the frequency of overt and covert appraisals in general; as Alba-Juez (2017: 83) remarks, "broadsheets are considered more serious and objective", while tabloids are seen as "less serious and more subjective" and, in fact, this premise coincides with the findings in this study; that is, the majority of examples, such as that in (14) below, of inscribed evaluation are encountered in *The Sun*, a tabloid newspaper.[8]

(14) 'Ched Evans is *a scumbag rapist*' (*The Sun* 19/10/14)

To conclude, whilst this study offers some useful preliminary insights into how alleged sex offenders and, in this case, of celebrity status, alongside their (unknown) victims are represented in media discourse, it is by no means without its shortcomings. First and foremost, the identification of invoked and, even, inscribed appraisals, is somewhat subjective, which inevitably casts a degree of doubt over the reliability of one's findings in this type of research (Bednarek 2010: 37). One means by which to address this issue in future research, if only to an extent, is to use an inter-rater reliability approach in which several analysts carry out annotations of the same dataset and, subsequently, debate and resolve problematic cases together.

A final point worth raising concerns the fact that this study has focused on one specific case in which the accused is a high-profile celebrity; as such, the results would be more readily generalisable if other similar incidents (e.g. the Alex Hepburn rape case) are examined in future research, adopting a CADS approach that will assist in determining whether the appraisal patterns identified here are consistent in press coverage of comparable cases. Alternatively, triangulation (i.e.

8 Due to space constraints, a comparison across newspapers is not covered here.

the use of different analytical frameworks to analyse the same dataset) (Baker/Egbert 2016) may also be implemented in future work for the purposes of verifying the findings obtained thus far.

References

Adampa, Vasiliki. 1999. Reporting of a violent crime in three newspaper articles. The representation of the female victim and the male perpetrator and their actions: A critical news analysis. *Centre for Language in Social Life Working Paper No 108*. Department of Linguistics and Modern English Language Lancaster University.

Alba-Juez, Laura. 2017. Evaluation in the headlines of tabloids and broadsheets: A comparative study. In Breeze, Ruth/Olza, Inés (eds.) *Evaluation in media discourse: European perspectives. Linguistics Insights Series, Volume 207.* Bern: Peter Lang, 81–119.

Baker, Paul/Egbert, Jesse. 2016. *Triangulating methodological approaches in corpus-linguistic research*. New York/London: Routledge.

Baker, Paul/Gabrielatos, Costas/Khosravinik, Majid/McEnery, Tony/Wodak, Ruth. 2008. A useful methodological synergy? Combining critical discourse analysis and corpus linguistics to examine discourses of refugees and asylum seekers in the UK press. *Discourse & Society* 19/3, 273–306.

Bartley, Leanne. 2016. Girl A: The truth about the Rochdale sex ring by the individual who stopped them. A CDA of a rape victim's testimony. *Applied Linguistics* 39/3, 1–22.

Bartley, Leanne/Hidalgo-Tenorio, Encarnación. 2016. 'To be Irish, gay, and on the outside': A critical discourse analysis of the Other after the Celtic Tiger period. *Journal of Language and Sexuality* 5/1, 1–36.

Bednarek, Monika. 2008. *Emotion talk across corpora*. Houndmills/New York: Palgrave Macmillan.

Bednarek, Monika. 2010. Evaluation in the news: A methodological framework for analysing evaluative language in journalism. *Australian Journal of Communication* 37/2, 15–50.

Blauenfeldt, Anne. 2014. *Violent rapists and depraved paedophiles: Linguistic representation of sex offenders in the British Tabloid Press: A comparative corpus-based study*. Malmö University, Sweden: Unpublished Thesis.

Clark, Kate. 1992. The linguistics of blame: Representations of women in *The Sun*'s reporting of crimes and sexual violence. In Toolan, Michael (ed.) *Language, text and context: Essays in stylistics*. London: Routledge, 208–224.

Coffin, Caroline/O'Halloran, Keiran. 2006. The role of appraisal and corpora in detecting covert evaluation. *Functions of language* 13/1, 77–110.

Cotterill, Janet. 2007. *The language of sexual crime*. Basingstoke: Palgrave MacMillan.

Estrich, Susan. 1987. *Real rape*. Cambridge, MA: Harvard University Press.

Fairclough, Norman. 1989. *Language and power*. Harlow: Longman.

Fairclough, Norman. 1992. *Discourse and social change*. Cambridge: Polity Press.

Fairclough, Norman. 1995. *Critical discourse analysis: The critical study of language*. London: Longman.

Fowler, Roger. 1986. *Linguistic criticism*. London: Oxford University Press.

Fowler, Roger. 1991. *Language in the news. Discourse and ideology in the press*. London/New York: Routledge.

Fowler, Roger/Hodge, Bob/Kress, Gunther/Trew, Tony. 1979. *Language and control*. London: Routledge.

Gabrielatos, Costas/Baker, Paul. 2008. Fleeing, sneaking, flooding: A corpus analysis of discursive constructions of refugees and asylum seekers in the UK Press 1996–2005. *Journal of English Linguistics* 36(1), 5–38.

Gomez-Jimenez, Eva María. 2018. 'An insufferable burden on businesses?' On changing attitudes to maternity leave and economic-related issues in the *Times* and *Daily Mail*. *Discourse, Context & Media* 26, 100–107.

Halliday, Michael Alexander Kirkwood/Matthiessen, Christian Matthias Ingemar Martin. 2014. *Halliday's introduction to functional grammar*. London: Routledge.

Lorenzo-Dus, Nuria/Izura, Cristina. 2017. "Cause ur special": Understanding trust and complimenting behaviour in online grooming discourse. *Journal of Pragmatics* 112, 68–82.

Macken-Horarik, Mary/Isaac, Anne. 2014. Appraising Appraisal. In Thompson, Geoff/Alba-Juez, Laura (eds.) *Evaluation in context*. Amsterdam/Philadelphia: John Benjamins, 67–92.

Martin, James Robert/White, Peter Robert Rupert. 2005. *The language of evaluation: Appraisal in English*. Basingstoke: Palgrave MacMillan.

Meyer, Anneke. 2010. Evil monsters and cunning perverts: representing and regulating the dangerous paedophile. *Sociology of Crime, Law and Deviance* 14, 195–217.

O'Donnell, Michael. 2016. The UAM Corpus Tool 3.3. Retrieved 3 November 2018 from <http://www.corpustool.com>

O'Halloran, Keith/Coffin, Caroline. 2004. Checking overinterpretation and underinterpretation: Help from corpora in Critical Linguistics. In Coffin, Caroline/Hewings, Ann/O'Halloran, Keiran (eds.) *Applying English grammar: Corpus and functional approaches*. London: Arnold, 275–297.

O'Hara, Shannon. 2012. Monsters, playboys, virgins and whores: Rape myths in the news media's coverage of sexual violence. *Language and Literature* 21(3), 247–259.

Oteíza, Teresa. 2017. The appraisal framework and discourse analysis. In Bartlett, Tom/O'Grady, Gerard (eds.) *The Routledge handbook of systemic functional linguistics*. London/New York: Routledge, 457–472.

Rentel, Nadine. 2012. Subjectivity in academic discourse. A cross-linguistic comparison of the author´s presence in French, Italian and German research articles in linguistics. In Baumgarten, Nicole/Du Bois, Inke/House, Juliane (eds.) *Subjectivity in language and in discourse*. Bingley: Emerald, 339–354.

Statham, Simon. 2016. *Redefining trial by media: Towards a critical-forensic linguistic interface*. Amsterdam: John Benjamins.

van Dijk, Teun A. 2001. Multidisciplinary CDA. In Wodak, Ruth/Meyer, Michael (eds.) *Methods of critical discourse analysis. First Edition*. London: Sage, 95–120.

White, Peter Robert Rupert. 2004. Subjectivity, evaluation and point of view in media discourse. In Coffin, Caroline/O'Halloran,

Keiran (eds.) *Grammar, text and context: A reader.* London/ New York: Arnold, 229–257.

Wodak, Ruth/Chilton, Paul. 2005. *A new agenda in (Critical) Discourse Analysis: Theory, methodology and interdisciplinarity.* Amsterdam: John Benjamins.

Sergio Maruenda-Bataller

The role of news values in the discursive construction of the female victim in media outlets: A comparative study[1]

1 Introduction

In this chapter, I analyse the way media outlets discursively represent female victims of *violence against women* (VAW) contrastively in two Spanish and two British quality dailies in a purpose-built corpus of 19,560 articles over a 10-year period (2005–2015), drawing upon a CADS framework. By identifying the news values used to portray female victims, I aim to compare the treatment these newspapers give to female victims of VAW episodes in their news. I believe that news values can provide an insight into a culture-specific set of beliefs, attitudes and representations that are essential to the meaning re-signifying of the concept *woman* (as female victim) and, more generally, of the construction of women's identity in society.

Some research has recently focused on the ideological nature of news values in various social and political discourses (see Baker et al. 2013; Baker/Levon 2015; Huan 2016; Fruttaldo/Venuti 2018; Lorenzo-Dus/Smith 2018; Molek-Kozakowska 2018; Formato 2019).

1 This research is part of the project "News values and ideology: The discursive, cross-cultural construction of gender and social inequalities in (digital) press through online, real time corpus linguistic tools: *The Gender Gap Tracker* and *Kaleidographic*" (Ref. PID-2019-110863GB-100), funded by the Spanish Ministry of Science and Innovation.

However, there is lack of scholarly research on how media outlets use news values to construct female victims of VAW. This study aims to fill that gap. Besides, the present chapter contributes a cross-cultural study of VAW press discourse by synergizing corpus linguistics and the Discursive News Values Analysis (DNVA) (Bednarek/Caple 2017). In doing so, I explore the ways in which gender-related identities are built across socio-cultural and linguistic contexts, and thus take the opportunity to apply the DNVA framework to news stories in different languages and different cultures (Bednarek/Caple 2017: 137; Caple/Huan/Bednarek 2020: 14–15).

2 The representation of female victims in the media: from the private to the public sphere

2.1 News as social construction

Media are primary sources of definitions and images of social reality and, thus, of social meanings. Through their treatment of social issues, media crucially form and register the way culture, politics and social life are constructed through discourse (Bell 1998; Cotter 2010). Hence, it can be argued that news stories convey cultural scripts and ideologies which shape and control societal perceptions and representations of events and social actors (van Dijk 1988).

News production is regarded as a process whereby events and texts mutually influence each other, and thus construct ideologies about the events, topics and actors being discussed by virtue of the semiotic means they use to represent news actors, identities and relations between social groups. Hence, while the media often transmit what is socially accepted or legitimised, it is also a fact that a great deal of it is sanctioned and reinforced by media coverage.

The study of news texts as ideology-bearing discourse(s) has been widely researched in CDA (see, for instance, Bell 1991; Fowler 1991; Bell/Garrett 1998; van Dijk 1998; Richardson 2007). Such analysis is key to understanding their influence on public perceptions of dominant topics, groups and events (Fairclough 1995). In this regard, the present research is concerned with the unveiling of ideology in news reporting on VAW through the analysis of the role of news values in constructing female victims.

2.2 News discourse

From a constructivist view, news is defined as the end-product of a complex process of selection of events and topics guided by a socially-forged set of categories: news values. Events, however, are not in themselves newsworthy. The selection of what counts as news involves an act of interpretation whose discursive presentation involves political, economic and social factors. Thus, news is a practice in the sense that it intervenes in the social construction of reality (see Cole/Harcup 2010; Cotter 2010).

In this social construal, several crucial aspects are involved. First, news does not report events objectively but construct or manufacture a representation thereof in order to make stories newsworthy for a given audience (Durant/Lambrou 2009). Thus, newsmakers *frame* news stories in order to spotlight certain issues or states of affairs, based on specific news sources and ideologies. Second, as a corollary, news also constructs audiences by presuming their interests, often blurring the lines between mere consumption and their right to be informed (Tabbert 2016). Finally, language is only seemingly objective. As stated by Wodak/Meyer (2001), the purported neutrality of media institutions emanates from their scope for public discourse and their impartiality on perceptions and arguments "while they often have hidden political agendas that lie at the heart of the matter" (Wodak/Busch 2004: 109).

From journalism studies, however, Cole/Harcup (2010) argue that CDA's views on ideological hues often disregard newsroom practice and the "complex ways" in which audiences may receive texts and approach their language (un)critically (but see Cotter 2010). Aware of this latter outlook, the present paper, however, aligns with a CDA approach to news discourse by assuming that media portrayal of VAW may well have important implications on beliefs, perceptions and social and public policing (Carlyle/Slater/Chakroff 2008).

2.3 News discourse on VAW

In recent years, VAW has become a major issue in political, social and institutional discourses, hence permeating the agenda of the newsroom. Undoubtedly, media have played a decisive role in ensuring visibility to this social problem and contributing to sensitising citizenship. However, this is not without a potential ethical cost (see Tabbert 2016 on the 'craft ethos'). Media coverage of VAW often focuses on impact, in terms of newsworthiness, for the community, which frames a particular portrayal of VAW and can "confirm and debunk myths surrounding it by choosing certain topics, facts and words over others" (Bullock/Cubert 2002: 479).

With regard to this framing, audience research suggests that media portrayals can encourage and legitimise particular views and attitudes towards VAW (Wozniak/McCloskey 2010; Easteal/Holland/Judd 2015; Fairbairn 2015). In this respect, some scholars have underscored that media coverage tends to overrepresent femicide, while other more common forms of aggression, mistreatment, physical and sexual violence are downplayed as 'less newsworthy' (Benedict 1992; Meyers 1997; Carter/Steiner 2004; Fairbairn 2015; Formato 2019). This may contribute to the routinisation of some forms of violence over others in the news and, in fact, distort and manipulate audience perceptions (Carter/Steiner 2004). Besides, as Fairbairn/Dawson (2013) point out, news accounts of VAW often engage in subtle or overt victim blaming or pathologize the perpetrators by focusing on mental illnesses.

In view of this, it seems that, in spite of increased media attention, news framing and coverage of VAW "present significant challenges as well as opportunities for VAW work" and become "an important area of feminist engagement and critique moving forwards" (Fairbairn 2015: 80). Against this background, the present work aims to develop an understanding of how Spanish and British news media construct female victims of VAW through specific discourse practices.

3 News values

News values (henceforth, NV) is a multifaceted concept that has been identified with those features that determine who or what count as news (i.e. newsworthiness) and how these are covered by news reporters. Cotter (2010: 74) states that NV "function as a heuristic, as a guide that is viable at different stages of the news process", "fundamental decision-making parameters" that provide internal or cross-professional criteria for the selection of what constitutes news (see also Cole/Harcup 2010).

Upon the basis of the earliest attempt to provide an inventory of NV as a set of criteria to determine newsworthiness (Galtung/Ruge 1965), the literature to date has put forth a wealth of labels that applies to the different dimensions of news production, namely the selection process (Cotter 2010; PROXIMITY, IMPACT, CHANGE, CONFLICT, USEFULNESS), the potential newsworthiness of the event (Harcup/O'Neill 2001; Cole/Harcup 2010; THE POWER ELITE, CELEBRITY, ENTERTAINMENT, SURPRISE, MAGNITUDE, RELEVANCE), the news text (Bell 1991; Bednarek/Caple 2012; NEGATIVITY, TIMELINESS, PROXIMITY, PROMINENCE, CONSONANCE, IMPACT, NOVELTY). This heterogeneity of categories only shows that they are not a closed set, but a list of potential options for researchers to apply and adapt to their own work (Harcup/O'Neill 2016; Fuster-Márquez/Gregori-Signes 2019).

Research on news discourse has considered NV as key ideological factors that govern the decisions of news reporters regarding the focus and contours of news stories (van Dijk 1988; Bell 1991; Fowler 1991; Richardson 2007; Cotter 2010; Bednarek/Caple 2012, 2014). Thus, NV shape the text by reinforcing an ideology of what counts as news in specific contexts and, consequently, by organising story design for audiences (Cotter 2010). For Bednarek/Caple (2014), it is precisely this relationship between texts, NV and audiences that configures NV as socially-negotiated constructs and enables them to convey and disseminate ideologies through discourse. Despite this, NV have scarcely been the focus of critical linguistic analyses of news discourse (Bednarek/Caple 2014: 137).

For a linguistic and discursive approach, Bednarek/Caple (2017) argue that the variability of definitions and dimensions diminishes the theoretical significance of NV, especially when these are conflated. In their review of the extant research, these scholars put forth an understanding of NV through four complementary dimensions that interact in various ways and cross-cut research lines within NV studies: (1) material (ethnographic); (2) social; (3) cognitive and (4) discursive. Following Bednarek/Caple (2017: 43), I briefly account here for the first three dimensions and deal more extendedly with the discursive dimension – the one I adopt in the present chapter – in section 4.

In the material dimension (see Bell 1991; O'Neill/Harcup 2008; Cole/Harcup 2010; Cotter 2010), NV are regarded as a series of 'internalised' selection criteria that are applied to an event to determine its potential newsworthiness for a given community. In the cognitive dimension, NV are conceived as a series of 'heuristics' that enable journalists and audiences to perceive events and actors as newsworthy. In their social dimension, these NV are applied as selection criteria in journalistic routines and practices and, therefore, research examines "how news workers apply NV as criteria in selecting what events to cover" (Bednarek/Caple 2017: 43).

In the latter dimension, labelled as Discursive News Values Analysis (DNVA), newsworthiness "can be communicated through discourse" (Bednarek/Caple 2017: 42). This approach argues that NV are used to discursively construct an event as newsworthy for a given community (Bednarek/Caple 2012, 2014, 2017; Caple/Bednarek 2013). Thus, for terminological precision, Bednarek/Caple (2017: 41) distinguish NV (*semiotic* resources that construct newsworthiness in discourse) from "news writing objectives" and "news selection factors", as some of their constituents are not concerned with newsworthiness.

4 Discursive News Values Analysis (DNVA)

The aim of DNVA is to provide a framework for an in-depth analysis of how specific events and actors are discursively constructed in a news text (Bednarek/Caple 2014: 137). This system identifies an inventory of semiotic resources that interact to potentially communicate NV (and convey ideological implications). Tab. 1 shows the list of NV used in the DNVA framework, with some linguistic devices and examples[2].

DNVA is a growing field of research that has been mainly applied in a series of recent studies that bring in an ideological dimension from a wide range of topics: environmental issues (Caple/Bednarek 2016; Bednarek/Caple 2017), NV in the marketisation reform of the Chinese press (Huan 2016), the interplay between verbal and visual representations of climate stories (Dahl/Flottum 2017), popularity-driven science journalism and climate change (Molek-Kozakowska 2018), crime news reports in Iran (Makki 2019), the visual construction of political crises in the UK (Lorenzo-Dus/Smith 2018), press vs. social media on same-sex marriage court ruling (Venuti/Fruttaldo 2019), the representation of male schizophrenia in UK news reports (Perkins 2019), or the NV analysis of tourism-phobia in Spanish newspapers in 2017 (Fuster-Márquez/Gregori-Signes 2019).

However, research that applies the DNVA framework to the study of gender and social inequality is still lacking (but see Fruttaldo/Venuti 2018). The analysis of newsworthiness on these topics has alternatively been addressed from other theories (see Fairbairn/Dawson 2013). As regards social inequality, Baker et al. (2013) use evaluation to compare the discursive representation of Muslims in British mainstream tabloids and broadsheets. Their results unveil a recursive association of this social community with cases of terrorism and conflict. More recently, Baker/Levon (2015) analyse the representation of masculine identities in more traditional UK press. Their results point to a high presence of stereotypical traits that clearly reproduce ideological standpoints. These traits might be said to be conveyed through negativity and consonance.

Thus, while DNVA has been used to explore a range of topics on gender and social inequality, this approach has not been applied to date to news reporting on VAW. It is the aim of the present research to address this gap by providing a DNVA analysis drawing upon Computer-Assisted Discourse Studies (CADS).

---

2 Whenever possible, I have replaced examples in the original by my own corpus examples.

News value	*Linguistic devices and examples*
Consonance ([stereo]typical)	References to stereotypical attributes or preconceptions; assessments of expectedness/typicality (*typical; known for*); similarity with past (*yet another case of, another episode of domestic violence at the hands of her partner*); explicit references to general knowledge/traditions, etc. (*well-known*).
Eliteness (of high fame and status)	Various status markers, including role labels (*Judge Martínez, The State Observatory on VAW in Spain, experts*); status-indicating adjectives (*the prestigious. , top diplomats*); recognised names (*Pedro Sánchez, Greta Thunberg*); descriptions of achievements/fame (*were gathering thousands of people in their meetings*).
Impact (having significant effects or consequences)	Assessments of significance (*momentous, historical, crucial*); representation of actual/non-actual significant/relevant consequences, including abstract, material or mental effects (*stabs wounds everywhere; deadly wounds were inflicted*).
Negativity/Positivity (negative/positive)	References to negative/positive emotion and attitude *(suffer, condemn, survive*); negative/positive evaluative language (*torment, brilliant)*; negative/positive lexis (*assault, violence, death, success, win, help*); description of negative (e.g. norm-breaking) or positive behaviour (*has broken his promise, unveiled a cabinet with an equal number of men and women*).
Personalisation (having a personal/ human face)	References to 'ordinary' people, their emotions, experiences (*Debbie Hodgkiss' body was found; murdered by her ex-partner, Brian Tedds, 46; despite extensive searches of the body of Gracia Morton, an Argentinian-born violinist*).
Proximity (geographically or culturally near)	Explicit references to place or nationality near the target community (*Valencia, mujer madrileña*); references to the nation/community via deictics, generic place references, adjectives (*here, the nation's capital, home grown*); inclusive first-person plural pronouns (*our women*).
Superlativeness (of high intensity/large scope)	Intensifiers (*severe, dramatically*); quantifiers (*thousands, huge*); intensified lexis (*panic, smash*); metaphor and simile (*a tsunami of crime; like a World War II battle*); comparison (*the largest drug ring in Detroit history*); repetition (*building after building flattened*); lexis of growth (*a growing list of; scaling up efforts*); *only/just/alone/already* + time/distance or related lexis (*only hours after*).

Tab. 1: Continued

Tab. 1. Continued

News value	*Linguistic devices and examples*
TIMELINESS (recent, ongoing, about to happen, new, current, seasonal)	Temporal references (*today, yesterday's, within days, now*); present and present perfect (*has suffered serious male violence in her life*); implicit time references through lexis (*never report the abuses committed*); reference to current trends, seasonality, change/newness (*1.4 % of women in... suffered serious male violence this year*).
UNEXPECTEDNESS (unexpected)	Evaluations of unexpectedness (*different, astonishing, strange*), reference to surprise/expectations (*the episode shocked the community*); comparisons that indicate unusuality (*for the first time since 1997*); references to unusual happenings (*British man survives 15-storey plummet*).

Tab. 1. The DNVA framework (adapted from Bednarek/Caple 2017: 79–80)

5 Methodology

This research aligns with current trends in Critical Discourse Studies, specifically in what is known as Corpus-Assisted Discourse Studies (CADS) (see Partington et al. 2013; Gabrielatos/Duguid 2014), which advocates for the interrelation of quantitative and qualitative methods using Corpus Linguistics (CL) tools. This synergy has proved its value in unveiling recurrent discourse patterns that construe and sustain ideologies, engender conflict and promote social inequality.

5.1 Corpus description

In this study I use a purpose-built corpus of 14.5 million words of news on VAW from two Spanish and two British mainstream dailies over a 10-year period (2005–2015), gathered using the online news database Nexis UK. The corpus is divided into four different data sets: El País (EP), El Mundo (EM), The Guardian (TG) and The Times (TT). A summary of the corpus data is shown in Tab. 2.

Newspaper	n. of articles (2005–2015)	n. of words (2005–2015)
EP	7,400	3,994,097
EM	4,379	2,971,097
Total SP	**11,779**	**6,965,194**
TG	5,084	5,483,308
TT	2,697	2,062,411
Total UK	**7,781**	**7,545,719**
Total	**19,560**	**14,511,223**

Tab. 2. Corpus data per dataset, number of articles and number of words

5.2 Procedure

This study relies on Potts et al.'s (2015) exploratory use of corpus-based methods to retrieve linguistic *pointers* as potentially conveying NV. In this regard, I aim to gain insights into how NV are used to construct ideological discourses on female victims of VAW. The same procedure is replicated in the four datasets for comparative purposes.

Firstly, I use *AntConc* software (Anthony 2019) to retrieve and analyse the most frequent content collocates (N=100) for the search lemma(s): VICTIM*/VÍCTIMA*. The minimum collocate frequency is set at 3, and frequencies are normalised per million words. I then manually classify them according to the potential NV they convey. Secondly, I use concordances of these content collocates to adjust prior assignment of NV in order to provide a more accurate portrayal of the discourse(s) built around victims of VAW by exploring context and co-text (see Graph 1). There are three reasons for this: (1) to account for the context-dependence of NV (i.e. the same linguistic devices can construct different NV for different audiences), (2) to highlight potential multiple coding (i.e. the same linguistic device can simultaneously build different NV) (Bednarek/Caple 2017), and (3) to avoid the allocation of the same NV to comparable node words in Spanish and English, thus addressing one of the challenges of cross-linguistic studies on CADS (Taylor 2014).

The final step involves the classification of the results according to the DNVA framework. Here, I provide a group of linguistic devices that emerge from the data analysis. The aim is theoretical: to provide

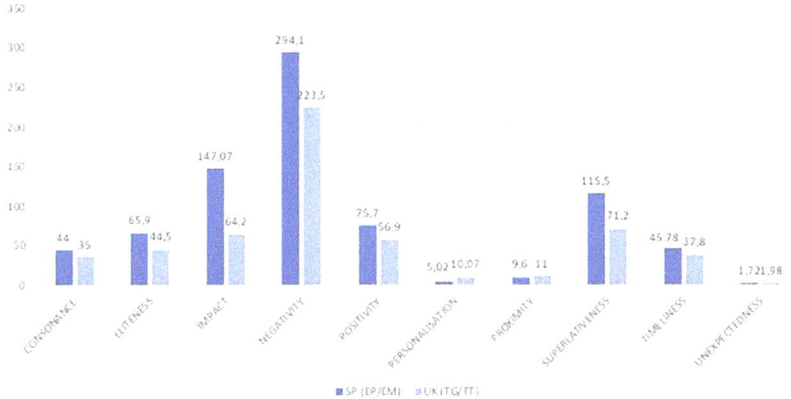

Graph 1. Normalised frequency of NV occurrences in the four sub-corpora (results show frequency of collocates + concordances).

DNVA with a more fine-grained toolkit to analyse NV in VAW news reports. As Bednarek/Caple (2014) state, the list of devices is far from exhaustive and needs further testing cross-linguistically and in other areas of discourse to continue developing the model and the field of DNVA. In this study, I put forth a set of linguistic devices or sub-categories in each of four NV in the corpus: NEGATIVITY, IMPACT, POSITIVITY and ELITENESS, the most common NV found in the corpus[3].

Against this backdrop, the present study aims to address the following research question: How do Spanish and UK press use NV to represent female victims of VAW?

6 Results and discussion

Generally, the results of the analysis unveil the presence of two contrasting yet interdependent discourses. On the one hand, female victims are

3 I deliberately exclude SUPERLATIVENESS from the analysis due to the fact that, for VAW reporting, intensified lexical resources and repetition have a cumulative effect that more likely constructs NEGATIVITY.

typically associated with death, violence and extreme suffering, which are conveyed mainly through NEGATIVITY and IMPACT. Comparatively, these NV encode a wider plethora of occurrences in the four datasets. On the other hand, female victims are surrounded by a discourse that conveys social and institutional care and support, but which portrays them mainly as passive individuals. This is mostly expressed through POSITIVITY and ELITENESS.

The results from the four datasets corroborate that NEGATIVITY has come to be routinised public and social rhetoric in news reports to frame women as victims of male violence. This seemingly encodes, I argue, a culture-specific narrative that news outlets construct around VAW that has become normalised through the routine reporting of ordinary cases (Cameron 2020). In the present research, this narrative is built through the combination of NEGATIVITY with other NV (see below). This may point to a hierarchy of NV that is evinced by the potential multiple coding of some linguistic realisations.

Tab. 3 shows the linguistic devices identified for NEGATIVITY, the most recurrent NV in the corpus, along with some examples of node words. These devices clearly exhibit a discourse of violence, death and emotional suffering, the intensity of which is often shown cumulatively in the lexis, as illustrated in (1). Pointers that convey this NV are seen to relate to[4]:

(1) **EP 08.03.2008 – El silencio se vuelve cómplice de la violencia contra las mujeres**[5]

> (...) La violencia machista todavía se percibe, mayoritariamente, como un asunto de la esfera privada, a pesar de que, hoy en día, es ya una de las grandes <u>lacras</u> para todas las sociedades. Porque cuando una mujer es <u>asaltada, violada, insultada, golpeada o asesinada</u>, es todo el cuerpo social el que es <u>maltratado y herido</u>.

4 Due to space restrictions, I use examples in English when reporting on general findings in all sub-corpora. Otherwise, I provide illustration in their original language. Spanish examples are translated where appropriate.

5 Own translation: Silence is an accomplice of violence against women (...) Male violence is still mostly perceived as a private issue, despite that it is today one of the greatest *scourges* for all societies. When a woman is *assaulted, raped, abused, battered or killed*, it is society as a whole that is *mistreated and hurt*.

NEGATIVITY	
Linguistic devices	**Examples**
Inflicted physical violence (specific episodes)	stalked; battered; raped; forced; killed, injured, forced, etc.
Negative emotions/endurance	terrifying, horrible, trauma; torture; vulnerable; blaming, etc.
Forms of aggression (N)	harassment; rape; crime; assault; abuse; murder; battering, etc.

Tab. 3. Linguistic devices for NEGATIVITY and examples from the corpus data

Despite a remarkably higher number of pointers in SP dailies for each subcategory (Graph 2), the qualitative inspection displays similar portrayals of the victims in the four datasets.

These linguistic pointers convey a negative prosody that includes the after-effects of acts of violence [adj.] (Eng. 'raped', 'killed', 'abused', 'battered', 'murdered'; Sp. 'violada', 'asesinada', 'agredida', 'maltratada', 'muerta'), violent acts [nouns] (Eng. 'rape', 'sexual abuse', 'mistreatment', 'murder', 'aggression'; Sp. 'violación', 'abuso sexual', 'maltrato', 'crimen', 'agresión'), and verbs denoting inflicted severe physical harm (Eng. 'kill', 'rape', 'stab', 'decapitate', 'murder', 'burn'; Sp. 'matar', 'violar', 'apuñalar', 'decapitar', 'asesinar', 'calcinar')[6].

As regards explicit negative emotions, NEGATIVITY combines with TIMELINESS to construct female victims' emotional endurance as timely and current affairs by reporting on particular events. Although UK and SP dailies qualitatively portray victims in similar terms, significant differences are found in the four datasets concerning the number of linguistic pointers to the said linguistic devices (see Graph 3). Interestingly, this tendency has reversed over the years. Thus, while the number of instances has increased in UK dailies since 2005 (N=139) to 2015 (N=215), this has decreased in SP dailies (2005, N=365; 2015, N= 292).

6 These are retrieved from the concordance, file-view analysis, and classified by part of speech.

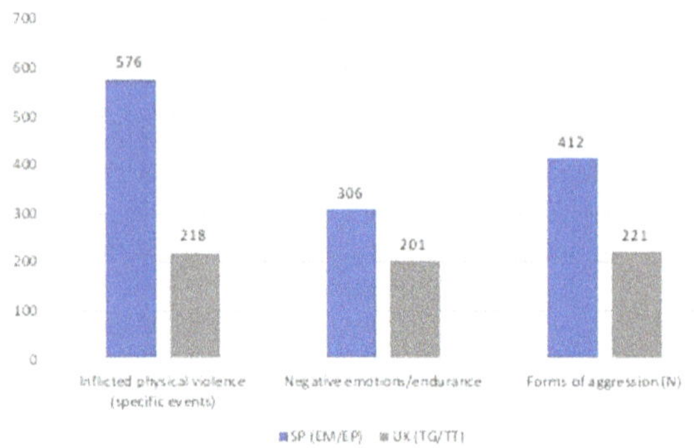

Graph 2. Number of linguistic pointers to NEGATIVITY per linguistic device (data shown per language).

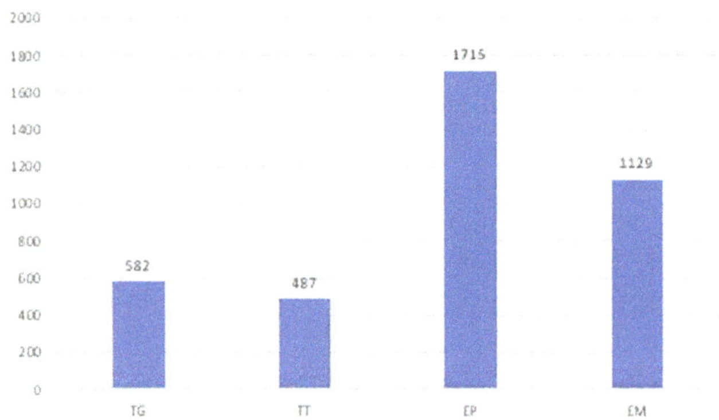

Graph 3. Absolute number of pointers to the linguistic device of negative emotions/ endurance (results shown per newspaper).

When dealing with explicit (authorial) negative emotion, a notable difference between SP and UK dailies lies in what the focus of the news report is. The SP data show a tendency to display the inner emotional suffering of the victims ('letal' ['deadly'], 'crueldad' ['cruelty'], 'trágico' ['tragic'], 'tormento' ['torment'], etc.). In UK dailies, the use of evaluative language to judge victims' emotional endurance often qualifies the abuse [adjs.] ('*dreadful* early life experiences', '*disproportionally* violent conduct', '*extraordinary* pain', '*tremendous* abuse', '*horrific* domestic violence', etc.). These differences may be evidence of a conscious or ideological decision by news outlets on how to report on the victims' emotional suffering (perhaps a sensationalist view in SP dailies). Although beyond the scope of this chapter, these results may be the starting point of a more in-depth study that includes interview with journalists.

The linguistic pointers to the NV of IMPACT typically collocate in the corpus data with the lemmas BODY/CUERPO or CORPSE/CADÁVER of the female victim (see Tab. 4). The results also show that IMPACT most frequently combines with PROXIMITY and NEGATIVITY to convey 'geographical location/identification' and 'signs of extreme violence'. Thus, more nuanced interpretations can be made by breaking down this NV into:

IMPACT [+body, +corpse]	
Linguistic devices	**Examples**
Geographical location/ identification (+ PROXIMITY)	found her body in [place]; the corpse was found in [place]; hidden; concealed; rescued (body), etc.
Signs of extreme violence (+ NEGATIVITY)	charred; stabbed; bruised; beaten; hung; burnt, decapitated, dismembered; emaciated; abrasions; etc.

Tab. 4. Linguistic devices for IMPACT and examples of collocates with the lemma BODY/CORPSE

The treatment of the deceased victims stands as one further point of divergence between UK and SP reports on VAW. Besides the disparate number of collocates with the said lemmas (see Graph 4), simple file view of the four data sets using concordance tools shows that there is a marked preference in SP dailies to communicate IMPACT through words or phrases that refer to 'signs of extreme violence' (see Graph 5). Some retrieved examples of this proclivity are: 'apuñalado' ['stabbed'], 'ensangrentado' ['covered in blood'], 'desgarros vaginales' ['vaginal tears'], 'golpes' ['blows'], 'magulladuras' ['bruises'], 'calcinado' ['charred'], 'desmembrado' ['dismembered'], 'quemado' ['burned'], 'acribillado' ['shot']. In contrast, UK dailies show a marked inclination to convey 'geographical location/identification' (N=243) ('the body was found', 'the body was discovered', 'the body of [name + age]', etc.).

This contrast is illustrated in examples (2) and (3) below. The SP news report clearly spotlights the atrocity and savagery of the crime by giving details of the wounds inflicted. In contrast, the UK news report scarcely mentions signs of violence. This may point to a sanitisation of violence in UK dailies when considering the full corpus.

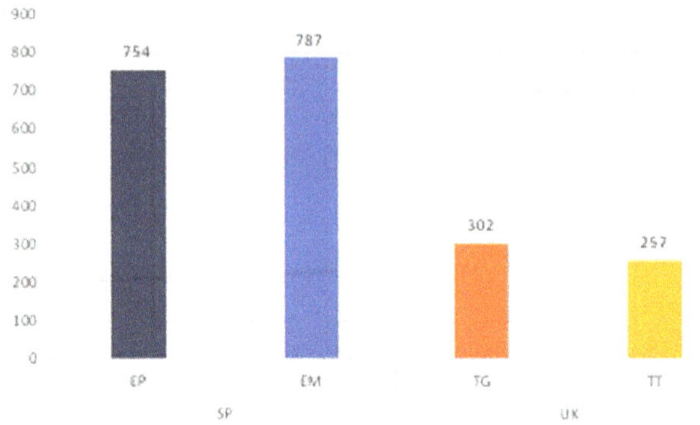

Graph 4. Total number of collocates with the lemmas BODY/CUERPO and CORPSE/CADÁVER per newspaper.

(2) **EM 17.10.2008 – Encuentran muerta a una mujer de nacionalidad rusa con 20 heridas de arma blanca**[7]

El primer informe de la autopsia es tremendo. Revela que el autor del crimen se ensañó con la chica de forma salvaje. El cuerpo tiene puñaladas por todas partes: en la espalda, cabeza, piernas, cuellos y brazos. Con todo, las heridas mortales son las que recibió en el cuello y el corazón.

7 Own translation: EM 17.10.2018 – Russian woman found dead with 20 stab wounds. The first autopsy report is devastating. The perpetrator attacked the woman savagely. The body has *stab wounds everywhere*: *in her back, head, legs, neck and arms*. Nevertheless, *deadly wounds were inflicted in her neck and heart*.

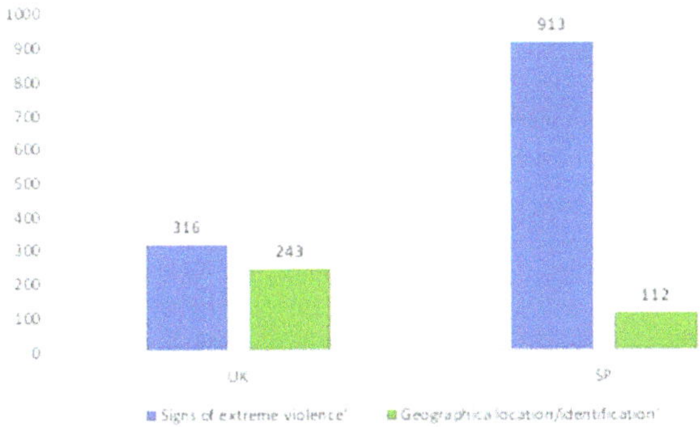

Graph 5. Total number of collocates with the lemmas BODY/CUERPO and CORPSE/CADÁVER per linguistic device.

(3) **TT 02.09.2009 – Man who killed girl in lorry had abused his wife; Tests may find out if the victim was 'touched sexually'**

> Police investigating the murder of a 19-year-old girl <u>whose body was found</u> in a parked lorry are examining a possible <u>sexual motive</u> for her killing. Detectives have ruled out <u>a full sexual assault</u> on Stacey Lawrence, who <u>was found strangled</u> in the cab of a lorry driven by her mother's boyfriend (. . .)

The linguistic pointers that may be indexed as ELITENESS in the corpus data typically refer to what may be classified as "high-status role labels" (Bednarek/Caple 2017: 82–83), which include political, social and legal institutions. However, "eliteness is scalar and dependent on the target audience" (58) and, therefore, it is conceptualized broadly to incorporate "various types of Eliteness that can be discursively construed: status, expertise, authority, celebrity, fame, or stardom" (58). Thus, for more precise labelling and analysis of the results obtained, I put forth the following linguistic devices in order to properly account for the different authority voices that construct newsworthiness across the data:

ELITENESS	
Linguistic devices	**Examples**
Reference to associations/groups	services to women experiencing violence; services to victims of domestic violence; battered women associations; etc.
Law and order	police officers, justice, judge + PN; special courts; gender violence court; etc.
Political institutions	parliament; minister(s); government; cabinet; etc.
Women-related (inter)national organisations	EU feminist movement; Women Institute; Observatory for Gender Violence; EU Institute for Gender Violence; etc.

Tab. 5. Linguistic devices for ELITENESS and examples of institutions and bodies shown in the data

The results show that ELITENESS is used in the corpus data to enshrine female victims in a protective fabric embodied by social and political institutions, protective actions, legal measures, social security, etc., in an attempt to construct a more positive discourse that counters the devastating effects of VAW. The analysis of collocations provides similar numbers for the linguistic devices identified, but with a significantly lower presence of women-related (inter)national organisations in the UK press (see Graph 6). The political and social measures approved in Spain seem to have favoured the emergence of a series of bodies that attest to more social activism and women in more active roles.

POSITIVITY often combines with ELITENESS to construct a discourse of safety and protection for female victims. However, there is a caveat here that concerns the contextual dimension of the results. While it is evident that the lemmas found in the corpus are positive for this type of discourse, these cannot be labelled as positive by simply attending to their encoded (semantic) meaning.

The linguistic devices identified are the following:

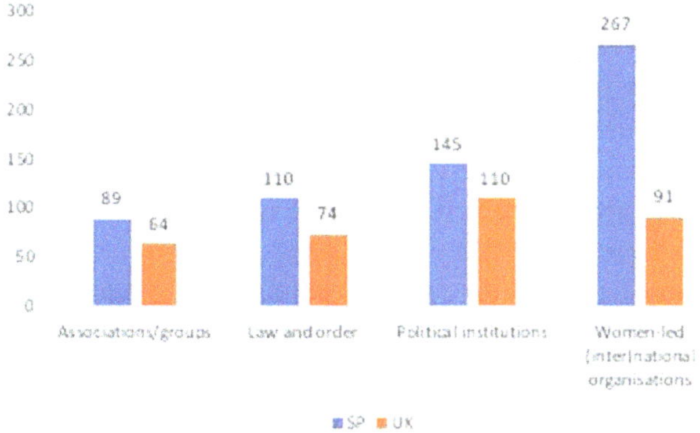

Graph 6. Total numbers of pointers to ELITENESS (per linguistic device).

POSITIVITY*	
Linguistic devices	**Examples**
Reference to protective actions	aid; help; refuge; protection; shelter; protection; safeguard; defend; etc.
Reference to legal measures	women's rights; equality; protection laws; prevention of domestic violence acts; etc.
Reference to social activism	women rights campaigns; fight against domestic violence; condemn male violence; etc.
Reference to social security	healthcare to women; medical assistance; psychological support, etc.

Tab. 6. Linguistic devices for POSITIVITY and examples

7 Conclusions

This chapter has examined the way news reporters portray female victims of VAW in a purpose-built corpus from UK and SP dailies over a 10-year period. Drawing on CADS, my aim has been to gain insights into how NV are used comparatively to construct female victims. In particular, the study applies DNVA (Bednarek/Caple 2017) in order to unveil potential ideological discourse(s). Besides the application of DNVA specifically to news reporting on VAW, this research presents a comparative study that sheds light on (dis)similarities in the ways NV are used to convey newsworthiness cross-linguistically.

The DNVA framework has been particularly useful in identifying and coding recurrent linguistic pointers that articulate certain discursive constructions of female victims in the corpus analysed. However, the qualitative analysis has revealed the need to populate the DNVA model with some further linguistic devices for more nuanced analyses. The aim of these is to capture the evaluative meaning potential of some NV for particular audiences. Specifically, this has been done by qualitatively identifying particular prosodies among the linguistic pointers.

In response to the research question (i.e. how do Spanish and British press use NV to represent female victims of VAW?), the results have substantiated the uneven presence of two complementary discourses: a discourse of death, violence and suffering and another of institutional and social support, which may construct a media narrative around VAW victims in the newspapers analysed. Notwithstanding this, two issues have arisen in the study that may deserve further consideration. First, from the role of NV in the construction of this narrative, I wonder if it is possible to talk about a hierarchy of NV in discourse(s). The patterns show that NEGATIVITY is the most pervasive NV in the data (perhaps given the nature of the corpus), while these patterns may help build expectations about the language used, the structure, the tone, the style, etc. (i.e. CONSONANCE) in news reporting on VAW that are endorsed by media outlets. Thus, these two NV may be said to become properties of the *event*. Second, the potential multiple coding of examples hinders the clear-cut delimitation of the linguistic devices identified. This may be a limitation of the methodology used.

The analysis has shown that NV convey more condemnatory overtones in SP news reports. As for negative emotions, however, the higher number of collocates in SP dailies (see Graph 3) may imply certain sensationalism that aims to exploit audiences' interest in crime and violence. As regards NEGATIVITY + IMPACT (see Graph 5), UK dailies seem less permeable to images of extreme violence, in spite of a slight increase over the years (data not shown). Besides, the collocates with the lemmas BODY/CUERPO or CORPSE/CADÁVER in SP dailies provide further evidence for more dramatic and explicit stories about physical violence. Further research may be needed to appraise whether these events are concealed in more condemnatory nuances.

The study has some limitations derived from the size of the corpus and the adopted methodology. As regards the former, the number of articles has made manual coding of all collocates virtually impossible. Perhaps a more definite focus on the reporting of VAW *crimes* would produce more accurate analyses on the specific role of some NV but this would certainly compromise representativeness. As for the latter, inter-coder reliability has only been used in a previous pilot study. Thus, much of the NV-coding is still open to subjective perception.

All in all, NV have also provided insights into a culturally-shared set of beliefs, attitudes and representations that are key to the meaning re-signifying of women, but which are partly created and partly reproduced by the Western press. This may lead to further research on the (re-)configuration of their identities in today's society.

References

Anthony, Lawrence. 2019. *AntConc* (version 3.5.8) [computer software]. Tokyo, Japan: Waseda University. Available from: https://www.laurenceanthony.net/software. Accessed 19 March 2020.

Baker, Paul. 2010. *Sociolinguistics and Corpus Linguistics*. Edinburgh: Edinburgh University Press.

Baker, Paul/Levon, Erez. 2015. Picking the right cherries? A comparison of corpus-based and qualitative analyses of news articles about masculinity. *Discourse & Communication* 9(2), 221–236.

Baker, Paul/Gabrielatos, Costas/McEnery, Tony. 2013. *Discourse Analysis and Media Attitudes: The Representation of Islam in the British Press*. Cambridge: Cambridge University Press.

Bednarek, Monika/Caple, Helen. 2012. 'Value added': Language, image and news values. *Discourse, Context & Media* 1(2–3), 103–113.

Bednarek, Monika/Caple, Helen. 2014. Why do news values matter? Towards a new methodological framework for analysing news discourse in Critical Discourse Analysis and beyond. *Discourse & Society* 25(2), 135–158.

Bednarek, Monika/Caple, Helen. 2017. *The Discourse of News Values: How Organisations Create Newsworthiness*. Oxford: Oxford University Press.

Bell, Alan. 1991. *The Language of News Media*. Oxford: Blackwell.

Bell, Alan. 1998. The discourse structure of news stories. In Bell, Alan/ Garrett, Peter (eds.) *Approaches to Media Discourse*. Oxford & Malden, MA: Blackwell, 64–104.

Bell, Alan/ Garrett, Peter (eds.) 1998. *Approaches to Media Discourse*. Oxford & Malden, MA: Blackwell.

Benedict, Hellen. 1992. *Virgin or Vamp: How the Press Covers Sex Crimes*. Oxford: Oxford University Press.

Bullock, Cathy/Cubert, Jason. 2002. Coverage of domestic violence fatalities by newspapers in Washington State. *Journal of Interpersonal Violence* 17, 475–499.

Cameron, Deborah. 2020. Isolated incidents [Blog post]. Retrieved from: https://debuk.wordpress.com/2020/07/11/isolated-incidents/. Accessed 20 March 2020.

Caple, Helen/Bednarek, Monika. 2013. Delving into the discourse: Approaches to news values in journalism studies and beyond. Working Paper. Oxford: Reuters Institute for the Study of Journalism. Available at https://reutersinstitute.politics.ox.ac.uk/ publications/risj.working-papers.html

Caple, Helen/Huan, Changpeng/Bednarek, Monika. 2020. *Multimodal News Analysis Across Cultures*. Cambridge: Cambridge University Press.

Carlyle, Kellie E./Slater, Michael D./Chakroff, Jennifer L. 2008. Newspaper coverage of intimate partner violence: Skewing representations of risk. *Journal of Communication* 58, 168–186.

Carter, Cynthia/Linda Steiner. 2004. Introduction to critical readings: Media and gender. In Carter, Cynthia/Linda Steiner (eds.) *Critical Readings: Media and Gender*, Maidenhead: Open University Press, 1–10.

Cole, Peter/Tony Harcup. 2010. *Newspaper Journalism*. London: Sage.

Cotter, Colleen. 2010. *News Talk: Investigating the Language of Journalism*. Cambridge: Cambridge University Press.

Dahl, Trine/Flottum, Kjersti. 2017. Verbal-visual harmony or dissonance? A news values analysis of multimodal texts on climate change. *Discourse, Context & Media* 20, 124–131.

Durant, Alan/Lambrou, Marina. 2009. *Language and Media: A Resource Book for Students*. London & New York: Routledge.

Easteal, Patricia/Holland, Kate/Judd, Keziah 2015. Enduring themes and silences in media portrayals of violence against women. *Women's Studies International Forum* 48, 103–113.

Fairbairn, Jordan. 2015. *Ecologies of Change: Violence Against Women Prevention, Feminist Public Sociology and Social Media*. PhD Thesis. Carleton University.

Fairbairn, Jordan/Myrna Dawson. 2013. Canadian news coverage of intimate partner homicide: Analyzing changes over time. *Feminist Criminology* 8(3), 147–176.

Fairclough, Norman. 1995. *Critical Discourse Analysis*. Boston: Addison Wesley.

Formato, Federica. 2019. *Gender, Discourse and Ideology in Italian*. Switzerland: Palgrave Macmillan.

Fowler, Roger. 1991. *Language in the News. Discourse and Ideology in the Press*. London & New York: Routledge.

Fruttaldo, Antonio/Venuti, Marco. 2018. A cross-cultural discursive approach to news values in the press in the US, the UK and Italy: The case of the Supreme Court ruling on same-sex marriage. *ESP Across Cultures* 14, 81–97.

Fuster-Márquez, Miguel/Gregori-Signes, Carmen. 2019. La construcción discursiva del turismo en la prensa española (verano de 2017). *Discurso y Sociedad* 13(2), 195–224.

Gabrielatos, Costas/Alison Duguid. 2014. Corpus Linguistics and CDA: A critical look at *synergy*. *CDA20+ Symposium*, University of Amsterdam, 9 September 2014.

Galtung, John/Ruge, Mari 1965. The structure of foreign news. *Journal of Peace Research* 2(1), 64–91.

Harcup, Tony/Deirdre O'Neill. 2001. What is news? Galtung and Ruge revisited. *Journalism Studies* 2(2), 261–280.

Huan, Changpeng. 2016. Leaders or readers, whom to please? News values in the transition of the Chinese press. *Discourse, Context & Media* 13, 114–121.

Lorenzo-Dus, Nuria/Smith, Philippa. 2018. The visual construction of political crises: A news values approach. In Patrona, Marianna (ed.) *Crisis and the Media. Narratives of Crisis across Cultural Settings and Media Genres*, Amsterdam/Philadelphia: John Benjamins, 151–176.

Makki, Mohammad. 2019. Discursive news values analysis of Iranian crime news reports: Perspectives from the culture. *Discourse & Communication* 13(4), 437–460.

Meyers, Marian. 1997. *News Coverage of Violence Against Women: Engendering Blame*. Newbury Park: Sage Publications.

Molek-Kozakowska, Katarzyna. 2018. Popularity-driven science journalism and climate change: A critical discourse analysis of the unsaid. *Discourse, Context & Media* 21, 73–81.

Partington, Alan/Duguid, Alison/Taylor, Charlotte. 2013. *Patterns and Meanings in Discourse: Theory and Practice in Corpus-Assisted Discourse Studies (CADS)*. Amsterdam/Philadelphia: John Benjamins.

Perkins, Keighley. 2019. *A News Values Analysis of Representations of Male Schizophrenia in UK National Newspapers (2013–2016)*. MPhil Thesis. Swansea University.

Potts, Amanda/Bednarek, Monika/Caple, Helen. 2015. How can computer-based methods help researchers to investigate news values in large datasets? A corpus linguistic study of the construction of newsworthiness in the reporting of Hurricane Katrina. *Discourse and Communication* 9(2), 149–172.

Richardson, John E. 2007. *Analysing Newspapers: An Approach from Critical Discourse Analysis*. Basingstoke: Palgrave Macmillan.

Tabbert, Ulrike. 2016. *Language and Crime: Constructing Offenders and Victims in Newspaper Reports*. Basingstoke: Palgrave Macmillan.

Taylor, Charlotte. 2014. Investigating the representation of migrants in the UK and Italian press: A cross-linguistic corpus-assisted discourse analysis. *International Journal of Corpus Linguistics* 19(3), 368–400.

van Dijk, Teun A. 1988. *News as Discourse*. Hillsdale: Lawrence Erlbaum Associates Inc.

van Dijk, Teun A. 1998. *Ideology*. London: Sage.

Venuti, Marco/Antonio Fruttaldo. 2019. Contrasting news values in newspaper articles and social media: A discursive approach to the US ruling on same-sex marriage. In Lewandowska-Tomaszczyk, Barbara (ed.) *Contacts and Contrasts in Cultures and Languages*. Cham: Springer, 147–161.

Wodak, Ruth/Brigitta Busch. 2004. Approaches to media texts. In Downing, John D. H. et al. (eds.) *The Sage Handbook of Media Studies*. London: Sage, 105–123.

Wodak, Ruth/Michael Meyer. 2001. *Methods of Critical Discourse Analysis*. London: Sage.

Wozniak, Jessica A./McCloskey, Kathy A. 2010. Fact or fiction? Gender issues related to newspaper reports on intimate partner homicide. *Violence Against Women* 16, 934–952.

Alfonso Sánchez-Moya

How does violence-motivated online discourse differ from its non-violent counterpart? Insights from a CADS approach

1 Introduction

Gender-related killings of women and girls continue to entail a pervasive social problem across countries worldwide. According to recent figures published by the United Nations Office on Drugs and Crime (UNODC 2018), an estimate of 87,000 women were intentionally killed across the globe in 2017. Strikingly, this global study suggests that women are more likely to be murdered by someone they know, and more than a third (30,000) of these women were killed by their current or former intimate partner. Quite undeniably, countries have adopted measures of many kinds to address violence of this sort, yet the number of casualties remains practically the same. Despite the many controversies around this social issue, the main reason why figures are far from decreasing lies in the very complex nature of Intimate Partner Violence (IPV henceforth). As argued by Ali / Naylor (2013), a solid comprehension of IPV does necessarily require a multifarious approach to it, which in itself constitutes a firm justification for the attempt to better understand it from a wider multidisciplinary perspective.

As a matter of fact, this is the main objective that this study has in mind. In what follows, this chapter seeks to provide insights into the discourse of female survivors of Intimate Partner Violence. Findings discussed here are embedded within a broader exploration of this type of discourse underpinned in both quantitative and qualitative explorations (Sánchez-Moya 2018). Nonetheless, and based upon Corpus-assisted Discourse Studies (CADS), this chapter provides a sentiment analysis of online forum messages by women who are undergoing IPV-related experiences. More specifically, this study looks at how this violence-motivated discourse differs from its non-violent counterpart in order to contrast how female online users contributing to this online forum are characterized by a different discursive style when compared to women writing in fora across less specific domains. To this end, this chapter first informs of the main theoretical sources sustaining this research, examining the connection between IPV and CADS and describing LIWC, the text analysis software used for the purposes of this study. Core methodological details are then outlined, paying special attention to issues of data collection and analysis. After this, relevant findings are presented and discussed; and concluding remarks ultimately wrap up the chapter.

2 Literature review

2.1 Exploring Intimate Partner Violence (IPV) from Corpus-Assisted Discourse Studies (CADS)

As already hinted in the previous section, my stance as a researcher advocates a multidisciplinary approach to the understanding of IPV in order to shed as much light as possible on this worrying phenomenon. Unsurprisingly, most attempts to investigate this type of violence spring from areas that can be seen as more connected to an issue of this kind, such as psychology and health sciences, sociology, or even law. Nevertheless, insights from discourse related research are to date more limited. This dearth of research is in itself very significant if we bear in mind that one of the main drives in critical discourse analysis is to explore social phenomena in which power imbalances play a central role, especially when this lack of equilibrium brings about discrimination and inequality in society (Koller 2012). Nevertheless, and somehow mirroring the more central position that IPV has achieved in socio-political agendas worldwide, interesting explorations have started to bloom over the last years (Holmes et al. 2007; Hester 2012; Bou-Franch 2013; 2016; Santaemilia/Maruenda 2016). Similarly, this study keeps contributing to recent explorations of discourse by female survivors of IPV in online contexts and through the lens of corpus linguistics and sentiment analysis (Sánchez-Moya 2017, 2018).

This study is mostly influenced by Corpus-assisted Discourse Studies (Partington et al. 2013), which defends a rather eclectic approach to incorporating techniques from corpus linguistics in order to better understand the discursive components of social phenomena. In fact, the aim of the CADS is 'the uncovering, in the discourse type under study, of what we might call "non-obvious meaning", that is, meaning which might not be readily available for the naked-eyed perusal' (Partington et al. 2013: 11). In contrast with the tendency among traditional corpus linguists (especially those interested in general linguistics) to privilege the quantitative approach, the whole motivation behind the incorporation of corpus techniques in CADS is 'to acquaint ourselves as much as possible with the discourse type(s) in hand' (Partington et al. 2013: 12). To this end, a wide range of tools becomes available for discourse-oriented researchers to gain a better understanding of how things are done linguistically in the discourse-type being studied (Partington et al. 2013). Additionally, a common tendency among CADS research is the *ad hoc* compilation of specialized corpora, since chances are that there exists no previously available collection of the discourse type under scrutiny (Partington et al. 2013). In a similar vein, CADS is also characterized for being comparative in nature. As suggested by Partington et al. (2013), contrast can be established either between more local levels (especially when seeking to evaluate the distinctive features of a discourse type with similar kinds) or larger, more heterogeneric corpora.

2.2 LIWC as a text analysis software tool and related studies

Out of the multiple possibilities available for CADS-related research, this study relies on *Linguistic Inquiry and Word Count* (LIWC henceforth)[1] as a text analysis software tool to investigate the discourse type at hand. It is noteworthy to consider that LIWC developers conceive language as 'the most common and reliable way for people to translate their internal thoughts and emotions into a form that others can understand' to the extent of seeing words and language as 'the medium by which cognitive, personality, clinical, and social psychologists attempt to understand human beings' (Tausczik/Pennebaker 2010: 25). Quite relatedly, LIWC developers assume that lexical choices made by people transmit psychological information over and above their literal meaning and independent of their semantic context (Pennebaker et al. 2007),[2] which can at the same time be used to make inferences about the dimensions of individuals' personalities (Tausczik/Pennebaker 2010).

Moving now to a more technical explanation, LIWC has two central features: the processing component and the internal dictionaries (Tausczik/Pennebaker 2010). Basically, LIWC analyses speech samples by identifying and classifying them according to the three internal dictionaries that the LIWC2015 version has, which consist of almost 6,400 words, words stems and selected emotions.[3] Each dictionary refers to the collection of words that define a particular category. LIWC provides the percentage-use scores of 80 standard linguistic categories of different types as they are represented in the scrutinized texts submitted by users. These linguistic categories include language variables (such as analytical thinking, authenticity, or emotional tone), 21 standard categories identifying function words (%of pronouns, articles, auxiliary verbs, etc.) and 41 semantic categories dealing with psychological constructs (such as affect, cognition, biological processes). Broadly speaking, this output measure is correlated to both personality and real-world outcome measures, which arguably capture people's social and psychological statuses as represented in their discursive production.

1 Information on this software tool can be found here: http://liwc.wpengine.com

2 'Semantic context' is seen here as 'meaning-constraining context, i.e., discourse context, experimental context, situational context within which a target word is uttered [or used]' (Rahman/Melinger 2009: 713).

3 This chapter is based on LIWC 2015 version. More details on the development and psychometric properties of it can be found in Pennebaker et al. (2015).

Nonetheless, as Tausczik / Pennebaker themselves claim (2010), language dimensions such as function words are more straightforward than others. This is not the case when dealing with dimensions related to emotions, which are definitely more subjective. In order to solve this slippery challenge, 'an initial selection of word candidates was gleaned from dictionaries, thesauruses, questionnaires, and lists made by research assistants [and] groups of three judges then independently rated whether each word candidate was appropriate to the overall word category' (Tausczik/Pennebaker 2010: 27). Reportedly, the final percentage of judges' agreement ranged from 93 % to 100 % after this rating phase (Tausczik/Pennebaker 2010: 28).

Due to both the uncomplicated methodological manoeuvring and the potential it has to provide a computerized exploration of texts according to their emotional characterization, it is possible to identify a rich profusion of studies that combine language-driven research and sentiment analysis via the application of LIWC. Interesting insights have been obtained after examining discourses pertaining to social relationships or health issues. For instance, there is evidence supporting the correlation between physical and/or emotional pain and a higher use of first-person singular pronouns (Rude et al. 2004). In a similar vein, research has also pointed out that verb tense differences (present or past) can also indicate increased psychological distance and a higher degree of resolution when speakers describe disclosed events in comparison to when they do the same with previously undisclosed events (Pasupathi 2007). Studies combining linguistic analyses and psychological processes in major social phenomena have proved that LIWC is capable of providing accurate identification of emotion in language use (Tausczik/Pennebaker 2010; Kahn et al. 2007) in contexts ranging from cancer talk (Bantum/Owen 2009) or narcissism (Holtzman et al. 2019). Moreover, there have been interesting attempts to examine narratives by IPV survivors. Based on 32 volunteers in offline contexts, Holmes et al. (2007) concluded that the higher use of emotion words, the bolder the perceived immersion in the traumatic event. Quite relatedly, Tani et al. (2016) also employed LIWC to explore IPV discourse, identifying, for instance, that women who experienced violence wrote longer narratives that contained proportionately more negative emotion words and more references to cognitions and physical/body issues.

3 Research design

As I specified in the first section, the main objective of this study is to investigate how violence-motivated online discourse differs from its non-violent counterpart in order to contrast how female users contributing to an online forum are characterized by a different discursive style if compared to women writing in fora in less specific domains. With this in mind, the overarching research question guiding this chapter can be worded as follows: based on their discursive characterization, to what extent do these online IPV communities differ from other non-violence motivated forum communities? Unlike related explorations (Sánchez-Moya 2018), the methodological approach adapted in this chapter is mainly quantitative, since it does not provide textual instances of the type of text under analysis. This is also the case due to the main objective of this chapter, and qualitative analysis would be envisaged here as the subsequent methodological approximation in order to obtain a more holistic understanding of the discourse at hand. In what follows, essential details of data collection and data analysis are put forward.

3.1 Data collection: corpora under scrutiny

This study is based on two different corpora, whose details are described below and summarized in Tab. 1 below. On the one hand, the main corpus (experimental) entails a total of 120,000 words collected from an online forum ascribed to British charity (*Women's Aid*) and aimed at assisting women who have experienced IPV during their life spans. This collection of words is called VIOL_CORPUS for referential purposes in this study. More specifically, and due to the overall objective of the project this research is embedded with, online messages were gathered from three different online communities within this online space. Thus, posts come from three subcommunities: *Is it abuse?* (SB1), where women describe the abusive relationship episodes they are witnessing without even knowing for sure, in some cases, if what they are going through can be considered abusive or not; *Getting out* (SB2), where women largely recognize the abuse in their relationships and seek to find mutual online support on how to proceed; and *Life after abuse* (SB3), where most women conceptualize themselves outside the abusive relationship and share their (mostly encouraging) experiences with other users.

In the attempt to strive for a comparable analysis, I decided to compile an *ad hoc* reference corpus based on allegedly similar discourse types (the NON_VIOL corpus henceforth) at the level of production and communicative context. To this end, the same amount of words was compiled from similar online contexts (forums): a forum related to female solo-travelling (NV1), posts included in a forum aimed at sharing experiences linked to wedding preparation (NV2), and forum posts included in an online site linked to a wide range of issues pertaining to motherhood (NV3). Far from the excitement one might expect in these communities, users engaged in communicative practices of different kinds, many of them narrating the dangers encountered when travelling alone, family argument when arranging wedding invitations, or the distress experienced by many first-time mothers. This was mostly done in order to control one of the most central variables for the purposes of this research, which presumed that the writers of these posts were women and would therefore bring the comparability of both corpora closer. Likewise, the fact that corpora compared here are nested in similar contexts of production and reproduction was thought to add internal validity to the study. Textual examples of each community are provided in the Appendix at the end of this chapter.

As previously pointed out, an essential requirement when creating this reference corpus was to collect posts produced in similar circumstances to those integrating the experimental corpus. To this end, posts were collected from online forums that fitted the multiple criteria suggested by Internet scholars (Bolander/Locher 2014; Markham/Buchanan 2015; Mackenzie 2017) in the attempt to comply with good research practice in ethical terms. In short, posts were not password protected, registration was not required, discourse data was anonymized to the furthest possible degree and a sensitive approach to data storage was equally adopted. Apart from this, forum users were informed by the different online sites of the public and open nature of the spaces to which they were contributing, and private-messaging was also available for users to communicative privately.

CORPUS UNDER SCRUTINY		
EXPERIMENTAL CORPUS (VIOL)	**POSTS**	**WORDS**
VIOL1_Is it abuse (SB1)	163	40,000
VIOL2_Getting out (SB2)	122	40,000
VIOL3_Life after abuse (SB3)	187	40,000
TOTAL_VIOL	472	120,000
CONTROL CORPUS (NON_VIOL)	POSTS	WORDS
NONVIOL1_Travelling (NV1)	244	40,000
NONVIOL2_Wedding (NV2)	299	40,000
NONVIOL3_Mothering (NV3)	217	40,000
TOTAL_NONVIOL	760	120,000
TOTAL CORPUS	1232	240,000

Tab. 1. Details of corpora under analysis for this study (VIOL and NONVIOL_CORPUS)

Once both the VIOL_CORPUS and the NONVIOL_CORPUS had been gathered, all posts were submitted to LIWC. Despite the numerous available categories researchers can select from, only some of the most relevant semantic categories for the purposes of this study were chosen. Thus, attention is paid to categories included within 'language variables' (namely 'analytical thinking', 'WPS', 'authenticity' and 'tone') and those corresponding to emotionality ('positive emotions', 'negative emotions'; and more specifically 'anxiety', 'anger' and 'sadness'). Categories concerning pronominal distribution, as well as some other categories, are part of differently-motivated studies (Sánchez-Moya 2017). A more detailed explanation of the categories employed in this study is provided in the next section.

3.2 Data analysis

Among the many categories LIWC uses to classify words, seven of them are considered 'summary language variables' (Pennebaker et al. 2015). Thus, LIWC supplies scores related to analytical thinking ('Analytic'), authenticity ('Authentic') and emotional tone ('Tone'). It can further explore more syntactic correlations on the basis of the number of words included per sentence ('WPS'). These are the categories that this study will be focusing on, as explained in what follows.

Firstly, attention is paid to 'analytical thinking' and 'WPS' (words per sentence) in order to investigate complexity of thinking styles. High scores in 'Analytic' are thought to indicate formal, logical and hierarchical thinking patterns (LIWC 2017; Pennebaker et al. 2014), whereas low percentages may imply using language in more narrative ways, focusing on the here-and-now and leave more room for personal experiences (Pennebaker et al. 2014). 'WPS' is thought to psychologically correlate with a higher ability to engage in verbal fluency and exude cognitive complexity (Hancock et al. 2007). Secondly, high figures in 'authenticity' tend to be indicative of people expressing in honest and personal ways, while lower numbers may evidence a more guarded, distanced form of discourse (Newman et al. 2003; Pennebaker et al. 2015; Peslak 2018). Lastly, emotional 'tone' seems to be more straightforward in interpretative issues, since the higher the percentage, the more positive the tone (Cohn et al. 2004; Pennebaker et al. 2015).

Influenced by the type of discourse under scrutiny, and the possibilities that LIWC offers to provide a fine-grained analysis of how emotionality is displayed in discourse, special emphasis is put on positive and negative emotions. Furthermore, LIWC can detect three subtypes of negative emotions ('anxiety', 'anger' and 'sadness'). In contrast to those described before, these categories need less explanation. Scores here represent the percentage of words in each online community that LIWC identifies for each category.

4 Results and discussion

This section presents the results obtained after running the text software tool LIWC through the corpora under scrutiny. More specifically, this section focuses on comparing the six online communities at the kernel of this chapter: SB1, SB2 and SB3 in the VIOL_CORPUS;

LIWC language variables	VIOL_CORPUS vs. NONVIOL_CORPUS			
	VIOL_CORPUS		NONVIOL_CORPUS	
	N	%	N	%
Analytical	22,608	18.8	49,656	41.3
WPS	25,608	21.3	22,476	18.7
Authenticity	84,180	70.1	85,740	71.4
Tone	11,880	9.9	21,435	52.5

Tab. 2. LIWC language variables (raw numbers and %): VIOL_CORPUS vs. NONVIOL_CORPUS

and NV1, NV2 and NV3 in the NONVIOL_CORPUS. To start with, Tab. 2 contrasts the LIWC scores obtained for both the VIOL_CORPUS and the NONVIOL_CORPUS as far as language variables are considered.

On these grounds, it seems sensible to establish two different trends. If results obtained for both corpora are borne in mind, two variables seem to behave less differently in these two discourse types. To start with, both corpora present very similar 'authenticity' scores. This is surely influenced by the high figure that the online travelling community (NV1) offers (89.9 %), suggesting that users in this community communicate in less guarded and/or distanced ways then the rest. A very slight divergence rate (2.6 %) is also spotted in 'WPS'. This would then point out to a higher cognitive complexity in IPV-related discourse, which was also within the expected results. Nevertheless, curious interpretations may be reached if the six subcorpora are juxtaposed.

LIWC scores obtained in the 'analytical' and the 'tone' variables suggest broader divergences between IPV-related discourse and its counterpart. On the one hand, different thinking/writing styles in both corpora are observed. Thus, online users' discourse in the NONVIOL_CORPUS can be said to be more logical and integrated by more hierarchical thinking patterns, whereas IPV survivors' discourse is allegedly narrative-oriented, personal, and focused on the here and now. On the other hand, the most drastic divergence between two corpora is that concerning 'tone' (42.6 %). Such a divergence between both corpora highlights the

	LIWC language variables (%)			
Online community	**ANALYTIC**	**WPS**	**AUTHENTIC**	**TONE**
SB1	17.6	22.1	62.7	6.2
SB2	18.4	21.2	70.5	10.5
SB3	20.4	20.8	76.4	14
NV1	57.1	17.3	89.9	71.8
NV2	42	18.4	59.1	60.2
NV3	26.3	20.9	57.5	25.8

Tab. 3. Explored language variables across six online communities under scrutiny (in %)

pessimistic tone governing the IPV online communities under scrutiny. Nonetheless, more insights along these lines can be gained if percentages obtained in each of the six subcorpora are contrasted.

In fact, the possibility of juxtaposing the six online communities can reinforce some of the claims already made and provide more fine-grained interpretations, as shown in Tab. 3. Similarly, Fig. 1 below offers a comparison based on raw numbers so that readers can assess the differences among communities. As anticipated in previous paragraphs, a less remarkable difference is observed as far as 'WPS' and 'authenticity' are concerned. First, 'WPS' scores gradually decrease from SB1 (22.1 %) to NV1 (17.3 %). This pattern reinforces the complexity in cognitive-emotional terms that discourse reflected by women trying to find out if they are being abused. Interestingly, however, this same complexity seems to be more central in discourses around motherhood (NV3) than in women's accounts of 'Life after abuse' (SB3), which may also point at the many difficulties faced by women in the process of motherhood. This can explain the reason why the lowest percentage for 'authenticity' is associated with NV3, which suggests a more guarded discursive style. As will be further elaborated in this chapter, the discursive style associated with motherhood experiences does not seem too distant from the IPV-related one.

Previous claims associated with the variables 'analytical' and 'tone' are strengthened by means of this detailed presentation of results.

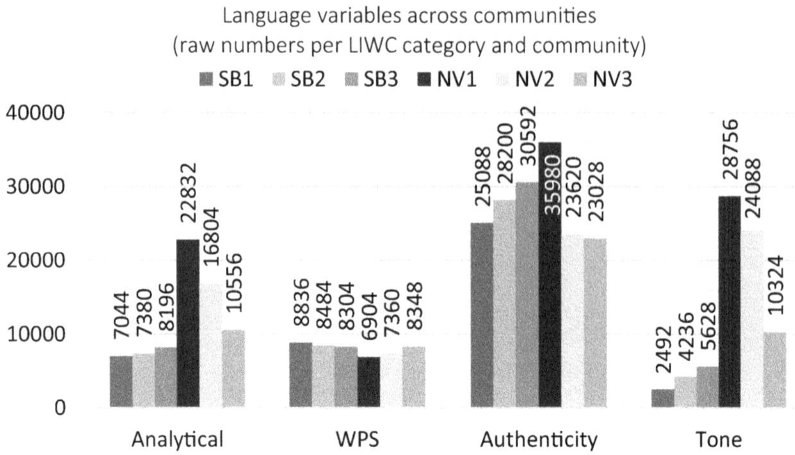

Fig. 1. | LIWC language variables across communities (raw numbers)

Thus, LIWC scores in these two cases are arranged exactly in the same way. Judging from percentages in 'analytical', it is possible to claim that more narrative writing styles are encountered as SB1 is approached (which is accompanied by an inverted progression if cognitive complexity is at issue). A similar (though more drastic) pattern is spotted in 'tone', which at the same time entails the most severe decline if the highest score (71.8 % in NV1) is compared with the lowest one (6.2 % in SB1). As a matter of fact, this remarkable difference was one of the main reasons why a more detailed account of discursive emotionality between these two corpora was worth analysing, which is what the next section endeavours to examine.

As the previous section indicated, there is a sharp contrast between percentages measuring the emotional tone of each corpus. Hence, a closer analysis of both corpora's (discursive) emotionality is worth pursuing. Therefore, Tab. 4 below illustrates LIWC specific measurements for emotionality in the corpus under inspection.

Broadly speaking, the control corpus displays a higher score if emphasis is placed on positive emotions, a tendency that is reverted if negative emotions are taken into account. Focusing now on the three specific categories overarched by the 'negative emotions', it is interesting to observe the ways in which 'anxiety', 'anger' and 'sadness'

Emotionality (LIWC)	VIOL_CORPUS vs. NONVIOL_CORPUS			
	VIOL_CORPUS (N=120,000)		NONVIOL_CORPUS (N=120,000)	
	N	%	*N*	%
Positive emotions	2,820	2.4	3,804	3.2
Negative emotions	4,344	3.6	2,100	1.8
Anxiety	900	0.8	636	0.6
Anger	1,404	1.2	312	0.3
Sadness	912	0.8	564	0.5

Tab. 4. | Emotionality in LIWC: VIOL_CORPUS vs. NONVIOL_CORPUS (raw numbers and %)

are distributed across the VIOL and the NONVIOL corpora. Although differences are observed if 'anxiety' and 'sadness' are contrasted, the sharpest divergence is found in the discursive expression of 'anger'.

Moving now to the cross-community comparison, Tab. 5 below includes all the percentages obtained for each LIWC categories concerning emotionality in the six subcorpora representing the online communities under investigation. Likewise, Fig. 2 offers a graphic representation of results based on raw numbers. It should be noted again that each community contains 40,000. In contrast to the previous section, low raw figures are a consequence of the greater degree of specificity when dealing with lexical items included within these categories.

Bearing all these indicators in mind, several interpretations can be reached at this point. Overall, forum communities engaged in non-violent communicative scenarios and emphasize the very little room that online communities around IPV leave for positive emotions. Nonetheless, it seems that users in SB3 ('Life after abuse') make use of more positive discourse than online users sharing their experiences with motherhood (NV3). What seems clear, however, is the very few instances of lexical items echoing positive emotions in users contributing to SB1 ('Is it abuse?'). This is also validated if the scores for negative emotions are paid attention to, since SB1 takes in this case the top position. Notice however that the second highest score for negative emotions is that shown in SB3, which becomes a rather controversial

	Discursive emotionality (%)				
Online community	**POS_EM**	**NEG_EM**	**ANX**	**ANGER**	**SAD**
SB1	2	3.8	0.7	1.3	0.8
SB2	2.3	3.5	0.8	1	0.7
SB3	2.8	3.6	0.8	1	0.8
NV1	3.9	1.4	0.5	0.2	0.6
NV2	3.2	1.4	0.4	0.2	0.4
NV3	2.4	2.4	0.7	0.4	0.5

Tab. 5. | Discursive emotionality across six online communities under scrutiny (in %)

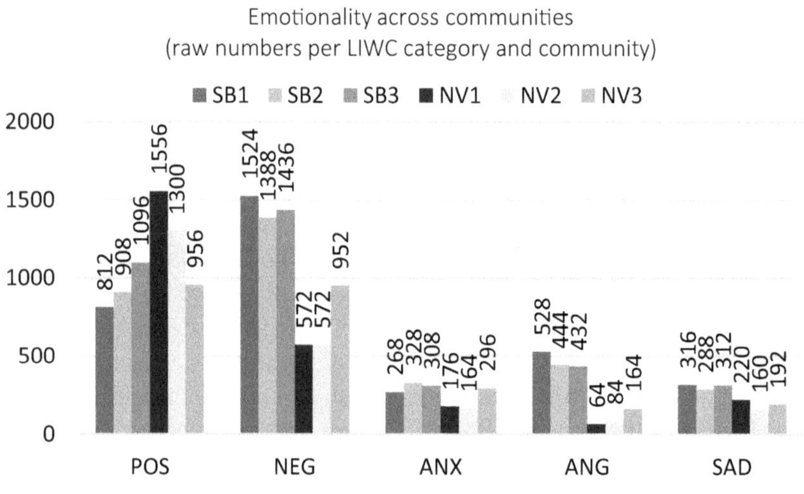

Fig. 2. | Discursive emotionality across six online communities under scrutiny (N)

result considering that SB3 proved to be the most positive online community within the VIOL_CORPUS. This could be explored further by a more qualitative exploration of the ways in which LIWC carries out this type of sentiment analysis, which was not an available feature and one of the most noticeable limitations of the tool at the time of analysis. Nonetheless, this caveat can be mitigated if the percentage-distribution of the three negative emotions across the six communities is examined.

The three subcorpora integrating the VIOL_CORPUS take the top positions as far as negative emotions are concerned. Judging from the results obtained, these users' online discourse shows higher instances of lexical anxiety in experiences connected with motherhood than at a very initial stage within an abusive relationship. In order to better understand the relevance of this, it should be noted that percentages for 'anxiety' in either the travelling or the wedding preparation communities oscillate between 0.5 % and 0.4 %, respectively, whereas the highest point for anxiety in fact doubles in SB2 (0.8 %). A very similar pattern is observed is percentages ascribed to 'sadness'. The three online communities linked to IPV show very similar figures. Although this may suggest that lexical sadness is uniformly scattered throughout the VIOL_CORPUS, a comparison with the control corpus does not seem to suggest so. As a matter of fact, the lowest indicator for sadness (0.4 % in NV2) almost doubles in its highest counterpart (0.8 % in SB1).

Despite this, it is not until the category 'anger' is examined when the most telling results are observed. As shown above, women contributing to the online travel forum show a rather insignificant degree of lexical anger (0.2 %). Overall then, this represents the sharpest contrast between the online community in which lexical anger is used the least (0.2 % in NV1) compared to where it is used the most (1.3 % in SB1). Consequently, and based on previous considerations, this suggests that discourse generated around IPV is characterized by a higher inclusion of lexical anger than by certainly interrelated negative emotions such as anxiety or sadness. This claim gains prominence if online instances of discourse in forums not connected with IPV itself are taken into account.

Overall, this section has provided interesting insights into the way emotionality is discursively expressed in the corpora under investigation. Interestingly, findings of this sort have been achieved by previous research, identifying insightful correlations between the distribution of these categories and aspects related to cancer narratives (Bantum/Owen 2009) or childhood trauma (Luterek et al. 2005). Some other studies have shown a correction between negative emotion words and some other discursive features that a LIWC analysis can offer, which hints at the necessary incorporation of qualitative explorations to an analysis of this kind.

5 Concluding remarks

Through the application of LIWC, a text analysis software tool for sentiment analysis, this study has sought to offer insights from a CADS approach into the different discursive characterization of IPV online communities and non-violence motivated ones. As pointed out before, the main research question that this chapter has attempted to answer is the following: based on their discursive characterization, to what extent do these online IPV communities differ from other non-violence motivated forum communities?

Paying attention to LIWC language variables first ('authenticity', 'analytical thinking', 'WPS' and 'tone'), both the VIOL_CORPUS and the NONVIOL_CORPUS present similar scores if 'authenticity' is at issue. A detailed analysis of all corpora suggests that discourses around motherhood score remarkably higher than discourse used by users in IPV communities. Based on 'WPS' scores, IPV-related discourse shows a higher degree of cognitive-emotional complexity, especially that employed by users in SB1 (Is it abuse?). Interestingly, however, discourses around motherhood are closer to IPV-related discourse than that of some other, non-violent contexts. As far as analytical thinking is concerned, IPV online communities are especially characterized by a discursive style that is more narrative-oriented and personal, focusing more on the here-and-now. However, non-violence motivated online communities are generally more logical and hierarchical. The sharpest contrast between both corpora is obtained in 'tone'. This manifest a very remarkable difference in the way emotional tone is used, highlighting the severely pessimistic type of discourse found in SB1 if compared to non-violent online communities.

In terms of emotionality, forum communities engaged in non-violent communicative contexts are discursively characterized more by a more positive emotionality than IPV-related communities. The opposite pattern is found if 'negative' emotions are at stake. If all subcorpora are compared, claims about IPV-related negative emotions and their discursive characterization are validated. It is striking, however, to find out that the discourse generated around IPV is characterized by a higher inclusion of lexical anger than by certainly interrelated negative emotions such as anxiety or sadness, findings that provide textual-based evidence when shedding light onto women survivors' emotional situation.

To conclude, it is convenient to identify the most salient limitations of this study and some of possibilities that future research along these lines could consider. As already suggested throughout the text, one of the main shortcomings of this chapter is related to the absence of qualitative insights into the discourse under investigation. Nonetheless, as pointed out elsewhere, this quantitative exploration is mostly understood here as the first examination of the corpora, which in turn assists discourse-driven researchers to build more solid assumptions. In other words, and as advocated by Baker / McEnery (2015), corpus linguistics in general and CADS in particular are not regarded as the panacea for all issues concerning discourse analysts' biases but as useful pathways to equip them with assistance for more empirically-grounded claims. Further research should hence encourage to incorporate text-based instances of the discourse under examination, which would surely provide a more holistic understanding of the discursive (and therefore social) phenomenon at hand.

References

Ali, Parvenn A./Naylor, Paul B. 2013. Intimate partner violence: A narrative review of the feminist, social and ecological explanations for its causation. *Aggression and Violent Behavior* 18(6), 611–619.

Baker, Paul/McEnery, Tony. (eds.) 2015. *Corpora and discourse studies: Integrating discourse and corpora*. London: Palgrave.

Bantum, Erin O./Owen, Jason E. 2009. Evaluating the validity of computerized content analysis programs for identification of emotional expression in cancer narrative. *Psychological Assessment* 21, 79–88.

Bolander, Brook/Locher, Miriam A. 2014. Doing sociolinguistic research on computer-mediated data: A review of four methodological issues. *Discourse, Context & Media* 3, 14–26.

Bou-Franch, Patricia. 2013. Domestic violence and public participation in the media: The case of citizen journalism. *Gender and Language* 7(3), 275–302.

Bou-Franch, Patricia. (ed.) 2016. *Exploring language aggression against women*. Amsterdam: John Benjamins Publishing Company.

Cohn, Michael A./Mehl, Matthias R./Pennebaker, James W. 2004. Linguistic markers of psychological change surrounding September 11, 2001. *Psychological Science* 15(10), 687–693.

Hancock, Jeffrey T./Landrigan, Christopher/Silver, Courtney. 2007. Expressing emotion in text-based communication. In *Proceedings of the CHI'07 conference on human factors in computing systems*. New York: Association for Computing Machinery Press, 929–932.

Hester, Marianne. 2012. Portrayal of women as intimate partner domestic violence perpetrators. *Violence against Women* 18, 1067–82.

Holmes, Danielle/Alpers, Georg W./Ismailji, Tasneem/Classen, Catherine/Wales, Talor/Cheasty, Valerie/Koopman, Cheryl. 2007. Cognitive and emotional processing in narratives of women abused by intimate partners. *Violence against Women* 13(11), 1192–1205.

Holtzman, Nicholas S./Tackman, Allison M./Carey, Angela L./Brucks Melanie S./Küfner, Albrecht C./Deters, Fenne G/Mehl, Mitja R. 2019. Linguistic markers of grandiose narcissism: A LIWC analysis of 15 samples. *Journal of Language and Social Psychology* 38(5–6), 773–786.

Kahn, Jeffrey H./Tobin, Renee M/Massey, Audra E/Anderson, Jennifer A. 2007. Measuring emotional expression with the linguistic inquiry and word count. *The American Journal of Psychology* 120(2), 263–286.

Koller, Veronika. 2012. How to analyse collective identity in discourse – Textual and contextual parameters. *Critical Approaches to Discourse Analysis Across Disciplines* 5(2), 19–38.

Luterek, Jane/Orsillo, Susan/Marx, Brian. 2005. An experimental examination of emotional experience, expression and disclosure in women reporting a history of childhood sexual abuse. *Journal of Traumatic Stress* 18, 237–244.

Mackenzie, Jai. 2017. Identifying informational norms in Mumsnet talk: a reflexive-linguistic approach to internet research ethics. *Applied Linguistics Review* 8(2–3), 293–314.

Markham, Annette/Buchanan, Elizabeth. 2015. Internet research: Ethical concerns. In Wright, J.D. (ed.) *International encyclopedia of the social and behavioral sciences.* Amsterdam: Elsevier, 606–613.

Newman, Matthew L./Pennebaker, James W./Berry, Diane S./Richards, Jane M. 2003. Lying words: Predicting deception from linguistic styles. *Personality and Social Psychology Bulletin* 29(5), 665–675.

Partington, Alan/Duguid, Alison/Taylor, Charlotte. 2013. *Patterns and meanings in discourse: Theory and practice in corpus-assisted discourse studies (CADS).* Amsterdam: John Benjamins.

Pasupathi, Monisha. 2007. Telling and the remembered self: Linguistic differences in memories for previously disclosed and previously undisclosed events. *Memory* 15(3), 258–270.

Pennebaker, James W./Booth, Roger J./Francis, Martha E. 2007. *Linguistic Inquiry and Word Count (LIWC): LIWC2007.* Austin, TX: University of Texas at Austin. Retrieved from: http://liwc.wpengine.com. Accessed 4 December 2019.

Pennebaker, James W./Chung, Cindy K./Frazee, Joey/Lavergne, Gary M./Beaver, David I. 2014. When small words foretell academic success: The case of college admissions essays. *PloS One*, 9(12), e115844.

Pennebaker, James W./Boyd, Ryan L./Jordan, Kayla/Blackburn, Kate. 2015. *The development and psychometric properties of LIWC2015.* Austin, TX: University of Texas at Austin.

Peslak, Alan R. 2018. Facebook fanatics: A linguistic and sentiment analysis of the most "fanned" Facebook pages. *Journal of Information Systems Applied Research* 11(1), 23–33.

Rahman, Rasha A./Melinger, Alissa. 2009. Semantic context effects in language production: a swinging lexical network proposal and a review. *Language and Cognitive Processes* 24(5), 713–734.

Rude, Stephanie/Gortner, Eva-Maria/Pennebaker, James W. 2004. Language use of depressed and depression-vulnerable college students. *Cognition & Emotion* 18, 1121–1133.

Santaemilia, José/Maruenda, Sergio. 2016. The linguistic representation of gender violence in (written) media discourse. *Journal of Language Aggression and Conflict* 2(2), 249–273.

Sánchez-Moya, Alfonso. 2017. Corpus-driven insights into the discourse of women survivors of Intimate Partner Violence. *Quaderns de Filologia-Estudis Lingüístics* 22(22), 215–243.

Sánchez-Moya, Alfonso. 2018. *Exploring digital discourse on Intimate Partner Violence: a socio-cognitive approach*. PhD dissertation. Universidad Complutense de Madrid/Vrije Universiteit Amsterdam.

Tani, Franca/Peterson, Carole/Smorti, Martina. 2016. The words of violence: Autobiographical narratives of abused women. *Journal of Family Violence* 31(7), 885–896.

Tausczik, Yla R./Pennebaker, James W. 2010. The psychological meaning of words: LIWC and computerized text analysis methods. *Journal of Language and Social Psychology* 29(1), 24–54.

UNODC 2018. *Global Study on Homicide 2018*. Vienna: United Nations. Retrieved from: https://bit.ly/2PVnppd. Accessed 25 November 2019.

Appendix

TEXTUAL EXAMPLES	
EXPERIMENTALFORUM POST CORPUS (VIOL)	
VIOL1 Is it abuse (SB1)	Hi I'm new here and feel silly I been with my husband for (removed by moderator) in the beginning he was the model bf loving affectionate, etc., then his rages started! He's never hit me but screams insults me calls ne all the names under the sun. We have a little girl who's 3 too. When he gets in his rage he smashes things I mine my phone twice! He's pushed my but says its my fault I walked into him! Don't know what to do!
VIOL2 Getting out (SB2)	I have had enough and don't think o can take another day. I've woke up this morn with a heavy heart as my partner finished nights this morn and that always means I'm in for a bad night tonight as he will be tired later and will take everything out on me. I don't think my body or brain can take anymore [crying_ emoji] Xx Why can't I do it and get us out and be free? X x x

TEXTUAL EXAMPLES	
VIOL3 Life after abuse (SB3)	I did something I deem brave. . .and during my time with my family I ventured into the local town and had coffee at a coffee shop with a friend [smiley_emoji] I felt nervous as I was waiting in the town centre with relatives for my friend but after that I felt fine, relaxed. Not on edge or anxious. It was definitely the right time for me to go back to my hometown and into the town centre and I'm so proud that I did it. Of course I had to clear it with my DC and wasn't allowed to take public transport or be alone at all, but it still felt freeing and so good. After all this time away, in a refuge, and too afraid to go back. . .I finally did it. I smelt the sea again <3 and it was amazing! Love to all. (removed by moderator) xx
CONTROL CORPUS (NON_VIOL)	FORUM POST
NONVIOL1 Travelling (NV1)	Hi everybody, I'm a 21 years old girl who is planning her first solo travel in London (city where I've never been before). You could imagine how excited and at the time scared I am. I have visited many solo travel blogs lately to find useful tips; many of them say that I shouldn't tell anybody I meet on the road of my solo condition because it could be dangerous. However, in some kind of situations (when you're in hostel, when you're alone in a pub and don't wanna spend the whole evening by yourself, on a guided visit of the city) I find that tell that that I'm travelling by myself could be an opportunity to push people I met to involve me in their activities. But I've never travelled alone before, so I can't really say if I am right or not and I don't wanna compromise at all my safety. Any advice?
NONVIOL2 Wedding (NV2)	Hi guys, I have a venue a little far away book but it was just what i was looking for, I had a call this morning to say they have had a problem with their roof and are not sure if the venue will be available now in August when i'm getting married!! So i am now back to square one with my venue and i am stressing out so much, can anyone help. I need a venue that can hold 120 people, dry hire in London for as cheap as possible. Any help would be very much appreciated. Kind Regards One very stressed out bride to be!

TEXTUAL EXAMPLES	
NONVIOL3 Mothering (NV3)	Help! Exhausted new mum over here. My baby is 12 days old, and seems to be struggling and straining in his sleep, and during feeding. He is having some expressed milk in the mornings and then formula throughout the day/night, He settles in his basket, bouncer and sleeps perfect on me, but then within 5–10 minutes he's in pain again with a red face and seems to be forcing out trapped gas making whinging noises. We have tried dentinox in his bottles (as was suggested by a family member) but doesn't seem to make a difference and it's really disturbing his sleep and ours even more 😭, wakes him up eventually. He is Having dirty Nappies at least once a day also. And suggestions how to relieve his pains?

Nuria Lorenzo-Dus and Anina Kinzel

'We'll watch TV and do other stuff': A corpus-assisted discourse study of vague language use in online child sexual grooming

1 Introduction

In 2014 the UK child protection charity National Society for the Prevention of Cruelty to Children (NSPCC) launched the campaign 'A Flaw in the Law', demanding that it be made a criminal offence for an adult to send a sexual message to a child. The campaign was successful, contributing to changes made to Section 15A of the 'Sexual Offences Acts' (2003) that, from 3rd April 2017, would:

> criminalise a person aged 18 or over who intentionally communicates with a child under 16, who the adult does not reasonably believe to be 16 or over, if the communication is sexual or if it is intended to encourage the child to make a communication which is sexual. The offence will be committed whether or not the child communicates with the adult.[1]

The relevance of these legislative changes to the present study is two-fold. Firstly, they concern communication, specifically the communicative act of an adult sending a message to a child for the purpose of obtaining sexual gratification. The message may be

1 https://www.gov.uk/government/publications/circular-201701-sexual-communication-with-a-child-implementation-of-s67-of-the-serious-crime-act-2015

written language and/or images; it may be sent via different media, including the Internet. This is crucial given that online child sexual grooming (OCSG, hereafter) is an Internet-enabled *communicative* process of entrapment (see Section 2). Secondly, the offence of sexual communication with a minor covers messages in which sexual intent is conveyed but does not state that sexual intent needs to be explicitly stated. Again, this is important because some victims of OCSG struggle to recognise actual sexual abuse, believing themselves instead to be involved in a friendship/romantic relationship with the grooming adults (Davidson/Gottschalk 2011; Larner 2018). Groomers' use of non-sexually explicit means of communication likely contributes to these beliefs.

2 The communicative process of online child sexual grooming

Despite a considerable body of scholarship in Criminology, Psychology and, to a lesser extent, the Computer Sciences (see, e.g., O'Connell 2003; Whittle/Hamilton-Giachristis/Beech/Collings 2013; Williams/Elliott/Beech 2013; Vartapetiance/Gilliam 2014; Cano Basave/Fernández/Alani 2014; Van Gijn-Grosvenor/Lamb 2016; Quayle/Newman 2017; Winters/Kaylor/Jeglie 2017; Kloess/Hamilton-Giachritsis/Beech 2017), Linguistics scholarship into OCSG is still 'in its infancy' (Chiang/Grant 2018: 2). This is surprising given that OCSG is 'an internet-enabled communicative process of entrapment in which an adult uses language and other semiotic modes (e.g. images) to lure a minor into taking part in sexual activities online and, at times, also offline' (Lorenzo-Dus/Kinzel/Di Cristofaro 2020: 15–6).

The first model of OCSG *discourse* (see Fig. 1) developed in 2016 (Lorenzo-Dus/Izura/Pérez-Tattam 2016), used a Computer Mediated Discourse Analysis (Herring 2004, 2013) framework to identify the tactics used by adults convicted of online child sexual offending. The corpus (c. 75,000 words) was extracted from the Perverted Justice website,

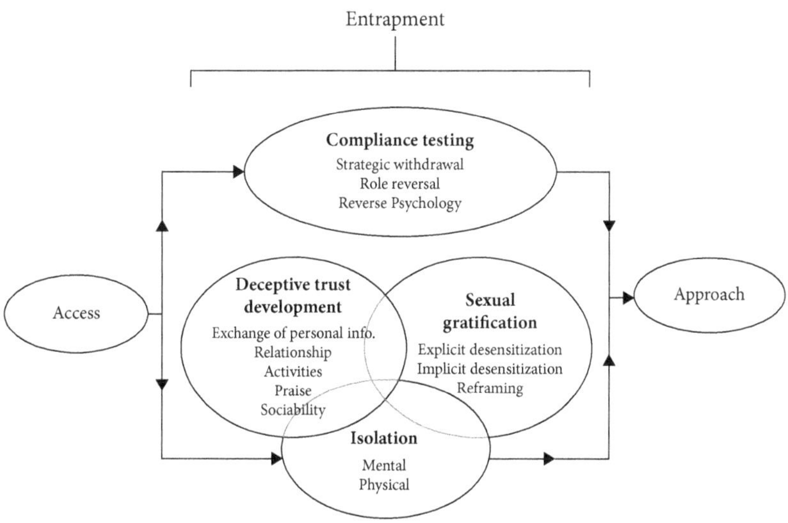

Fig. 1. A model of OCSG discourse (Lorenzo-Dus et al. 2016)

which is operated by the publicly available Perverted Justice Foundation, a not for profit organisation that collaborates with law enforcement to capture and convict online child sexual offenders.[2]

OCSG has three main phases: access, entrapment and approach. The access phase pertains to the groomers' initial contact with their target online, the approach phase concerns offline access to the target for the purpose of sexual abuse. The entrapment phase includes four processes: Deceptive Trust Development (DTD), Compliance Testing (CT), Isolation (I), and Sexual Gratification (SG). DTD entails groomers using language to establish a trust-based bond with their targets, for example via paying compliments, engaging in seemingly innocent small talk, exchanging personal details (e.g. location) and discussing

2 Perverted Justice Inc. trains adult volunteers to enter social media and public chat rooms with child profiles. If the volunteers (decoys) are approached by an online groomer and the conversation turns sexual, they work with law enforcement to get the groomer convicted. Chat logs of successful convictions are subsequently uploaded to the Perverted Justice website.

relationships and hobbies. Through CT groomers discursively gauge the likelihood of their targets going along with different behaviours proposed to them, including of a sexual nature. To do this, groomers may adopt strategies such as role reversal, where they appear to be concerned about their targets' safety, strategic withdrawal, where they may appear suddenly no longer interested in the proposed behaviour, and reverse psychology. Isolation entails groomers' communicative attempts at establishing the groomer-target relationship as exclusive and distancing their targets emotionally and physically from their support networks. SG concerns groomers' discursively desensitising their targets to the idea of performing sexual activities online and, in some cases, also offline.

In a follow-up study, Lorenzo-Dus et al. (2019) adopted a CADS methodology to identify regular language structures (three word collocations) used by > 600 adults whose chat logs were uploaded to the Perverted Justice website (approximately 3.3 million words). They then mapped these language structures onto the components of the OCSG discourse model, such as 'can't_wait_hold' (e.g. 'can't wait to hold u in my arms as we sleep' – DTD process) and 'older_guys_like' (e.g. 'or do u like older guys?' – SG (implicit desensitisation)). The study found that a third of the linguistic patterns served to advance the SG process. Importantly for the present study, not all of them used sexually explicit language. Additionally, 20 % of the collocations were used to realise discursive strategies within the DTD process and thus falsely emphasised the romantic/friendship goal of the groomers' discourse. These collocations were often used in interactional segments in which sexual intent was connoted, rather than denoted. Whereas these findings are not to be taken as indicative of the absence of explicit, even coercive, communication of sexual intent in OCSG (see Chiang/Grant 2018; and Schneevogt et al. 2018), they highlight the importance that implicitness plays in the communication of sexual intent within OCSG. It is to the linguistic conceptualisation of this notion that we therefore turn next.

3 Communicating meaning implicitly: A focus on vague language

Although implicitness is a central concept term in Linguistics, it is also

> a blanket term that researchers use intuitively with regard to the "hidden aspects of meaning" (Bertuccelli Papi 2009:140). These include, amongst other, different types of presuppositions, entailments, implicatures and implicitures, explicatures, as well as a (growing) number of more specialized concepts denoting specific inferential schemata in different languages (Cap/Dynel 2017: 1).

Various theoretical approaches have been applied to understanding implicitness, which overall agree on both its richness from an analytic perspective and the need for a 'bottom-up, data driven agenda' to guide further research into it (Cap/Dynel 2017: 11). Our rationale for focusing on a specific manifestation of implicitness, namely vague language, is data-driven, too. Use of vague language has been noted in the OCSG literature (e.g. Kloess et al. 2017; Chiang/Grant 2017; 2018, Lorenzo-Dus/Kinzel 2019; Lorenzo-Dus et al. 2020). Yet, to our knowledge, it has not been systematically examined. Moreover, research into vague language in interaction has been shown to display a positive correlation with levels of topical sensitivity. Zhang (2013), for instance, has demonstrated that as topical sensitivity increases, so does the use of vague language overall and of certain vague language categories in particular, namely Vague Category Identifiers and Subjectivisers (see below for definitions). Sexuality both features centrally in OCSG and is a sensitive topic, thus justifying our analytic focus on vague language use in the discourse of online child sexual groomers.

The first (general) definition of vagueness speaks of a language feature that is 'a matter of degree', unlike 'accuracy [which] is an ideal limit.' (Russell 1923: 90). Since then, a considerable number of studies have sought to explain and/or categorise vagueness, either in general language use or within specific discourse genres (e.g. Channell 1994; Cheng/Warren 2001, 2003; Cutting 2000, 2012; Carter/McCarthy 2006; Cheng 2007; Ruzaitė 2007). Within this research, Zhang's (1998, 2011, 2013) work offers a comprehensive theoretical and empirical account of vague language. Zhang (2013: 88) characterises vague language as

> a linguistic unit (word, phrase or utterance) that has an unspecified meaning boundary, so that its interpretation is elastic in the sense that it can be stretched or shrunk according to the strategic need of communication.

This definition is underpinned by a theory of elasticity – a view of (vague) language as being capable of stretching or shrinking strategically in locally-instantiated contexts of communication according to negotiable and fluid communicative purposes. The elasticity of language has been demonstrated, amongst other, in relation to speech acts. For instance, Glinert (2010) shows how the choice of a particular realisation for the speech act of apologising (e.g. 'we apologise', rather than, say, 'we're very sorry' in the context of political diplomacy) is adaptable, rather than governed by fixed general language rules. This elasticity, which is described via 'imagery of stretching [a] rubber band', operates according to complex and evolving face work considerations (Glinert 2010: 57–58).

Using a similar metaphor, in her case that of vague language being like a slingshot, Zhang (2011: 578–9) suggests one principal maxim and four specific vague language elasticity maxims:

> Principal Maxim: 'stretch language elastically in discursive negotiations to achieve communicative goals.'
>
> Specific maxims:
>
> 1. Go just right: provide the right amount of information (e.g. That <u>tall</u> woman is very <u>kind</u>.)
> 2. Go general: speak in general terms (e.g. Do you have any convictions <u>or anything</u>?)
> 3. Go hypothetical: speak in hypothetical terms (e.g., It <u>could</u> be him.)
> 4. Go subjective: speak in subjective terms (e.g. <u>I think</u> she is dishonest.)

Zhang's (2013) approach highlights the interconnectedness of patterns of strategic elasticity, between the above maxims and both their linguistic realisations and pragmatic functions. In other words, certain linguistic categories of vague language tend to perform particular pragmatic functions and thus to conform to certain maxims. The actual pragmatic functions and linguistic realisations are listed in Tab. 1.

Vague language realisation category		Example	Pragmatic function
Approximator	Expresses an inexact amount, such as 'about 50', '50-ish', 'a few', 'many', 'several'	'I have *many* friends.'	Approximation
Possibility & Plausibility Indicator	Expresses something possible or that could be valid, such as 'possible', 'seem', 'appear', 'maybe', 'probable'	'I *probably* won't be drinking'	Uncertainty
Vague Category Identifier	Indicates an unspecified category, such as 'stuff', 'thing', 'and all that', 'things like that', 'or something'	'I bought apples, pears and *things like that.*'	Avoidance
Intensifier	Expresses vaguely a high intensity degree and increase the tone of speech, such as 'very', 'really', 'extremely'	'She is *very* smart.'	Strengthening
De-intensifier	Expresses vaguely a low intensity degree and decrease the tone of speech, such as 'sort of', 'fairly', 'a bit', 'somewhat'	'You are *a bit* blunt.'	Downtoning
Subjectiviser	Expresses speaker's low certainty or commitment, such as 'I think', 'I guess', 'we believe', 'it seems'	'*It seems* that she wouldn't mind doing that.'	Shielding

Tab. 1. A taxonomy of linguistic realisations and pragmatic functions of vague language (based on Zhang 2013: 50 and Zhang 2011: 90)

It is worth noting that research into vague language has tended to focus on a subset of linguistic categories, primarily general nouns and general extenders, with 'general verbs and indefinite pronouns hav[ing] received less [attention]' (Cutting 2012: 24). This is reflected in the vague language realisation categories in Tab. 1, in which hedges, adverbials, nouns and only a few verbal phrases are included.

The range of factors that account for how easily we may be able to trace putative intentions in conversational interaction has been examined too. Culpeper / Haugh (2014), for instance, have shown that illocutionary force transparency, semantic content and target can all affect the degree of pragmatic explicitness of a given implicature. Potentially, therefore, they may also affect the degree of pragmatic explicitness in contexts in which vague language is used. Haugh (2015) has further demonstrated that speaker commitment to and/or accountability for an implicature can also affect pragmatic explicitness. For this author (2017), the 'inferential substrate' – that is 'the subtext' – of a conversation can either remain embedded or become exposed. An inferential substrate remains embedded when interlocutors do not make inferences about it the focus of their interaction. Embedded substrates are therefore 'less analytically tractable as they often rely on particular background assumptions, experiences and so on that may only be known or knowable to those participants in question'. In contrast, an inferential substrate becomes exposed when interlocutors make the relevant inference/s 'the focus of interactional business' (2017: 287). It is important to note that interlocutors – rather than only speakers – jointly work to make inferences embedded and/or exposed. In other words, inferences are 'a form of social action that is tied through recurrent interactional practices, such as prompting, to the inferential substrate in which they are grounded.' (2017: 299).

4 Methodology

4.1 Data

Our corpus consists of approximately 3.3 million words, which comprise all the groomer contributions to the >600 chatlogs available on the Perverted Justice website at the time of data collection (February 2018). Each chat log contains all the chat sessions between a groomer and one or more decoy(s) over a period of interaction that ranged from seventeen to 10,597 minutes. The chat logs were uploaded to the website between 2004 and 2016.

4.2 Procedure and framework

The corpus was analysed using a CADS methodology, which entails 'the investigation and comparison of features of particular discourse types, integrating into the analysis, where appropriate, techniques and tools developed within corpus linguistics' (Partington 2010: 88; see also Taylor/Marchi 2018). The analytic steps that we adopted within our CADS framework are summarised below:

Data extraction and formatting:

The chat logs were scraped from the Perverted Justice website using a custom Python script, transferred to a data frame, and saved to different csv files (one for each chat session within a given chat log). Another custom Python script was then used to (1) convert the extracted csv files into XML, which is the format supported by the software that we used for the analysis (CQPweb)[3]; (2) identify and replace emoticons with their respective labels (e.g., ☺ ➔ smiley face); (3) separate groomer and decoy contributions. Only the groomer contributions were analysed. The software VARD 2.5.4[4] was used to standardise the spelling in the corpus.

Data analysis:

We firstly conducted a lexical frequency and dispersion analysis. This required loading the plain text files containing the groomer corpus into the software #LancsBox (Brezina, McEnery and Wattam 2015), where lexical dispersion values (DP_{Norm} scores) were calculated. DP_{Norm} scores indicate the normalised dispersion of given words in a corpus, based on their individual frequency and the number of elements (texts) in which these words appear (Gries 2008). The score ranges from zero to one. Values around zero mean that 'the relative frequencies of occurrence of the linguistic expression in the corpus are directly proportional to the sizes of the corpus parts whereas large values close to 1 mean the linguistic expression is distributed very unevenly among the corpus parts' (Gries 2010: 274–5).

As there is no agreed upon cut-off point for DP_{Norm} values, after manually considering the DP_{Norm} scores for our corpus, we decided to

3 https://cqpweb.lancs.ac.uk/

4 http://ucrel.lancs.ac.uk/vard/about/

focus our subsequent analysis on words with a DP_{Norm} score <0.6, which ensured that subsequent analyses were based on sufficiently dispersed terms. From the resulting list we manually identified and extracted those terms that could be used to convey sexual intent. This list comprised thirty-five items, including content words (e.g., nouns like 'bed', adjectives like 'cute' and verbs like 'hold'), as well as different types of function words, such as pronouns (e.g. 'it'), delexicalized verbs (e.g. 'do'), modal verbs (e.g. 'may') and minimisers/boosters (e.g. 'just'). Having calculated the collocates for each of these thirty-five words and examined concordance lines containing these collocations, we manually selected those that did convey sexual intent in context, discarding examples where this was not the case (e.g., use of 'do' as an auxiliary verb in questions). This resulted in a final list of vague language terms used frequently across the corpus to advance OCSG goals (see Tab. 2 in Section 5.1), which we further analysed qualitatively. To do so, we extracted twenty random concordances for each of these terms and coded them using Zhang's (2013) vague language framework (see Tab. 1).

5 Results

5.1 Vague language in online child sexual grooming

Tab. 2 lists the result of the analysis of all the sampled concordance lines that contained vague language terms used frequently across the corpus to advance OCSG goals (i.e., specific OCSG discourse processes).

Three of the linguistic realisation categories in Zhang's (2013) framework featured in our corpus, too: Approximator (*like*, *hold*, *fun*, *bed*, *feel*, *love*, *kiss*), Vague Category Identifier (*stuff*, *thing*) and De-intensifier (*cute*, *pretty*, *sweet*, *nice*). The Approximator category primarily concerned referencing an inexact characteristic or condition – rather than an inexact quantity, which was the case in Zhang's (2013) study. We henceforth refer to this category in our corpus as Approximator – Quality. In the example in Tab. 2, the meaning in context of *like* in 'So

Vague language linguistic realisation category	**Pragmatic function**	**Vague language terms**	**Illustrative example from the groomer corpus**
Approximator – Quality	Approximation	*like, hold, fun, bed, feel, love, kiss*	G: So you *like* older guys?
Vague Category Identifier	Avoidance	*stuff, thing*	G: But I'll teach you about foreplay and other *stuff* if you wanna learn that
Explicit-Vague Category Identifier	Partial avoidance	*sex stuff, sexual thing*	G: and do you want to do the *sex thing*
De-intensifier	Downtoning	*cute, pretty, sweet, nice*	G: Like I said before you are young but you are also *cute* if I may say so
General Verb	Avoidance	*do, get*	G: Do you want to just *do* touchy feely stuff, maybe take some things off?

Tab. 2. Vague language terms in the corpus: linguistic realisation and pragmatic functions

you like older guys' is that of being sexually attracted to rather than being interested in older guys in a non-sexual way. Use of 'to like', which can cover both meanings, is strategic – indeed manipulative: the groomers may argue that the latter meaning, which carries neither moral nor legal risks for them as adults, was the one intended.

Two of the vague language terms in the groomer corpus were used frequently to connote sexual activity via the use of the Vague Category Identifiers: *stuff* and *thing*. In the example in Tab. 2, 'other *stuff*' helps the groomer to avoid specifying sexual actions that are linked to an antecedent – the noun 'foreplay' – that does denote sexual intent. Although foreplay is a type of sexual activity, it takes place *before* the sexual act. The groomers may therefore strategically use it to mitigate the potential face-threatening and explicitly illegal act of engaging in sexual activity ('foreplay and other stuff') with a minor (here, a decoy).

As for the De-intensifier category, it comprised four adjectives (*cute*, *sweet*, *pretty* and *nice*) – rather than noun-based hedges (*sort of*, *a bit*) and adverbials (*fairly*, *somewhat*), as identified in Zhang's (2013) taxonomy (Tab. 1). In terms of evaluative and/or pragmatic force, these adjectives are not in the upper limit of a given quality (beauty, likeability), that is to say, they are not superlative adjectives. Nor do they carry sexual meaning linked to either physical appearance or personality (unlike, for example, *hot* or *sexy*). This may explain their being used as a means to mitigate the potential face threat of complimenting targets on sexual attributes.

Two vague language categories, not identified in Zhang's framework, emerged from the analysis of the groomer corpus: General Verb (*do*, *get*) and Explicit-Vague Category Identifiers (*sex stuff*, *sexual thing*). The general verbs *do* and *get* were used frequently by groomers to refer to different sexual actions. In the example in Tab. 2, *do + touchy feely stuff*, avoids the use of a sexually explicit noun (sex) and is further mitigated via the hedge 'just'.

Finally, our analysis also identified a particular use of the Vague Category Identifier category, whereby the vague term (*stuff*, *thing*) would follow – and collocate with – a sexually explicit noun or adjective (*sex*, *sexual*). The resulting collocations were thus both explicit (the sexual intent was overtly expressed) and yet vague (the actual action – having sex – was avoided through nominalisation and made unspecific). We treated this as a separate category, which we labelled 'Explicit-Vague Category Identifier.'

As for the frequency of use of the vague language realisation categories and their pragmatic functions, these are respectively shown in Figures 2a and 2b.

As shown in Figures 2a and 2b, Approximator-Quality (54 % of the total) was the most frequent vague language category, a finding that is consistent with the results of Zhang's (2013) study. The next most frequent terms were De-intensifiers (26 %) and the Vague Category Identifiers (13 %). The two other categories – General Verbs and Explicit-Vague Category Identifiers – displayed considerably lower frequencies of use. In terms of pragmatic function, Vague Category Identifiers (13 %), General Verbs (3 %) and Explicit-Vague Category Identifiers (4 %) were used as avoidance mechanisms. Collectively,

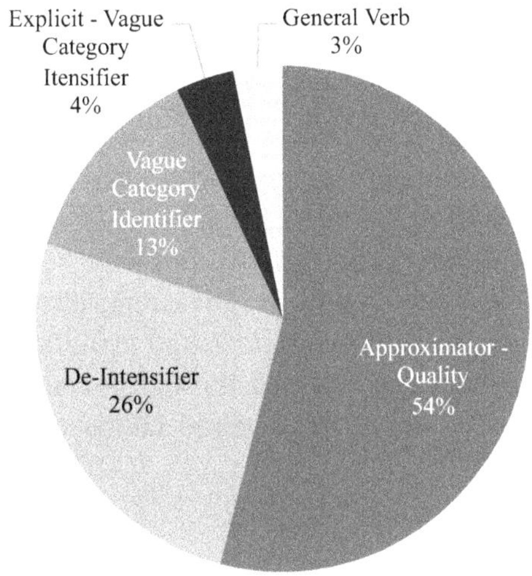

Fig. 2a. Frequency of use (%) of vague language categories in the corpus

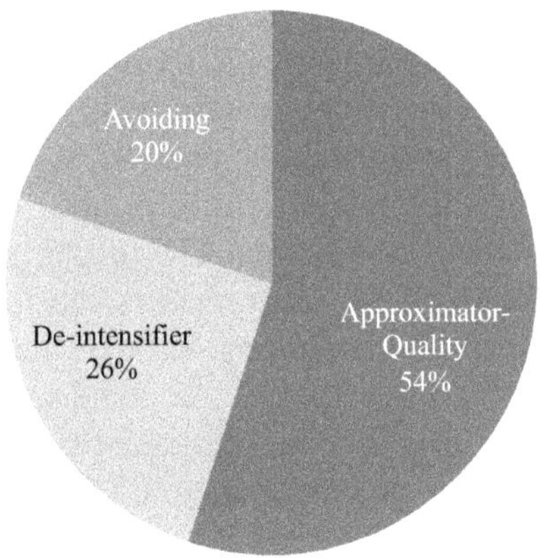

Fig. 2b. Frequency of use (%) of pragmatic function of vague language terms in the corpus

therefore, the pragmatic function of avoiding accounted for 20 % of the three pragmatic functions realised by the various vague language categories in the corpus. Downtoning – which was realised via the De-intensifier category – accounted for a similar proportion of use

(26 %). Approaching implicitly sexual content – which was realised via Approximator – Quality terms – remained the most frequent function (54 %) in the corpus.

Overall, then, use of vague language in OCSG served primarily an approximating function and was realised via the verbs *like, hold, feel,* love and *kiss*, as well as the nouns *fun* and *bed.* These terms served to broach and reference sexual activity covertly. The two other pragmatic functions were downtoning sexual intent, through de-intensifier adjectives (*cute, pretty, sweet* and *nice*), and avoiding explicit mention of sexual intent, which was realised through a combination of vague nouns, generic verbs and explicit-vague collocational noun-phrases (*stuff, thing, do, get*).

5.2 Retrieving sexual intent from vague language use in online child sexual grooming

In order to determine how straightforward it may be to interpret the inferential substrate of vague language terms, we manually examined all the sampled concordance lines containing instances of the most frequent vague language category in the corpus (Approximator-Quality). We noted whether their inferential substrates (i.e., sexual intent) stayed embedded or became exposed therein. The results showed a fairly balanced picture: in 53 % of the concordances the inferential substrate remained embedded; in the remaining 47 % of the concordances, the inferential substrate became exposed. As noted in Section 3, in those interactional contexts in which the inferential substrate stays embedded, meaning retrieval is more challenging. The slight prevalence of embedded inferential substrate cases in our data thus offers some support to the thesis that use of vague language terms contributed to victims of OCSG struggling to realise (for some time) that they are being sexually groomed, believing themselves instead to be involved in a friendship/romantic relationship.

As for those cases in which the groomers exposed the inferential substrate (47 %) behind their use of Approximator-Quality terms, they strategically combined sexual covertness and overtness. Their strategy was similar to the use of 'push-pull structures' in other interactional contexts (Montgomery 2006). Push-pull structures are intercalated discourse units the pragmatic force of which is opposite: assertiveness ('push structure'), on the one hand, and tentativeness ('pull structure'), on the other. In live two-way news interviews, for instance, push-pull structures, such as 'he will certainly resign, I think', help to engage – draw in – audiences within a highly competitive media environment. The 'push' component conveys the facts via strong assertions ('he will certainly resign') and it is thus used for 'doing facticity', even if the grounds for it may be rather speculative, which explains the use of the 'pull component', which hedges the assertiveness of those very facts ('I think').

In our data, concordance lines in which the sexual inferential substrate was exposed also revealed this strategic use of pragmatic force contrast. In these cases, the push-like component was the explicit sexual term and the pull-like component was the Approximator-Quality term. The former was used for 'doing sexual desensitisation', that is, for advancing the SG process in OCSG. The latter was used for 'doing avoidance of face-threat' and hence contributed to the DTD process in OCSG. In 43 % of the cases of exposed inferential substrate, push-pull structures entailed two lexical units, and hence collocational use of a sexually explicit and a vague language term, as illustrated in Extract 1:

Extract 1:

01	Groomer	lol
02		sounds fun to me ha
03		but I doubt it does to u
04		fuck & fun

In line 04, the groomer places a sexually explicit term ('fuck') and an Approximator-Quality term ('fun') alongside each other, linking them explicitly via the ampersand sign ('&'). The inferential substrate is thus clearly exposed – sexual intent on the groomer's part is overtly stated. However, the focus is placed on the approximator ('fun'), which is the evaluation that he is discursively engaged with in lines 01–03. Within the OGSG communicative process of entrapment, this strategic use of push-pull structures serves to advance the SG process through explicit sexual desensitisation. It also serves to advance the DTD process by framing sexual activity in non-sexual terms – in Extract 1, for example, evaluating sexual behaviour in terms that make it seem appealing because it leads to enjoyment ('fun').

In the 57 % of the remaining cases that we examined, push-pull structures involved more than two lexical items, and developed either over the course of a single interactional turn (whether represented as one or several written turns), as illustrated in Extract 2, or over a longer dyadic exchange with the decoy, as illustrated in Extract 3.

Extract 2

01	Groomer	you think it would be romantic for us to both be in a bed naked
02		kissing and feeling and fondling each other

In line 02 the groomer references sexual behaviours: 'kissing, and feeling fondling each other'. All three verbal actions are illegal between a minor and an adult, not least in the context he describes in line 01 ('for us to both be in a bed naked'). Yet, he deceptively presents this context as hypothetical (note the use of the modal verb 'would') and relationship rather than abuse driven ('romantic').

Extract 3

01	Groomer	and do u want to kiss and cuddle a little before i change ur clothes
02	Decoy	Yea
03	Groomer	and talk and get to know each other
04		and hold each other
05	Decoy	yessss yes
06	Groomer	and touch each other

In line 01, the groomer asks a question about the decoy's willingness to engage in particular activities, namely kissing and cuddling. These expose an inferential substrate of sexual intent. Note that at this point he minimises the potential face-threat of sexual intent through the hedge 'a little'. He then further exposes the inferential substrate of sexual intent on his part through the reference to 'chang[ing] ur clothes'. Having thus 'pushed' sexual intent in line 01, in line 03 the groomer 'pulls' it by referring to activities that are not sexual per se – 'talk and get to know each other'. Within the same interactional turn, the reference to 'hold[ing] each other' (line 04) moves progressively towards the next 'push' element, in line 06, where the sexual intent of the activity becomes clear ('touch each other') despite the lack of a sexually-explicit term.

6 Conclusion

The study reported in this chapter addresses both a crucial societal challenge – an escalation of cases of OCSG – and an important gap in academic scholarship in relation to this social challenge: approaching OCSG as a communicative process. In our work, we have focussed on one aspect of this scholarly gap, namely online child sexual groomers' use of vague language in order to achieve their manipulative goals. Using a combination of quantitative and qualitative linguistic analysis tools, we have shown that vague language is indeed strategically used to advance specific OCSG goals. We have also identified a list of vague language terms that exhibit statistical frequency and high dispersion values in a corpus of c. 3.3 million words from over 600 convicted online child sexual groomers. The linguistic realisations of these terms reveals that Quality-Approximators are the main vague language category in use, followed by Vague Identifiers and De-identifiers. Approximating, avoiding and downtoning sexual intent are – in decreasing frequency order – the three pragmatic functions that these terms fulfil in the context of OCSG. Our work has moreover examined the type of inferential substrate that groomers favour when seeking to convey sexual intent through approximation (Approximator – Quality). The findings reveal a broadly balanced combination of embedded and exposed inferential substrate and, within the latter, strategic use of push-pull structures that further embed sexual intent.

The overall picture that emerges is clearly one of communicative manipulation on the part of online child sexual groomers, which can be very confusing for their targets. Groomers resort to vague language terms to communicate sexual intent covertly, couching it in terms that make interpretation of friendship and romance likely, which in turn helps to develop trust of their deceiving goals. This is particularly concerning for it may lead to feelings of blame – in addition to those of hurt, disappointment, trauma, etc. – once the targets realise that sexual intent had been communicated to them, albeit that implicitly.

The findings of this work may be used to complement existing preventative work on child online safeguarding, which seeks to educate children about the importance of their taking an active role in their own Internet safety, as well as in engaging in healthy relations online. Training materials for professionals working with children could be developed, for instance, to raise awareness, and help recognise use, of embedded inferential substrate of sexual intent in groomers' discourse. The findings may also be used to inform multi-disciplinary efforts at developing OCSG detection software, in which the part played by vague language may be adequately accounted for. As a methodology that synergises use of quantitative and qualitative linguistic tools and operates at the language in use (i.e., discourse) level, CADS can – and should in our view – make a significant contribution to such applied research efforts.

Acknowledgements

The authors would like to thank Dr. Paiement, Dr. Di Cristofaro, Dr. Reitmaier and Mr. Morgan for their assistance processing the corpus data.

References

Bertuccelli Papi, Marcella. 2000. *Implicitness in Text and Discourse*. Pisa: Edizoni ETS.

Brezina, Vaclav/McEnery, Tony/Wattam, Stephen. 2015. Collocations in context: A new perspective on collocation networks. *International Journal of Corpus Linguistics* 20(2), 139–173.

Cano Basave, Amparo/Fernández, Miriam/Alani, Harith. 2014. Detecting child grooming behaviour patterns on social media. In *SociInfo 2014: The 6th International Conference on Social Informatics*, http://oro.open.ac.uk/41394/1/predatorBehaviour.pdf. Accessed 22 November 2019.

Cap, Piotr/Dynel, Marta. (eds.) 2017. *Implicitness: From lexis to discourse*. Amsterdam/Philadelphia: John Benjamins.

Carter, Ronald/McCarthy, Michael. 2006. *Cambridge Grammar of English: A Comprehensive Guide. Spoken and Written English Grammar and Usage*. Cambridge: Cambridge University Press.

Channell, Joanna. 1994. *Vague Language*. Oxford: Oxford University Press.

Cheng, Winnie. 2007. The use of vague language across spoken genres in an intercultural Hong Kong corpus. In Cutting, Joan (ed.) *Vague Language Explored*. New York: Palgrave Macmillan, 161–181.

Cheng, Winnie/Warren, Martin. 2001. The use of vague language in intercultural conversations in Hong Kong. *English World-Wide* 22(1), 81–104.

Cheng, Winnie/Warren, Martin. 2003. Indirectness, inexplicitness and vagueness made clearer. *Pragmatics* 13(3), 381–400.

Chiang, Emily/Grant, Tim. 2017. Online grooming: Moves and strategies. *Language and Law/Linguagem e Direito* 4(1), 103–141.

Chiang, Emily/Grant, Tim. 2018. Deceptive identity performance: Offender moves and multiple identities in online child abuse conversations. *Applied Linguistics* 40(4), 1–25.

Culpeper, Jonathan/Haugh, Michael. 2014. *Pragmatics and the English Language*. Basingstoke: Palgrave Macmillan.

Cutting, Joan. 2000. Vague language and international students. In Cutting, Joan (ed.) *The Grammar of Spoken English and EAP Teaching*. Sunderland: University of Sunderland Press, 39–54.

Cutting, Joan. 2012. Vague language in conference abstracts. *Journal of English for Academic Purposes* 11, 289–293.

Davidson, Julia/Gottschalk, Petter. 2011. Characteristics of the Internet for criminal child sexual abuse by online groomers. *Criminal Justice Studies* 24(1), 23–36.

Glinert, Lewis. 2010. Apologizing to China: Elastic apologies and the meta-discourse of American diplomats. *Intercultural Pragmatics* 7(1), 47–74.

Gries, Stefan T. 2008. Dispersions and adjusted frequencies in corpora. *International Journal of Corpus Linguistics* 13(4), 403–437.

Gries, Stefan T. 2010. Useful statistics for corpus linguistics. In Sánchez, A./Almeda, M. (eds.) *A Mosaic of Corpus Linguistics: Selected Approaches*. Frankfurt am Main: Peter Lang, 269–291.

Haugh, Michael. 2015. The role of English as a scientific metalanguage for research in pragmatics: Reflections on the metapragmatics of 'politeness' in Japanese. *East Asian Pragmatics* 1, 41–74.

Haugh, Michael. 2017. Implicature and the inferential substrate. In Cap, Piotr/Dynel, Marta (eds.) *Implicitness: From Lexis to Discourse*. Amsterdam/Philadelphia: John Benjamins, 281–304.

Herring, Susan C. 2004. Computer-mediated discourse analysis: An approach to researching online behaviour. In Barab, Sasha *et al.* (eds.) *Designing for Virtual Communities in the Service of Learning*. New York: Cambridge University Press, 338–376.

Herring, Susan C. 2013. Discourse in Web 2.0: familiar, reconfigured, and emergent. In Tannen, Deborah/Tester, Anna M. (eds.) *Georgetown University Round Table on Languages and Linguistics 2011: Discourse 2.0: Language and New Media*. Washington, DC: Georgetown University Press, 1–25.

Kloess, Juliana A./Hamilton-Giachritsis, Catherine E./Beech, Anthony R. 2017. Offense processes of online sexual grooming and abuse of children via internet communication platforms. *Sexual Abuse* 31(1), 1–24.

Larner, Samuel. 2018. Child sexual abuse: Hearing the cry for help is not always a simple task. *The Conversation*. http://theconversation.com/child-sexual-abuse-hearing-the-cry-for-help-is-not-always-a-simple-task-89599. Accessed 10th October 2019.

Lorenzo-Dus, Nuria/Kinzel, Anina. 2019. 'So is your mom as cute as you?': Examining patterns of language use by online sexual groomers. *Journal of Corpora and Discourse Studies* 2, 15–39.

Lorenzo-Dus, Nuria/Izura, Cristina/Pérez-Tattam, Rocío. 2016. Understanding grooming discourse in computer-mediated environments. *Discourse, Context and Media* 12, 40–50.

Lorenzo-Dus, Nuria/Kinzel, Anina/Di Cristofaro, Matteo. 2020. The communicative modus operandi of online child Sexual groomers: Recurring patterns in their language use. *Journal of Pragmatics* 155, 15–27.

Montgomery, Martin. 2006. Broadcast news, the live-two way and the case of Andrew Gilligan. *Media, Culture & Society* 28 (2), 233–259.

O'Connell, Rachel. 2003. *A typology of child cyber exploitation and online grooming practices*. Preston, England: University of Central Lancashire.

Partington, Alan. 2010. Modern Diachronic Corpus-Assisted Discourse Studies (MDCADS) on UK newspapers: An overview of the project. *Corpora* 5(2), 83–108.

Quayle, Ethel/Newman, Emily. 2017. An exploratory study of public reports to investigate patterns and themes of requests for sexual images of minors online. *Crime Science* 5(2), 1–12.

Russell, Bertrand. 1923. Vagueness. *Australian Journal of Philosophy and Psychology* 1, 84–92.

Ruzaitė, Jurate. 2007. *Vague Language in Educational Settings: Quantifiers and Approximators in British and American English*. Frankfurt am Main: Peter Lang.

Schneevogt, Daniela/Chiang, Emily/Grant, Tim. 2018. Do perverted justice chat logs contain examples of overt persuasion and sexual extortion? A research note responding to Chiang and Grant (2017, 2018). *Language and Law = Linguagem e Direito* 5(1), 97–102.

Taylor, Charlotte/Marchi, Anna. (eds.) 2018. *Corpus Approaches to Discourse: A Critical Review*. London/New York: Routledge.

van Gijn-Grosvenor, Evianne L./Lamb, Michael E. 2015. Behavioural differences between online sexual groomers approaching boys and girls. *Journal of Child Sexual Abuse* 25(5), 577–596.

Vartapetiance, Anna/Gillam, Lee. 2014. 'Our little secret': Pinpointing potential predators. *Security Informatics* 3(1), 1–19.

Whittle, Helen/Hamilton-Giachritsis, Catherine E./Beech, Anthony/Collings, Guy. 2013. A review of online grooming: Characteristics and concerns. *Aggression and Violent Behavior* 18, 62–70.

Williams, Rebecca./Elliott, Ian A./Beech, Anthony. 2013. Identifying sexual grooming themes used by internet sex offenders. *Deviant Behavior* 34(2), 135–152.

Winters, Georgia M./Kaylor, Leah E./Jeglic, Elizabeth L. 2017. Sexual offenders contacting children online: An examination of transcripts of sexual grooming. *Journal of Sexual Aggression* 23(1), 62–76.

Zhang, Grace. 2011. Elasticity of vague language. *Intercultural Pragmatics* 8(4), 571–599.

Zhang, Grace. 2013. The impact of touchy topics on vague language use. *Journal of Asian Pacific Communication* 23(1), 87–118.

Zhang, Qiao. 1998. Fuzziness–vagueness–generality–ambiguity. *Journal of Pragmatics* 29(1), 13–31.

Stefania M. Maci

The narrative of the anti-vax campaign on Twitter[1]

1 Introduction

Edward Jenner's work on vaccination contributed to the dissemination of vaccination information within the medical community from the late 18th century both in the UK and in the US. Yet in the 19th century vaccination resistance began in both countries: in the UK, the introduction of the Vaccination Act (1849–1898) was considered as a violation of civil liberty; in the US, vaccination laws were vigorously opposed by anti-vaccination movements (Wolfe/Sharp 2002).

A smallpox outbreak in the US made antivaccine activists be quiet until the 1980s when a TV program, the *DTP Vaccine roulette* put an emphasis on the alleged health risks caused by a triple vaccine for diphtheria (a bacterial infection), pertussis (whooping cough) and tetanus. Furthermore, in 1999, *The Lancet* published a study carried out by Wakefield et al. which demonstrated a correlation between the measles, mumps and rubella vaccine (MMR) and autism. This made anti-vaccination movements strongly revive. Yet this study was heavily distorted, as demonstrated by Taylor et al. (1999) and Miller et al. (1999). Indeed, Wakefield et al. (1999) selected the data they needed to suggest a vaccine-autism correlation; in addition, their study was funded by litigants

1 The research on which this study is based is part of the MIUR-funded research project of national interest (PRIN) *Knowledge Dissemination across media in English: continuity and change in discourse strategies, ideologies, and epistemology* (COFIN grant no. Prot. 2015TJ8ZAS_002), directed by prof. Marina Bondi of the University of Modena and Reggio Emilia – local coordinator, prof. Maurizio Gotti.

opposing vaccine manufacturers (Hussain et al. 2018), as discovered by Brian Deer, a *Sunday Times* journalist, in his reports written between 2004 and 2010. As a consequence, *The Lancet* (Editors 2010) retracted Wakefield et al.'s (1999) article in 2010. The absence of any correlation between MMR and autism has been further confirmed by recent medical studies which have underlined the genetic predisposition of autism (cf., for instance, Davidson 2017; Garcia 2019; Hviid et al. 2019; Omer/Yildirim 2019). Nevertheless, anti-vaccinists' support for Wakefield et al.'s (1999) study and the resistance to vaccination became so strong that vaccination dropped worldwide. Apparently, this depends on the easiness people can access information via the Net, which, in the case of doctor-patient communication, has radically changed its dynamics (Hussain et al. 2018): doctors are no longer the repository of medical information because information technology has not only granted the easy access to any type of medical information but also contributed to construct the shared decision-making process between patients and physicians (Hussain et al. 2018). Sharing decisions may help patients to cope better with health issues (Hunt/Koteyko 2005; Seale 2005), but in the case of vaccination, sharing decisions *and* medical information has facilitated the spreading of disinformation.

Investigations about popularization have been carried out by many scholars (cf., for instance, Bondi 2014; Calsamiglia/van Dijk 2004; Garzone 2006, 2012, 2014; Gotti 2013, 2014; Maci 2014a, 2014b), which implies aspects related to health literacy (Briones 2015), particularly when medical knowledge is disseminated through the digital media play (Luzón 2015; Tessuto 2015; Turnbull 2015a, 2015b.; Myers 2015; as to social media communication, cf. also Zappavigna 2012 and KhosraviNik 2018). Since to the best of our knowledge, no research has so far been carried out on Twitter as a communication medium for disseminating (mis)information about vaccination, in this study we will describe what discourse strategies are employed by anti-vaccine activists on Twitter to spread fake news about vaccination.[2] For this purpose,

2 This study is part of a larger project dealing with medical popularization and misinformation on Twitter. In the first phase of this investigation, not published here, we analysed the visuals of the same corpus drawing on a socio-semiotic

an investigation will be carried out on a small corpus of 16,768 tweets (75,960 running words) collected over ten days in October 2018, soon after the death of some children due to an upsurge of measles in New York City.

In order to carry out this investigation, the chapter will draw on a CDA applied to the collected tweets with a corpus-based (Tognini-Bonelli 2001) approach and a semantic annotation of the collected tweets. Semantic annotation can offer great insights into online discourse as it can provide key themes of the data, identifying "key comments within the thread, based on their containing the constituent words of those key semantic categories" (Collins 2015: 43). The chapter will develop in the following sections: an overview of how misinformation is constructed and how spread on online platforms will be offered in Section 2, followed by the methodology in Section 3; Section 4 will introduce the Twitter data analysis and interpretation; Section 5 will conclude the chapter. The results seem to indicate that the #antivax discourse is, as usual, constructed in an accessible way, apparently founded on scientific grounds, thus granting itself authority.

2 Background: Misinformation, fake news and the informed citizen

According to the AgCom report (2018), the audience's request of specialized information from the media industry surpasses the offer provided by the media themselves. In this context, the media industry tries to cope with this issue by offering specialized information written by non-specialized journalists (AgCom 2018: 21–22), thus running the risk of spreading misinformation. This is particularly true

and CDA approach with the purpose of revealing cognitive, social and institutional constructs of misinformation. Results are being published by *Languages Cultures Mediation as* a contribution entitled "Ideological dynamics and discourse strategies of fake news in the #anti-vax campaign".

in online contexts, which require immediate updates, where the adequateness of the required information can be jeopardized. If citizens realize that information from the media is compromised, they lose their trust towards the information system (AgCom 2018: 75), tend to contest scientific and/or official sources and support misconceptions while, at the same time, upholding their beliefs (AgCom 2018: 76). In this context, online platforms and, in particular, social media, are considered the main and objective sources of news where citizens can turn to and get information (Tandoc et al. 2018: 138). As the type of information is seldom verified with scientific sources, through social media the 'informed' citizen can propagate information as well as misinformation and fake news on polarizing topics (AgCom 2019: 6). Furthermore, the viral diffusion of this type of (fake) news is based on algorithms that bring people to similar news they have read before, creating vicious circles: what people read online is the same type of (fake) news offered by such algorithms, which in a self-predicting way tend to confirm what they believe. All this makes readers unable to discern real and fake news (Balmas 2014), *de facto* exposing them to unchecked and unreliable information. The fake news acquire legitimacy when the audience perceives it as real. Indeed, as claimed by Tandoc et al. (2017: 148): "[i]t is when audiences mistake it as real news that fake news is able to play with journalism's legitimacy".

3 Methodological approach

As explained in the *Introduction* section, the aim of this chapter is to describe what linguistic discourse strategies are employed by anti-vaccine activists on Twitter to spread fake news about vaccination. To carry out this analysis, the investigation will draw on CDA (Fairclough 2014) trying to reveal the implicit ideological shades and intricacies the discourse anti-vaccination has on a *corpus-based* approach (Tognini-Bonelli 2001).

The analysis will be quantitative and qualitative and based on the verbal elements of the tweets collected.[3]

Linguistic data has been collected by downloading all tweets with the hashtags #provax, #provaxxer(s), #vaccine, #antivax, #novax, #anti-vaxxer(s) or #vaxxed. The only filter applied was the use of the English language. Users' nationality, gender, or place was not taken into consideration. The analytic tool to download tweets was *Socialbearing.com* [06/10/18], a free Twitter analytics and search tool for tweets, timelines and twitter maps. The tools allowed a search by applying as a filter all English tweets and replies for 9 days working backwards and starting on 27 October 2018 (and therefore, tweets were downloaded from 18/10/2018 to 27/10/2018). The starting date was decided following some children's deaths due to a measles outbreak in NYC – see for instance some articles found in the *Independent*, as the one by Kristin Hugo *Measles outbreak in NYC: what you need to know about the highly contagious disease*, (18 October 2018), and, in the *New York Times*, the article by Alexandra S. Levine *NYC Today: Measles in Brooklyn* (22 October 2018). Overall, I was able to collect a corpus of 16,782 tweets (75,960 running words) which contain 3,737 pictures. For the purpose of this investigation, videos and links have not been taken into consideration, but pictures have.

The linguistic quantitative analysis has been carried out with WMatrix (Rayson 2008) key-semantic domains, to which the CDA approach has been applied for a qualitative interpretation of the resulting data. A semantic domain can be defined as a cluster of terms and texts that have a high level of lexical coherence. Key semantic domains are such because they are identified with keyness computation. WMatrix detects key semantic domains through the University Centre for Computer Corpus Research on Language's (UCREL's) semantic analysis system (USAS), based on Tom McArthur's Longman Lexicon of Contemporary English (McArthur 1981). The semantic tagset used by USAS 21 "has a multi-tier structure with major discourse fields (shown

3 The visual analysis of the same corpus has been investigated in the first part of this project. Results are being published by *Languages Cultures Mediation as* a contribution entitled "Ideological dynamics and discourse strategies of fake news in the #anti-vax campaign".

here on the right), subdivided, and with the possibility of further fine-grained subdivision in certain cases'[4] (cf. also Rayson 2008). A manual checking of the automatic tagging has been carried out to better contextualize the concordances within the various key semantic domains.

4 Data analysis: Key semantic domains in the #antivax campaign

As said above, the corpus collected in the verbal section comprises 16,768 tweets (75,960 running words). The sentiment analysis elaborated by *Socialbearing.com* and indicated in the histogram in Fig. 1, below, reveals that over 45 % of the tweets are neutral, roughly 35 % of the tweets convey negative feelings (bad and terrible), while just 20 % convey positive ones:

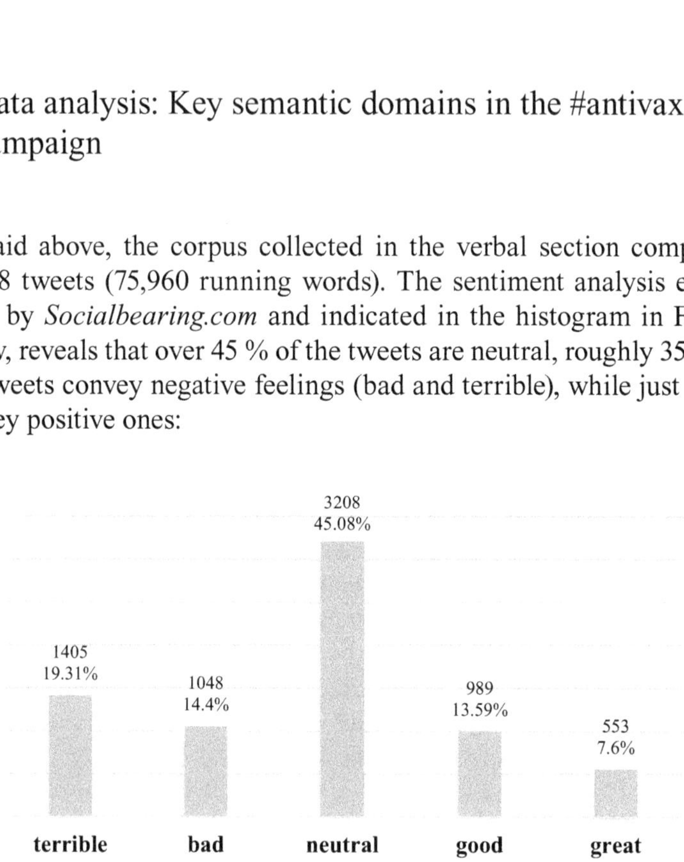

Fig. 1. Tweets sentiment analysis

Although negative feelings exceed positive ones by 15 %, almost half of the tweets are neutral. Nevertheless, while reading the whole

4 See http://ucrel.lancs.ac.uk/usas/ [24/03/2018].

corpus the impression one has is that of strongly negative emotions as far as vaccination is concerned. The sentiment analysis has a correspondence in the linguistic data, as the investigation with WMatrix suggests and revealed by the key semantic domain analysis. As explained in the introduction, the key semantic analysis can provide a more comprehensive account of the key themes of the data collected. In key semantic domains, what is analysed are not keywords in contexts but the context of the semantic prosody of words grouped under the semantic fields characterizing the corpus under investigation, by collating all members detected within the semantic domain.

Before using WMatrix, the corpus had to be manually checked because *Socialbearing.com* generally downloads tweets, retweets and mentions. While the retweets have not been taken into consideration in my investigation, because they are duplicates of what has already been said, mentions are, as they are replies to tweets starting with the name of the twitter user. This left me with 7,275 tweets (37,980 running words).

The analysis with WMatrix yielded 346 key semantic fields computed with a log-likelihood statistical test which is set by default. Of these, the 54 top semantic fields (listed in the *Appendix*) group more than 100 items in them. Apart from the semantic fields normally linked to medicine, disease and medical treatments, anatomy and physiology, science and technology, cause and effect, as it should be in a discourse centred around vaccination, and other fields that have not been regarded as particularly marked, such as those related to Twitter users' proper nouns, or geographical nouns, or even those associated with speech acts, or other grammatical markers such as pronouns, there are other semantic fields that are peculiar, as we can see in Tab. 1 below, since they do not seem to belong to the semantics of vaccination. For this reason, I will describe them in detail, by taking into consideration lexical items that have a frequency higher than 10 occurrences:

Semtag	*Frequency*	*Relative Frequency*	*Tagset*
S8+	175	0.46	Helping
X2.2+	166	0.44	Knowledgeable
S7.1+	157	0.41	In power
T3-	131	0.34	Change
L1-	126	0.33	Dead
S4	120	0.32	Kin
A5.1+	111	0.29	Evaluation: Good
A5.2+	111	0.29	Evaluation: True
X2.1	109	0.29	Thought, belief
G2.1	106	0.28	Law and order
X7+	101	0.27	Wanted

Tab. 1. Semtags of marked Semantic domains of the #antivax tweet campaign

As we can see from Tab. 1, above, in the first column, a *semtag* corresponds to a set of symbols used to identify a semantic field; in the second column, we have the raw frequency of the items included in that *semtag*, while in the third column there is an indication of the relative frequency normalized in comparison to a reference corpus, which in our case is the BNC spoken sampler – given that the tweets are seen as online conversation (Zappavigna 2012: 16).

Before analysing the semantic fields detected, a few words must be said about the *semtag S4 Kin* (120 occurrences, 0.32 relative frequency). The breakdown of this semantic field reveals that it comprises the items indicated in Tab. 2, below:

WORD	SEMTAG	Frequency	Relative Frequency
dad	S4	4	0.01
daughter	S4	5	0.01
daughters	S4	1	0.00
families	S4	3	0.01
families.	S4	1	0.00
family	S4	15	0.04
family.	S4	2	0.01
fatherly	S4	1	0.00
having kids	S4	1	0.00
husband	S4	3	0.01
maternal	S4	1	0.00
mom	S4	6	0.02
moms	S4	2	0.01
mother	S4	6	0.02
parent	S4	5	0.01
parental	S4	3	0.01
parents	S4	45	0.12
son	S4	9	0.02

Tab. 2. Breakdown of semtag S4 KIN

In particular, we have 50 occurrences of *parent*(*s*), and 19 occurrences of *family/families*, which indicates that vaccination is certainly a family or parental matter connected to *daughter*(s) (overall, 6 occurrences) and *son* (9 occurrences), but above all, this seems a motherly issue, since the items related to *mom*(*s*), *mother* and *maternal* indicate, in total, 15 occurrences, compared to the presence of *dad* (4 occurrences) and *fatherly* (1 occurrence), as can be seen from the table above and from some tweets reported below – which is also confirmed by the higher relative frequency of *mom*(*s*), *mother* and *maternal* compared to that of *dad* and *fatherly,* as also indicated in excerpts (1)-(6), below:

(1) This #autism **dad** has a warning for #antivaxxers;

(2) #Texas **Mom** Blamed for 4-Month-Old Daughter's Accidental #Gardasil #Vaccine Injury Loses Parental Rights

(3) Oh look, recently #vaccinated child spread #varicella #vaccine virus to **mother** while she was #pregnant.

(4) STUDY: Transmission of #Varicella-#Vaccine Virus from a Vaccinated Child to His Pregnant **Mother** that Ended Up with Abortion ncbi.nlm.nih.

(5) **Mom** Goes Anti #Vaccine After Her Infant Suffers Terrible Vaccine Reaction

(6) On a mom chat board recently an #antivax **mom** asked for #pediatrician recommendations near where I grew up. She wanted a doctor who would let her skip #vaccines.

In (1), *dad* warns antivaxxers. In (2)-(4), *mom* undergoes actions perpetrated by others, which have negative consequences: she is either blamed for another's fault because of vaccination, or she is infected despite vaccination and has an abortion. In (5)-(6), *mom* is proactive and decides to became an anti-vaccinist, though, as indicated in (5), this may be because of a negative personal experience. Not only is this a motherly issue, but also they are first and foremost very active when they have to deal with their children, compared to the fathers who do not take real actions themselves.

The same aspects are confirmed by *parent, parents* (45 and 5 hits, respectively), *parental* (3 occurencesI and *family/families* (respectively, 17 and 4 occurrences). According to #antivaxxers, parents must, first and foremost get informed:

(7) Dear **PARENTS**, read ALL #Vaccine Package Inserts (VPI)! Know the difference between CDC Statement &; VPI! vactruth. com/vaccine-insert &; #LearnTheRisk #vaccines #InformedConsent pic.

Indeed, vaccines are believed to be dangerous not only in terms of safety (vaccines can kill kids) but also in terms of legal rights. In this, the stress on the abuse people in power have is always there: anti-vaccinists cannot decide what they want for their kids because they can lose their *parental* authority, as can be seen in (8) and (9), below:

(8) Mother Faces Jury Trial As Texas Seeks to Terminate Her **Parental** Rights Over Daughter Injured by #Gardasil #Vaccine

(9) #Child Was Removed From **Family** At Gunpoint Because Dad Showed The World His Son s #Vaccine

If we look more in-depth at the type of items included in the semantic tags computed by WMatrix as seen in Tab. 2 above, we can detect the lexical items that have a frequency higher than 10 occurrences listed in Tab. 3 below:

SEMTAG	***word***	***frequency***	***relative frequency***
S8+ Helping	help	28	0.07
	protect	16	0.04
	support	14	0.04
	benefit(s) (vb/noun)	12	0.03
X2.2+ Knowledgeable	**know**	**37**	**0.10**
	news	23	0.06
	information	12	0.03
	info	11	0.03
S7.1+ Power	leading	13	0.03
T3- Change	**new**	**87**	**0.23**
	recent	13	0.03
L1- Dead	death	19	0.05
	deaths	17	0.04
	died	13	0.03
	die	11	0.03
	killed	10	0.03
S4 Kin	**parents**	**45**	**0.12**
	family	15	0.04
A5.1+ Evaluation: good	good	27	0.07
	great	22	0.06
A5.2+ Evaluation: true	evidence	20	0.05
	facts	16	0.04
	truth	14	0.04
	fact	10	0.03
X2.1 Belief	think	11	0.03
G2.1 Law and order	probation	13	0.03
	court	13	0.03
X7+ Want	want	17	0.04

Tab. 3. Most frequent semtags

Each lexical item will be discussed following, tagset. By tagset in the following paragraphs.

The *semtag S8+ Helping* includes 60 types (175 occurrences), all of them centring around the discourse of vaccination protection in neutral terms. For instance, we can find tweets like the following:

(10) #Chickenpox can be severe, even for healthy babies and #children. Here's why the #chickenpox #vaccine is the best **protection** against the #vaccdisease

Within this semantic group, however, the item benefit(s) (12 occurrences) is included as a key item in context (KIIC). Apparently, the logical coherence in the *Helping semtag* has to do with the governmental benefits or help people can have. Clearly, when used in this sense by the #anti-vaccine activists, the sense is negatively connoted, as we can see in (11) below:

(11) The word "lobby" implies a conscious goal focused on a tangible outcome that **benefits** the lobbyist

In all other cases, the term *benefits* as a plural noun collocates with *vaccine*, but the implications stemming from this collocation are negative. Indeed, the benefits do not seem to be deriving from the vaccination but are rather supposedly destroyed by vaccination itself, as can be seen in excerpt (12):

(12) Measles are expected and provide health **benefits** vaccines destroy #vaxxed #vaccinesworktiny

The *semtag X2.2+ Knowledgeable* groups 36 types (166 occurrences). Of these, the types with the highest frequency are: *know* (37 occurrences), *news* (23 occurrences), *information* (12 occurrences) and *info* (11 occurrences). The type of knowledge the #anti-vaccine activists indicate is either the absence of certain knowledge about the side-effects vaccines have, as indicated in (13), below, or about the fact that false news and information are spread among the population, as in (14):

(13) #Gardasil Was Fast-Tracked #Vaccine, So We Don't **know** Long-Term Side Effects

(14) More FAKE **NEWS** from CBS; Bought Dr David Agus on Shingles #vaccine shingrix saying falsely that it is 97 % effective; another big fat; Recommended by CDC which is Bought by corrupt Big Pharma which hides effective Vit-C therapy 5–15 % of all patients are non-responders. More insight on enigmatic stem cell memory T cell from human in vivo dynamics: compatible with long-lived immunological memory and #stemness. #Tscm #vaccine #stemcell #PLOSBiology dx.plos.org/10.1371/journal; Most interesting science at: immunology. immunologyconferences.org.

Their narrative is based on the assumption that nobody really knows the (long-term) side-effects caused by vaccination, since what is known is false or fake news.

The *semtag S7.1+* related to *Power* has 68 types (158 occurrences). Amongst these, the only item which occurs more than 10 times is the present participle *leading* (13 occurrences) used as a premodifier, normally collocating with *cause*(*s*), as we can see in (15) and (16), below:

(15) Vaccines are the **leading** cause of Ligma

(16) #Measles is a **leading** cause of death among young children even though a safe & effective #vaccine is available

While (15) is used by #anti-vaccine activists, sentences like (16) are used in reply to them. In both cases, the term is indicated as a synonym for *prominent* and accompanies the term *cause* of either a disease (if the *cause* is a 'vaccine') or of death (if the *cause* is a disease). In particular, when sentences like (16) are posted, the #anti-vaccine activists tend to reply as in (17), where we find again a term related to the semantic field *ST.1+* linked to *Power*:

(17) When babies are routinely injected w 4925 mcg of aluminum before their 2nd birthday, it's not surprising there is a negative impact. #vaccine promoters fail to seriously investigate #nonspecificeffects aka #unintendedconsequences twitter.com/cmsriresearch/; When children are maimed and murdered by **forced** administration of pharmaceutical products but the masses don't notice . . . When millions of . . . m. facebook. com/story. php?story; #instagram #media #breakingnews #KimKardashian #LymeDisease #vaccine #healthcare

In this case, *power* stands for the fact that people are exerting power over other people by forcing them to assume unwanted "pharmaceutical products". The fact is more serious given that the people who are forced are children, who are "maimed and murdered" as a consequence of this forced action, and they do not have the legal authority to oppose this mandatory action done by the administration.

The semantic domain connected to the idea of *Change*, *T3-*, includes 14 types which have 131 occurrences altogether. Among these, the most frequent one is the adjective *new*, which appears 87 times and tends to collocate with *study/studies, analysis*, *report*, and in general with terms that have to do with scientific investigation. If so, the trend is that of putting forward studies that either show the inefficacious role of vaccines, as in (18), or the problems vaccines may provoke, as in (19), or even the inadequacy of data as to the possibility of creating correct vaccine strategies, as in (20):

(18) **New** Studies Reveal #Vaccine Harm – Two pilot studies led by Anthony Mawson (an interdisciplinary epidemiologist w/a doctorate in public health) reveal vaccinated children have more health problems than unvaccinated children. #vaccinedangers

(19) **New** study shows vaccinated children have more CHRONIC illness than not-vaccinated children: worldmercuryproject.org/news/unvaccinated

(20) **New** analysis by Prof Harry Campbell @EdinUniUsher and colleagues identify [sic] major gaps in data from LMICs on the annual burden of seasonal #influenza, which limit the ability to develop appropriate #vaccine strategies

The *semtag L1-* related to the semantic field *dead* includes 25 types (126 occurrences), with the items *death* (19 occurrences) *deaths* (17 occurrences), *died* (13 occurrences), *die* (11 occurrences) and *killed* (10 occurrences) being the most frequent types.

The tweets containing these items reveal the #antivaxxers' narrative, as can be seen in examples (21)-(24) reported below: vaccines cause deaths and Big Pharma hides this fact; unfortunately, children are the victims.

(21) Document hidden by #BigPharma proves #vaccines have caused sudden **death** before.

(22) In addition to #vaccine injuries and **deaths**, there are now two drowned humans, and 3 million dead honeybees connected to our #CDC and #FDA

(23) A healthy 14-yo boy **died** next day after receiving #HPV #Vaccine #Gardasilsanevax. org

(24) #Vaccine **killed** 14 #children and permanently damaged thousands yet #BigPharma is still trying to figure out how to sell it

There is one single interesting occurrence in (25) where the anti-vaccine activists use the notion of herd immunity to convey a completely different meaning from what this notion generally has. Herd immunity is a form of protection from infectious disease whereby a large proportion of the population (or herd) has become immune to an infection thanks to vaccination; it also grants protection for individuals who are not immune and/or cannot be vaccinated. Herd immunity is possible only via vaccination. This idea, however, is seen as negatively connoted by the anti-vaccinists. Indeed, anti-vaxxers use the imagery of a herd by connecting it to that of sheep, and by an intertextual link (Isaiah

53:7) to the saying *like a lamb to the slaughter* to coin the expression found in (25):

(25) So sad #Vaccine #autism #sheep to **slaughter** twitter.com/vaccineepidemic

Exactly like a lamb to the slaughter, vaccinated people are like sheep to the slaughter: by getting vaccinated they are going towards death, which is what they argue vaccination causes.

In the case of the *semtag A5.1+ Evaluation: good*, the semantic field is apparently positive and it seems difficult to see how the anti-vaccine movement can use positive evaluation in condemning vaccination. This field contains 29 types (110 occurrences) – *good* (27 occurrences) and *great* (22 occurrences) are the only two types with more than 10 occurrences in this group. The item *good*, however, is used with negative polarity when condemning vaccination, as in (26), below:

(26) Editors of medical journals confirm: HPV vaccines cause more harm than **good**

If it is used with positive polarity, it is normally employed to highlight the qualities of those people who are in tune with it:

(27) We should all hope that **good** Doctors around the World PRAISE the **good** works of US President Trump in protecting the livelihood of Children and medical careers from unwanted influence by investigating #Vaccine Fraud

In the case of the *semtag A5.2+ Evaluation: true*,[5] there are 27 types (111 occurrences). The types that occur more than 10 times are *evidence* (20 occurrences), *facts* (16 occurrences), *truth* (14 occurrences) and *fact* (10 occurrences). This is a semantic field that groups together words related to the world of evidence the antivaxxers have collected to demonstrate that vaccines are dangerous, as can be seen in excerpts (28)-(29):

(28) #Vaccine Cartel Destroys Lives: **Evidence** thedailysheeple.com/vaccine-cartel #vaccinesKILL #BigPharma

(29) Thou Shalt not tell the whole vaccine **truth** or public will refuse

---

5 WMatrix does not classifies the *semtag A5.2+ Evaluation: true* in linguistics terms as Hunston and Thompson (2000) mean but rather as "evidential truth".

As to the *semtag X2.1 Belief*, there are 45 types (109 occurrences), but just one type occurs more than 10 times: *think* (11 occurrences):

(30) Not an anti-jab but **think** asbestos or mercury. People assured they were safe. The problem here is the #government is forcing your arm (literally).

Think is used to invite people to 'ponder' and 'consider' rather than to 'believe'. And what the antivaxxers are asked to *ponder* about is related to the danger of vaccine contents, namely "asbestos or mercury".

The *semtag G2.1 Law and order* includes 44 types (106 occurrences altogether), which reveal how doctors who refuse to give vaccinations have legal issues, as in excerpts (31) and (32), where the medics are on *probation* (13 occurrences), or which indicate what foreign and US *courts* (12 occurrences) do, with the implicit assumption that such truth is covered up by the US media, as indicated in both (33) and (34):

(31) Doctor on **probation** after exempting boy from vaccines

(32) Dr. Bob Sears placed on **probation** after exempting 2-year-old boy from all childhood vaccinations

(33) Italian **court** rules mercury and aluminum in vaccines cause autism: US media continues total blackout of medical truth

(34) @TIME **Court** ruling confirms #Gardasil #vaccine kills people; & scientific evidence beyond any doubt

The *semtag X7+ Want* contains 41 types (101 occurrences) and has *want* as the most frequent type with 17 hits. The item is used to show the government's policy regarding vaccination:

(35) The government created lyme disease, read Lab 257, now THEY **want** to create a #vaccine to make a profit off the disease

Vaccination, in other words, is created to make profits from a disease which has been propagated by the government itself. There is no way to talk to antivaccine activists: whenever something reasonable is offered, a counterclaim based on a conspiracy theory is put forward.

To conclude, from the analysis of the SemTags, the #antivax narrative can be summarized as follows: vaccination is primarily a motherly issue. In general, if parents want to protect their children, they must get informed about the risks connected to vaccines given that they have extremely dangerous active substances, such as mercury or aluminum. Vaccination is claimed to cause deaths and injuries, as new studies have revealed and as the courts have established, or as indicated by the fact that *good* doctors who refuse to vaccinate children are on probation; and despite the fact that BigPharma has denied or dismissed this, facts cannot be denied. People therefore must get informed before getting vaccinated – indeed, false diseases can also be generated by the government so that vaccines are created in order to make a profit. In other words, there is a conspiracy between the government and Big Pharma at the expense of the population.

5 Conclusions

As the semantic tag investigation has revealed, with data summarized in Tab. 3 above, where we can find the most frequent key *semtags* (more than 100 occurrences), and, within the *semtags*, the most frequent types (more than 10 hits), the story the antivax activists tell indicates a very precise ideology based on distortions and fake news.

The distortions to which the spread of such fake news can lead over Twitter and other social media are so evident that social media have begun a policy of social (fake) news site removal from their platforms "on the grounds that they violate policies against misleading contents" (Alcott/Gentzkow 2017: 233). Apart from that, there is also an urgent need for a new digital-health literacy on vaccination that can help people to develop trust in health professionals (Wolfe/Sharp 2002).

References

AgCom, A.p.l.G.n.C. 2018. News vs. Fake News nel sistema dell'informazione. Interim Report. Indagine conoscitiva del 309/16/cons.

AgCom, A.p.l.G.n.C. 2019. Osservatorio sulla Disinformazione Online. *Osservatorio sulla disinformazione* 1(19).

Allcott, Hunt/Matthew Gentzkow. 2017. Social Media and Fake News in the 2016 Election. *Journal of Economic Perspectives* 31(1), 211–236.

Balmas, Feital. 2014. When Fake News Become Real: Combined Exposure to Multiple News Sources and Political Attitudes of Inefficacy, Alienation, and Cynicism. *Communication Research* 41(3), 430–454.

Bondi, Marina. 2014. Connecting Science. Organizational Units in Specialist and Non-specialist Discourse. In Caliendo, Giuditta/Bongo, Giancarmine (eds.) *The Language of Popularization: Theoretical and Descriptive Models/Die Sprache der Popularisierung: Theoretische und deskriptive Modelle*. Bern: Peter Lang, 51–72

Briones, Rowena. 2015. Harnessing the Web: How E-Health and E-Health Literacy Impact Young Adults' Perceptions of Online Health Information. *Medicine 2.0* 4(2), 111–118.

Calsamiglia, Helena/van Dijk, Teun A. 2004. Popularization Discourse and Knowledge about the Genome. *Discourse and Society* 15(4), 369–389.

Collins, Luke. 2015. How Can Semantic Annotation Help Us to Analyse the Discourse of Climate Change in Online User Comments? *Linguistik Online* 70(1), 43–60.

Davidson, Michael. 2017. Vaccination as a Cause of Autism-Myths and Controversies. *Dialogues in Clinical Neuroscience* 19(4), 403–407.

Fairclough, Norman. 2014. *Language and Power*. London: Routledge

Garcia, Jennifer. 2019. Vaccination With MMR Does Not Increase Autism Risk. *Medscape*. https://emedicine.medscape.com/article/912781-workup. Accessed 18 November 2019.

Garzone, Giuliana E. 2006. *Perspectives on ESP and Popularization*. Milan: CUEM.

Garzone, Giuliana E. 2012. Sapere scientifico e divulgazione nella stampa quotidiana tra accessibilità e affidabilità. In Diani, G./Preite, C. (eds.) *La trasmissione del sapere nelle diverse comunità accademiche: una prospettiva plurilingue*. Roma: Officina, 38–46.

Garzone, Giuliana E. 2014. News Production and Scientific Knowledge: Exploring Popularization as a Process. In Bongo, G./Caliendo, G. (eds.) *The Language of Popularization: Die Sprache der Popularisierung*. Bern: Peter Lang, 73–107.

Gotti, Maurizio. 2013. The Analysis of Popularization Discourse: Conceptual Changes and Methodological Evolutions. In Kermas, Susan/Christiansen, Thomas (eds.) *The Popularization of Specialized Discourse and Knowledge across Communities and Cultures*. Bari: Edipuglia, 9–32.

Gotti, Maurizio. 2014. Reformulation and Recontextualization in Popularization Discourse. *Ibérica* 27, 15–34

Hunt, Daniel/Koteyko, Nelya. 2015. 'What Was Your Blood Sugar Reading This Morning?' Representing Diabetes Self-management on Facebook. *Discourse & Society* 26(4), 445–463.

Hussain, Azhar/Ali, Syed/Ahmed, Madiha/Hussain, Sheharyar. 2018. The Anti-vaccination Movement: A Regression in Modern Medicine. *Cureus* 10(7), e2919.

Hviid, Anders/Hansen, Jørgen Vinsløv/Frisch, Morten/Melbye, Mads. 2019. Measles, Mumps, Rubella Vaccination and Autism: A Nationwide Cohort Study Measles, Mumps, Rubella Vaccination and Autism. *Annals of Internal Medicine*, 05/03/2019.

KhosraviNik, Majid. 2018. Social Media-Critical Discourse Studies. In Flowerdew, John/Richardson, John E. (eds.) *The Routledge Handbook of Critical Discourse Studies*. London: Routledge, 582–596.

Luzón, Maria José. 2015. Recontextualizing Expert Discourse in Weblogs: Strategies to Communicate Health Research to Experts and the Interested Public. In Gotti, Maurizio/Maci, Stefania/Sala, Michele (eds.) *Insights into Medical Communication*. Bern: Peter Lang, 331–352.

Maci, Stefania M. 2014a. Institutional Popularization of Medical Knowledge: The Case of Pandemic Influenza A (H1N1). In Caliendo, Giuditta/Bongo, Giancarmine (eds.) *The Language of Popularization: Theoretical and Descriptive Models/Die Sprache der Popularisierung; teoretische und deskriptive Modelle*. Sprache in Kommunikation und Medien Series. Bern: Peter Lang, 165–190.

Maci, Stefania M. 2014b. The Popularisation of Scientific Discourse for the Academia from a Diachronic Perspective: The Case of Nobel Lectures. In Chiavetta, Eleonora/Sciarrino, Silvia (eds.) *Perspectives on the Popularisation of Natural Sciences in a Diachronic Overview*. Newcastle upon Tyne: Cambridge Scholars Publishing, 97–118.

McArthur, Tom. 1981. *Longman Lexicon of Contemporary English*. Harlow: Longman.

Miller, Elizabeth/Farrington, Paddy/Taylor, Brent. 1999. MMR Vaccination and Autism. *The Lancet* 354(9182), 950.

Myers, Greg. 2015. Social Media and the Professional Practice in Medical Twitter. In Gotti, Maurizio/Maci, Stefania/Sala, Michele (eds.) *Insights into Medical Communication*. Bern: Peter Lang, 51–69.

Omer, Saad B./Yildirim, Inci. 2019. Further Evidence of MMR Vaccine Safety: Scientific and Communications Considerations MMR Vaccine Safety: Scientific and Communications Considerations. *Annals of Internal Medicine,* 05/03/2019.

Rayson, Paul. 2008. From Key Words to Key Semantic Domains. *International Journal of Corpus Linguistics* 13(4), 519–549.

Seale, Clive. 2005. New Directions for Critical Internet Health Studies: Representing Cancer Experience on the Web. *Sociology of Health & Illness* 27(4), 515–540.

Socialbearing at: https://socialbearing.com/. Accessed 4 December 2019.

Tandoc, Edson C./Lim, Zheng Wei/Ling, Richard. 2018. Defining "Fake News". *Digital Journalism* 6(2), 137–153.

Taylor, Brent/Miller, Elizabeth/Farrington, C. Paddy/Petropoulos, Maria-Christina/Favot-Mayaud, Isabelle/Li, Jun/Waight, Pauline A. 1999. Autism and Measles, Mumps, and Rubella Vaccine: No Epidemiological Evidence for a Causal Association. *The Lancet* 353(9169), 2026–2029.

Tessuto, Girolamo. 2015. Empowering Patients to Self-care in Web-Mediated Communication: A Multimodal Discourse Analysis. In Gotti, Maurizio/Maci, Stefania/Sala, Michele (eds.) *Insights into Medical Communication.* Bern: Peter Lang, 213–246.

The Editors of *The Lancet* 2010. Retraction—Ileal-Lymphoid-Nodular Hyperplasia, Non-Specific Colitis, and Pervasive Developmental Disorder in Children. *The Lancet* 375(9713), 445.

Tognini-Bonelli, Elena. 2001. *Corpus Linguistics at Work.* Amsterdam/Philadelphia: John Benjamins.

Turnbull, Judith. 2015a. Living with Diabetes: The Discourse of Medical Information on the Internet for Young People. In Gotti, Maurizio/Maci, Stefania/Sala, Michele (eds.) *Insights into Medical Communication*, Bern: Peter Lang, 247–268.

Turnbull, Judith. 2015b. Knowledge Dissemination Online: The Case of Health Information. In Bondi, Marina/Cacchiani, Silvia/Mazzi, Davide (eds.) *Discourse In and Through the Media. Recontextualizing and Reconceptualzing Expert Discourse.* Newcastle: Cambridge Scholars, 290–314.

USAS. Available at: http://ucrel.lancs.ac.uk/usas/. Accessed 7 December 2019.

Wakefield, Andrew/Murch, Simon H./Anthony, Andrew/Linnell, John/Casson, David H./Malik, Mohsin/Berelowitz, Mark/Dhillon, Amar P./Thomson, Michael A./Harvey, Peter/Valentine, Alan/Davies, Susan E./Walker-Smith, John A. 1998. Ileal-Lymphoid-Nodular Hyperplasia, Non-Specific Colitis, and Pervasive Developmental Disorder in Children. RETRACTED. *The Lancet* 351(9103), 637–641.

Wolfe, Robert M./Sharp, Lisa K. 2002. Anti-Vaccinationists Past and Present. *BMJ* (*Clinical research edition*) 325(7361), 430–432.

Zappavigna, Michele. 2012. *The Discourse of Twitter and Social Media*. London: Continuum.

Appendix

Semtag	Tagset	Frequency	Relative Frequency
Z99	unmatched	11,225	29.56
Z5	grammatical bin	6,857	18.05
Z8	pronouns	1,672	4.40
N1	numbers	1191	3.14
B3	Medicines and medical treatment	756	1.99
A3+	Existing	730	1.92
04.1	General appearance and physical properties	672	1.77
B2-	Disease	632	1.66
C1	Arts and crafts	495	1.30
A2.2	Cause & Effect/Connection	339	0.89
A9+	Getting and possession	331	0.87
Q2.2	Speech acts	328	0.86
M6	Location and direction	321	0.85
A1.1.1	General actions/making	308	0.81
Z6	Negative	302	0.80
Z1	Personal names	301	0.79
Z4	Discourse Bin	299	0.79
S2	People	283	0.75
A7+	Likely	273	0.72
Z3	Other proper names	264	0.70

Semtag	Tagset	Frequency	Relative Frequency
Z2	Geographical names	208	0.55
P1	Education in general	194	0.51
Q2.1	Speech: Communicative	192	0.51
T1.3	Time: Period	188	0.49
B1	Anatomy and physiology	181	0.48
S8+	Helping	175	0.46
N5.1+	Entire; maximum	170	0.45
X2.2+	Knowledgeable	166	0.44
I1	Money generally (*)	160	0.42
M1	Moving, coming and going (**)	160	0.42
S7.1+	In power	157	0.41
N5	Quantities	144	0.38
A13.3	Degree: Boosters	143	0.38
S6+	Strong obligation or necessity	141	0.37
N5-	Quantities: little	138	0.36
X2.4	Investigate, examine, test, search	134	0.35
T3-	Change	131	0.34
A2.1+	Time: New and young	131	0.34
T1.1.2	Time: Present; simultaneous	130	0.34
L1-	Dead	126	0.33
A10+	Open; Finding; Showing	125	0.33
A9-	Giving	124	0.33
Q1.2	Paper documents and writing	124	0.33
S4	Kin	120	0.32
N5+	Quantities: many/much	119	0.31
A5.1+	Evaluation: Good	111	0.29
A5.2+	Evaluation: True	111	0.29
X2.1	Thought, belief	109	0.29
Y1	Science and technology in general	108	0.28
A4.1	General kinds, groups, examples	106	0.28
G2.1	Law and order	106	0.28
M2	Putting, pulling, pushing, transporting (**)	105	0.28
L2	Living creatures: animals, birds etc.	103	0.27
X7+	Wanted	101	0.27

(*) The I1 *semtag* contains items all preceded by the symbol '#' - hashtag. They have nothing to do with the category of money and therefore the *semtag* has been excluded from the analysis.

(**) The *semtags* M1 and M2 are related to movement, they refer to 'cell movement'; M1 may also refer to migration (and the discourse of vaccination is related to what vaccines migrants have or do not have). These *semtags* have been excluded from the analysis.

Nouf Alotaibi and Jane Mulderrig

Debating Saudi womanhood: A corpus-aided critical discourse analysis of the representation of Saudi women in the Twitter campaign against the 'Male Guardianship' system

1 Introduction

In Saudi Arabia, the law stipulates that no political parties, civil society organisations or marches are allowed. However, the impact made by social media sites during the 2011 Arab Spring made women's rights activists realize that they too could benefit from the power of social media to bring about socio-political change. It offered a public platform on which to highlight and contest the unequal social status of women in Saudi society. As a consequence, numerous social media campaigns have been launched by Saudi women (e.g. 'Women2Drive', 'Saudi Women Revolution', 'Baladi' [My Country][1]). Arguably the most high-profile of these has been the #EndMaleGuardianshipSystem Twitter campaign which, since its inception in 2016 has sparked widespread public debate about the Male Guardianship System (hereafter MGS), whereby Saudi women's freedoms and decision-making powers are subordinated to those of a male relative. This chapter presents a corpus-aided critical analysis of the linguistic strategies employed in that campaign.

1 All translations are the authors' own.

Saudi Arabia applies the Hanbali School doctrine to the interpretation of Islamic texts (Commins 2006). One of its regulations that has been enforced rigorously is the male 'guardianship' of women. According to the Hanbali School, this regulation applies in just two cases: within marriage and when travelling (al-Zuhayli 1999). However, the male guardianship system was extended to other institutions (e.g. universities, hospitals and so forth) in the 1980s, with the result that Saudi women are treated as legal minors, positioned as second-rate citizens and subjected to unprecedented legal restrictions. Under this system, a Saudi woman must have a male guardian, chosen from one of her close relatives (for example, her father, husband, brother), to provide written consent for her to participate in a wide variety of activities. Examples include enrolling in (higher) education, applying for official documents (e.g. passport, family ID, or personal ID), applying for a scholarship, being released from state institutions (e.g. prisons or rehabilitation centres), undergoing certain types of surgery (e.g. an abortion, a caesarean section or cosmetic surgery), accessing bank services (e.g. opening an account), working in the governmental and non-governmental sectors, and accessing the judicial system. The guardianship system is not enforced by the judiciary or royal decree, but instead through Saudi Arabia's powerful religious tier.

Two major events led to the establishment of this system: the Islamic Awakening movement from the 1960s onwards (Lacroix 2015) and the seizure of the holy mosque in Mecca in 1979 (Al-Fassi 2013). After this seizure in 1979, religious institutions began to wield power in the public sphere; subsequently, Saudi women were increasingly restricted in access to education, employment and freedom of movement, which resulted in a dramatic change in economic status for them (Al-Fassi 2013).

In 2016, female Saudi activists started an online campaign #سعوديات_نطالب_اسقاط_الولاية, or '#EndMaleGuardianshipSystem' in English, to eliminate the male guardianship system. In fact, the use of the word 'guardian' in the campaign's Arabic language hashtag is misleading. In Islam, the concept of a 'guardian' is specifically related to marriage -i.e. a guardian plays an essential role in completing a woman's marriage. Although the word choice was inaccurate, it had been used previously in official documents, in reference to this system for controlling women's freedoms. Despite its misleading terminology, the campaign has proven successful. The hashtag began trending daily and eventually led to a series of recent reforms in state regulation. This campaign was not the first to demand an end to this 'guardianship' system. The Saudi Ministry of Commerce in 2004 abolished a regulation requiring a male guardian for Saudi businesswomen after widespread criticism (Yamani 2008; Al-Fassi 2013). In addition, a July 2009 campaign *Treat Us Like Adult Citizens – Or We'll Leave the Country* was launched by a liberal Saudi women's rights activist, together with other Saudi female activists. The campaign, also calling for an end to the male guardianship system, received heavy criticism (Admon 2009). Furthermore, in 2011, the #SaudiWomenRevolution hashtag was used on Twitter by Saudi women campaigning for women's rights, including but not limited to, the end of the male guardianship system (Saudi Women's Rights Blog 2011).

The #EndMaleGuardianshipSystem campaign (hereafter #EMGC) generated an online petition that gathered 14,700 signatures from both Saudi men and women, along with their full names and ID numbers. The petition was sent to King Salman bin Abdulaziz on October 2016, and the hashtag continued trending daily until August 2019. Since then, new regulations have been enacted regarding the abolition of guardian consent across a variety of government offices. A royal order issued on August 2019 met an important demand of the campaign, and women above the age of 21 are now able to travel and have their passports issued without permission from a guardian.

2 Aim of the research

In a conservative society like Saudi Arabia, social movements which repudiate practices adopted by the Islamic culture are highly controversial, and they are even considered by many to be against God's law. It is therefore unsurprising that #EMGC led to polarised and heated debate in Saudi society. The original and main platform for the campaign has been Twitter (the focus of this chapter), although it extends to other public forums, notably YouTube and online newspapers. On one side of this debate are the female activists and more liberal clerics who support the campaign to end the male guardianship system (hereafter 'Anti-MGS'). On the other side of the debate are conservative clerics and their supporters (Saudi women among them) who oppose the campaign and wish to maintain the system (hereafter 'Pro-MGS'). #EMGC thus offers a window into the complex dynamics of power and gender in contemporary Saudi society, revealing the linguistic strategies whereby the status and role of Saudi women were debated, by women themselves, in this very visible and controversial public domain. This paper draws on corpus linguistics methods in order to investigate these strategies on Twitter and focuses on the *female* campaigners on each side of the debate. It asks the following questions: 1) who were the salient social actors in the discourse of #EMGC?; 2) how did the *female* campaigners represent Saudi women as social actors?; and 3) what were their most prominent actions?

3 Theoretical background

The study draws on a theory of social justice put forth by the feminist writer Nancy Fraser (1995), who, in distinguishing socioeconomic injustice from cultural injustice, noted that the former is rooted in the political-economic construction of a society, such as exploitation, economic marginalisation and deprivation, and the latter – including cultural domination, misrecognition and disrespect – is rooted in the social paradigms of representation, interpretation and communication. Of course, the two are intertwined and lead to overlapping demands, as shown in the descriptions of social movements in which demands for cultural change intermingle with demands for economic change. This intermingling is exemplified in the social campaign against male guardianship that has taken hold in Saudi Arabia. The campaign calls for both cultural and socioeconomic change, since from the former flows the latter. Under the existing system, Saudi women are treated as second-class citizens and are thereby also economically marginalised.

Cultural injustice generates cultural devaluation and the denial of legal rights, while socioeconomic injustice results in the inability to access, without a male guardian's permission, adequate economic benefits (such as full and equal access to employment in the public and private sectors, or rights to personal banking services and investment opportunities). According to Fraser, 'neither redistributive remedies alone nor recognition remedies alone will suffice. Bivalent collectivities need both' (1995: 78). The recognition remedy for cultural justice involves 'revaluing disrespected identities and the cultural products of maligned groups', and the redistributive remedy requires transforming the political-economic structure of a society and abolishing the repressive system (Fraser 1995: 73). Thus, for Fraser (1995), it is necessary to consider the politics of cultural recognition and redistributive equality as mutually inclusive.

In the case of Saudi women, cultural recognition has been granted recently by one of the elites in the country, Crown Prince Muhammad bin Salman. In interviews, he has openly acknowledged that Saudi women are currently being denied their full rights and has promised action to improve their status (CBS News 2018; TIME 2018; Bloomberg 2018). This recognition of women's rights is a barometer of a wider shift in Saudi public discourse, as manifested in #EMGC and explored below.

4 Methodological approach

In order to explore the role of language in shaping the public construal of women's rights in Saudi society, the study draws on a combined corpus-aided critical discourse approach. Critical Discourse Analysis (CDA) (Fairclough 2003, 2015) offers a conceptual framework through which to explore the role of #EMGC within the Saudi social formation. #EMGC discourse construes patterns of participation, role-relations, values and norms for Saudi women, and rests on implicit and complex ideologies which, in turn, intersect with a range of other religious, political and cultural discourses. The study also makes use of corpus linguistics tools to explore salient textual patterns in the online campaign (Tognini-Bonelli 2001). To facilitate comparison of the linguistic strategies used by the two sides of the campaign, two corpora were compiled from Twitter's #EMGC spanning a nine-month period, then analysed using the concordance software 'AntConc' (Anthony 2017). This quantitative approach to the data was combined with text analytical frameworks whose systemic functional theory of discourse is compatible with CDA's view of language as a social semiotic (Halliday/Matthiessen 2014), while offering a means of investigating patterns of linguistic choice in the representation of social actors and their actions (Van Leeuwen 2008).

In recent years, critical discourse analysts have made increasing use of corpus linguistics tools (e.g.: Baker et al. 2008; Mautner 2005; Mulderrig 2008). Their integration with CDA's textually oriented and theoretically grounded approach produces 'a relatively systematic and readily replicable approach to CDA' and one which 'direct[s] the analyst's gaze in unexpected and often fruitful directions' (Mulderrig 2014: 449). Such an integrated approach also enables the critical analyst to handle large bodies of textual data in order to track the development of social movements (like #EMGC), as in the larger project from which this chapter stems.

4.1 Data collection

Participant observation on Twitter was used as a first step in the data collection process, in order to gain an overall picture of the campaign and identify the users associated with its salient hashtags[2]. This method also provided an understanding of the context of the problem and the affordances of social media platforms with respect to the social problem under investigation (Unger et al. 2016). Consideration was also given to the algorithms underpinning Twitter, whereby the popularity

2 A number of hashtags exist, both in English and Arabic, relating to the guardianship system. However, the main hashtag which started the campaign was #424 سعوديات_نطلب_اسقاط_الولايه [#EndMaleGuardianshipSystem424]. This was selected for the analysis because it is the original, most widely followed and retweeted, and enduring.

Twitter Corpora	First filtering		Second filtering			Total
	Gender	Stance	Nationality	No. of followers	Original tweets	No. of tweets
Anti-MGS	Female	Campaigns against the guardianship system	Saudi	2,000 or more	Yes	1500
Pro-MGS	Female	Supports the system	Saudi		Yes	1500

Tab. 1: The two phases used to divide and filter the Twitter account list

of content is measured, thereby ultimately making it more influential in the public circulation of knowledge (Gillespie 2014: 185).

Following this research into the 'backstage' of the campaign, it was thus possible to compile a list of female[3] Twitter account users on either side of the debate. This was then further filtered in order to obtain metadata on gender, nationality (only self-identified Saudi users were included in analysis), number of followers (only the most 'popular' users were included), and original tweets (only original content was included). This filtering process yielded two final lists (see Tab. 1 below), which were used to compile a reliable and representative corpus of Tweets spanning 01/06/2016 to 28/02/2017. On the basis of these lists two corpora were compiled for each side of the debate: an Anti-MGS corpus (women campaigning to abolish the guardianship system) and a Pro-MGS corpus (women arguing in favour of the system).

4.2 Preparing and coding the Twitter corpus

According to Gries and Newman, corpus files 'always need to be cleaned up and standardised and they often need to be marked up and annotated' (2013: 263). The corpus was thus cleaned by removing irrelevant information (e.g. time, number of likes and retweets, non-standard spellings) and anonymised. It was also tagged using the

3 This chapter focuses only on female campaigners. The larger study from which it derives looks at both males and females.

Text Encoding Initiative (TEI Consortium 2016) to demarcate tweets. Finally, the corpus was annotated by adding a coding system linked to the research questions. In short, the study sought to identify how *social actors* are represented in the campaign. Thus, a coding system was devised in order to identify the actors referred to in the data. Codes are short phrases/words that 'symbolically assign a summative, salient, essence-capturing and/or evocative attribute for a portion of language-based or visual data' (Saldanha 2013: 3). Two 'code books' were thus created in order to identify the social actors in each corpus (see Appendix). The next step integrates CDA text analytical tools in order to determine not just *which* actors were represented, but *how*.

4.3 Analysing the representation of social actors

Van Leeuwen's (2008) socio-semantic approach offers a taxonomic model for analysing how social practice is represented in language. It was developed out of the important insight that sociological agency is not always realised by linguistic agency. Thus, the traditional categories of grammatical description, like nouns and verbs, cannot reveal much about the ideational and evaluative significance of linguistic choices when representing actors and their actions. The following two phrases uttered by a government minister during the 2020 pandemic represent essentially the same event: 'The government urged the public to stay at home' and 'Boris urged us to stay at home'. However, in each case the representational choices frame that event in subtly different terms: the second choice is more personalised, perhaps in order to achieve compliance by down-playing institutional authority. To capture this kind of semantic nuance, Van Leeuwen's model posits socio-semantic categories[4] like 'personalisation vs functionalisation'. These enable the critical discourse analyst to identify the linguistic strategies which help produce and reinforce power asymmetries, discrimination, inequality and injustice (Van Leeuwen 2009).

---

4 Precisely because it has a socio-semantic basis, this model can be applied to languages other than English (Van Leeuwen 2009).

Social actors who participate in social practices are represented as either included or excluded, in order to suit the interests and purposes of the intended readers (van Leeuwen 2008). The excluded social actors are either *suppressed*, when no references to them are included in the text, or *backgrounded*, when they are mentioned elsewhere in the text. A*ctivation* means that actors are used as active and dynamic forces within an action, whereas *passivation* means that they are portrayed as undergoing an activity or as being on the receiving end of an action (i.e. as beneficiaries). Social actors can be an individual, as in *individualisation,* or groups, as in *assimilation*. Assimilation has two typologies: *aggregation*, whereby actors are represented by quantifiers and treated as statistics, and *collectivisation*, whereby a group of actors is referred to using a noun denoting a group of individuals. *Association* is another way of representing groups of actors and occurs when two or more are grouped together due to common qualities (e.g. ethnic origin).

Social actors can be represented through the process of *categorisation*. Categorisation has three typologies: *functionalisation*, in which actors are referred to by an activity or function they perform (e.g. an occupation or role), *appraisement*, in which they are referred to in evaluative terms as good or bad, and *identification*, in which they are described in terms of what they are more or less permanently. Identification has three types: *classification* i.e. based on major categories generated by a society or an institution, *relational identification* i.e. according to their kinship, personal or work relations, and *physical identification*, i.e. according to their uniquely physical characteristics. In addition, social actors can be *impersonalized,* for example, by referring to their utterance (this representation is called *utterance autonomisation*).

4.4 Analysing the representation of social action

Halliday and Matthiessen (2014) proposed a transitivity model that encompasses the process realised by the verb and the participants of that process. Processes in the transitivity model are divided into six main types, namely, material, mental, relational, behavioural, verbal and existential, reflecting the cognitive categories used when we construct events happening around us linguistically. *Material processes* cover activities and actions (i.e. doing and happening) requiring the involvement of an *actor* who does the action, the *goal* the process is directed at, and the *beneficiary* of the action. *Mental processes* are concerned with events in our consciousness (i.e. thinking and feeling).

Relational processes are seeking to identify and characterise (i.e. being and having) and have two moods: *attributive*, whereby the carrier (i.e. an entity) is ascribed to the attribute (i.e. some class) and *identifying*, whereby the identified is to be distinguished by the identifier (i.e. what serves as an identity). Both are classified into intensive, circumstantial and possessive. In *intensive attribution processes*, the attribute refers to the carrier through a class or a criterion for class membership (i.e. a quality constituting the class). An *intensive identifying process* recognises the identified and the identifier as either token or value. Participants functioning as tokens represent lower expressions and those that function as value represent higher content. In this process, token represents value.

Circumstantial attribution processes have two forms. First, circumstance can be considered to be an attribute: in which case, the attribute is a circumstantial element in a propositional phrase or an adverbial group. Second, circumstance can be a process; here, the attribute is realized by a nominal group and the circumstantial relation is expressed by the verbal group. In *circumstantial identifying processes,* they have two patterns. First, circumstance can be expressed through the participants; in this case, the process is recognised semantically through the relationship between two participants (i.e. the identified and the identifier), in which both participants express circumstantial elements of time, place, manner and so on. Second, circumstance can be a process; here, the circumstantial relation is realized through circumstantial verbs conveying the circumstance of manner, accompaniment, time, place, and so forth.

The last category of relational process is the *possessive process*, whereby 'one entity possesses another' (Halliday/Matthiessen 2014: 294). Possessive attribution occurs when the possessed represents the attribute. Within the possessive identifying process, the two entities together represent the notion of possession.

Behavioural processes have no clear characteristics. However, their identified characteristics are similar to those of material and mental processes representing physiological and psychological behaviour, respectively. *Verbal processes* deal with saying and have a *sayer,* who is the initiator of the process, a *receiver,* who is the addressee and the *verbiage*, that represents the content of what is said (i.e. the event as it happened). The last process is an *existential process,* representing the existence of something through the use of the word *there*, which has no functional role in the transitivity structure.

5 Data analysis: Salient social actors in the #EMGC

During the processes of coding, twenty-eight codes, each representing a social actor, were identified in the female Anti-MGS corpus, and thirty-four codes were identified for the female Pro-MGS corpus. To answer the first question, the Word List tool in AntConc was used to identify the salient social actors in the #EMGC. Besides Saudi women, four social actors were the most frequent in both corpora: female Anti-MGS, male guardians, female Pro-MGS and the government.

The second and third questions investigate the representation of Saudi women as social actors in female Anti-MGS and Pro-MGS corpora and their most prominent actions, respectively; as such, these questions require a more in-depth analysis of the data. Therefore, making use of the concordance tool in AntConc constituted the next step. All concordance lines of Saudi women were downloaded in order to apply van Leeuwen's (2008) and Halliday and Matthiessen's (2014) frameworks.

5.1 Exclusion and inclusion of Saudi women

In van Leeuwen's (2008) model, social practices are conducted by sets of social actors represented as either included or excluded in order to serve their purposes and readers' interests. The exclusion of social actors can be done through backgrounding or suppression. Reasons for exclusion could have been that followers and recipients were familiar

Saudi women as Social actors	**Included**		**Excluded *(Backgrounded)***		**Excluded *(Suppressed)***	
	Freq.	**%**	**Freq.**	**%**	**Freq.**	**%**
Anti-MGS corpus n=1012	698	**69**	152	**15**	162	**16**
Pro-MGS corpus n=222	169	**76**	49	**22**	4	**2**

Tab. 2. Saudi women as social actors in the female Anti-MGS and Pro-MGS corpora

with the social actors, which made referring to them in detail unnecessary, or that Twitter limits the length of tweets to 140 characters. Tab. 2 reveals that 69 % of Saudi women's occurrences in the female Anti-MGS corpus and 76 % of their occurrences in the female Pro-MGS corpus are included as actors. The exclusion of Saudi women, however, is higher in the female Anti-MGS corpus (31 %); they were excluded in acts relating to 'degradation', for example.

The Saudi women included are mostly involved in material and relational processes (Fig. 1).

5.2 Representation of Saudi women: Material processes

Of all the types of social action, Saudi women are most frequently engaged in material processes (41 % of the total) in the female Anti-MGS corpus (Fig. 1). In these processes, social actors can be assigned three roles: being activated, passivated or beneficialised. The focus will be on the patterns in Saudi women's representations in these processes. Saudi women are activated in 115 instances, passivated in 132 instances and beneficialised in 14 instances. Saudi women in an active role (in total, 115 instances) are individualised 57 % of the time (63 instances). Of these instances, there are 29 in which Saudi women are classified in terms of gender (for example, 'young woman' and 'woman') and 18 in which they are classified in terms of nationality (i.e. provenance). They are also appraised four times as 'ambitious girls' and 'powerless and marginalised women', and they are identified by their relationships

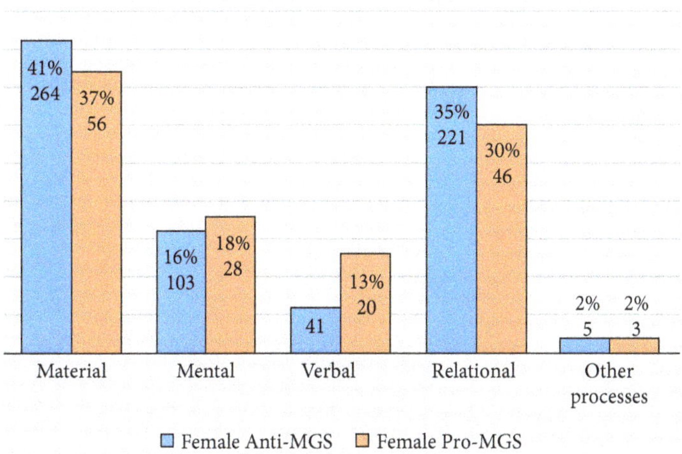

Fig. 1. Social actions taken by Saudi women in both corpora

with others four times, such as 'sisters', 'mothers' and 'married'. In ten instances, they are referred to by the pronoun 'she'. Saudi women in the active role are also represented collectively 35 % of the time (40 instances). These instances include 17 in which Saudi women are classified as 'Saudis' [+feminine] and ten in which they are classified as 'women'. They are also identified as 'daughters' and appraised as 'those who are deficient in mind and religion' a total of three times. They are referred to by the pronoun 'they' in ten instances (Fig. 2). Saudi women are also aggregated (7 %: nine times) and impersonalised (1 %: once) through utterance autonomisation – 'her scream'. The material processes from which Saudi women were said to be excluded without a male guardian's permission were 'travelling', 'working', 'studying', 'building a life' and 'participating in society'. As a result, female Anti-MGS were 'rebelling' against the system that gives male guardians power and control. Female Anti-MGS blamed the system for the 'escape' of Saudi women and their emigration to other countries.

Saudi women in the passive role (in total, 132 instances) are individualised 60 % of the time (79 instances). Within these instances, they are classified individually as a 'woman' or 'young woman' 55 times

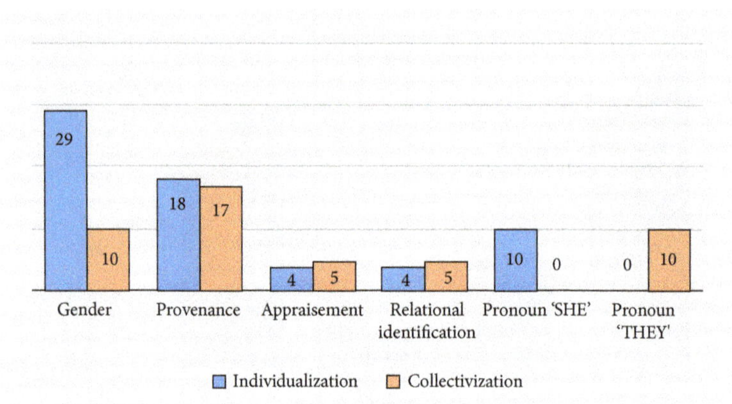

Fig. 2. The two prominent active representations of Saudi women in material processes in the female Anti-MGS corpus

and as 'Saudis' [+feminine] 13 times. They are also appraised as 'sane' four times, relationally identified as a 'daughter', 'wife' or 'victim' five times and functionalised twice, as 'queens' and as 'abused'. Saudi women are also represented collectively 30 % of the time (40 instances). In this group of instances, they are classified as 'women' or 'young women' 11 times, as 'Saudis' [+feminine] seven times and relationally identified as 'widows' or 'divorcees' three times. In 19 instances, they are represented by the pronoun 'they' (Fig. 3). They are also aggregated 10 % of the time (13 times), for example, as 'one half of society', 'millions of Saudi women' and 'many women'. In 42 instances, female Anti-MGS described Saudi women as being 'oppressed', 'enslaved', 'controlled' and 'guarded' by their male guardians. Consequently, female Anti-MGS demanded that Saudi women should be 'protected' by the law nine times and that they should be 'given their rights' ten times. Saudi women in beneficiary roles (in total, 14 instances) are individualised 64 % of the time (nine occurrences). They are referred to by the pronoun 'her' three times, classified as a 'woman' three times and as 'Saudi' [+feminine] twice and they are appraised as 'sane' once. Saudi women are represented collectively (29 %: four times) and aggregated (7 %: once). Female Anti-MGS railed against the male guardianship system by explaining what is happening to Saudi women because

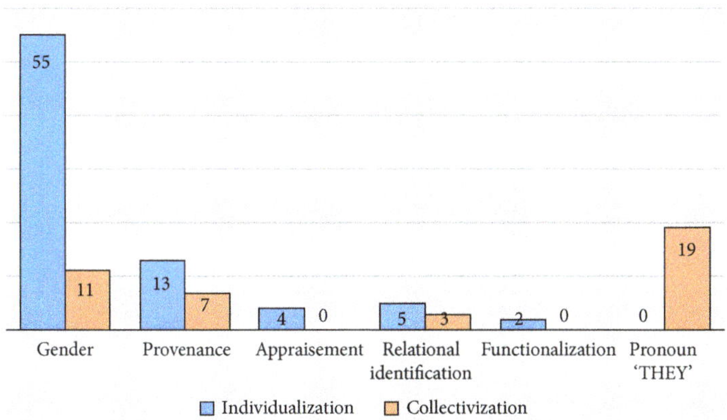

Fig. 3. The two prominent passive representations of Saudi women in material processes in the female Pro-MGS corpus

of it. Thus, Saudi women are apparently given passive roles more often than active ones.

As in the female Anti-MGS corpus, Saudi women are frequently involved in material processes (37 % of the total) in the female Pro-MGS corpus (Fig. 1). Saudi women are activated in 33 instances, passivated in 24 instances and beneficialised in eight instances. Saudi women in the active role (in total, 33 instances) are individualised 36 % of the time (12 instances). Within these instances, they are classified as a 'young woman', a 'woman' or as 'Saudi' [+feminine] five times, appraised as being a 'pearl' five times (i.e. precious) and relationally identified twice as a 'daughter' and 'sister'. They are also described collectively 48 % of the time (16 times). They are described as 'women' and 'Saudi women' six times and 'daughters of the Kingdom' four times. Saudi women are also represented by the pronoun 'they' six times (Fig. 4). They are aggregated (13 %: four instances) as, for example, 'millions/thousands of Saudi women' and represented associatively (3 %: once) as 'daughter', 'sister' and 'wife'. Saudi women were said to 'work' without their male guardian, to 'succeed' in their life without being obstructed by the system. Female Pro-MGS explained in their corpus that Saudi women cannot travel alone, justifying this with the

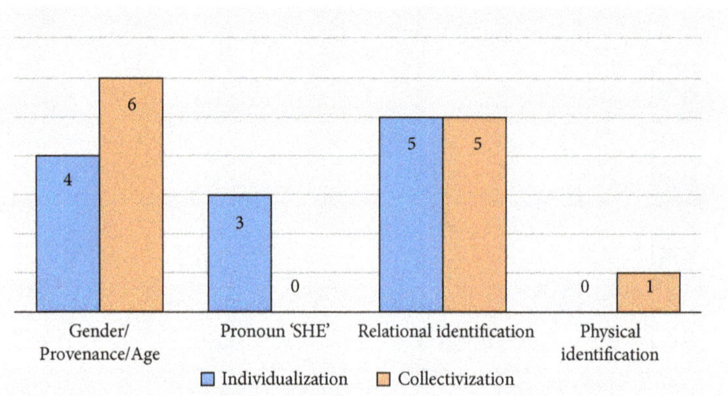

Fig. 4. The two prominent active representations of Saudi women in material processes in the female Pro-MGS corpus

Prophet's saying, 'A woman also may not travel with anyone except with a *Mahram* (relative)'[5] (Al-Asqalani 2003: 259).

Saudi women in the passive role (in total, 24 instances) are individualised 50 % of the time (twelve instances) as 'Saudi woman' and 'young woman' four times, 'daughter of men' five times, and three times by the pronoun 'she'. They are represented collectively 50 % of the time (a total of twelve times) as 'Muslim women' and 'Saudi women' six times, 'daughters of men' five times, and 'veiled women' once (Fig. 5). Saudi women in beneficiary roles (in total, eight instances) are individualised 38 % of the time (three times): twice through the pronoun 'her' and once as a 'woman'. Saudi women are represented collectively (62 %: five times) as 'Saudi women' twice and their 'daughters' or 'mothers' three times. Saudi women in the female Pro-MGS point of view need the 'protection' of their male guardians in order to avoid being 'killed' or 'abused'. Female Pro-MGS indicated that Saudi women were being used in a conspiracy that aimed to 'separate Saudi women from their families'.

5 In Islam, *mahram* refers to a male whom a female Muslim cannot marry.

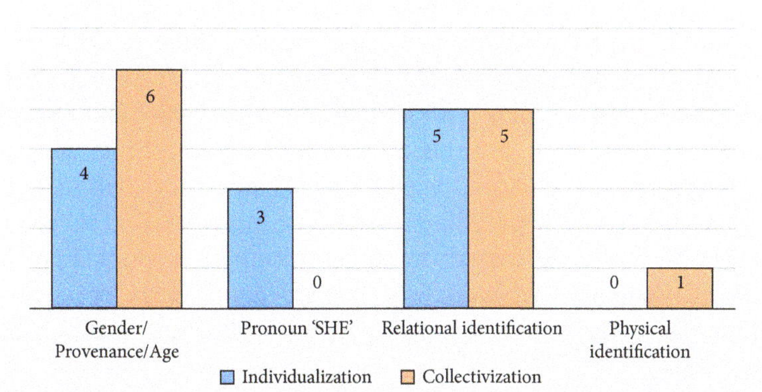

Fig. 5. The two prominent passive representations of Saudi women in material processes in the female Pro-MGS corpus

5.3 Representation of Saudi women: Relational processes

Of the different types of social action, relational processes occur second most frequently in both the female Anti-MGS and Pro-MGS corpora. In terms of identifying and characterising Saudi women in the female Anti-MGS corpus, Saudi women are identified and characterised in relational processes (35 % of the total). The patterns of Saudi women's representations in these processes will be examined according to the categories of the relational processes. In intensive attributive processes, Saudi women are classified as 'minors' 15 times, 'strugglers' three times and as 'abused' five times. However, they are also referred to as 'citizens' of Saudi Arabia who are 'brave, partners, educated, freewomen, independent and aware of their rights'. Female Anti-MGS clarified that Saudi women are neither 'queens' nor 'backward'. In intensive identifying processes, Saudi women are identified as 'second-class citizens', 'belonging to men', and when compared to women worldwide, 'the only women who are considered minors' and 'the only women who still demand for their human and legal rights'. It was argued that Saudi women should have their rights, because they are 'fully-fledged citizens' and 'one half of society'.

In possessive attributive processes, female Anti-MGS compared contemporary Saudi women with their grandmothers, who did not have male guardians. In these processes, Saudi women are required to 'have male guardians' (five occurrences) and 'needed them in order to live their life' (three occurrences). On 13 occasions, Saudi women are said to 'have no rights' to enjoy without their male guardian, and thus, they 'need a new regulation' to protect them. Female Anti-MGS suggested that talented Saudi scientists 'are lucky', because they 'had nice, kind and open-minded male guardians'. However, many are said to 'have the courage and power' to participate in contesting the system. In possessive identifying processes, Saudi women are identified as 'being owned by their male guardian' (five times); they 'possess nothing' for themselves.

In circumstantial attributive processes, Saudi women are characterised as 'depending on their male guardian and his mood, desire and conscience'. In circumstantial identifying processes, Saudi women are metaphorically treated as 'crazy' and 'minors'. Female Anti-MGS criticised the system, which categorised Saudi women as minors who required a chaperone and protector. They are also represented metaphorically as 'belongings' and 'concubines'.

Saudi women are identified and characterised in relational processes in about 30 % of all types of social action in the female Pro-MGS corpus (Fig. 1). They are given attributes such as 'being queens, stable, honourable, aware of the conspiracy, proud of their male guardian and good at handling their lives'. They are represented as not being 'slaves, weak, naïve, oppressed' and not being treated as 'commodities'. In intensive identifying processes, they are identified as 'the most respected women in the world', because of their decency and respect towards their families, being both 'hero makers' and 'mothers of men'. They are also considered to be misrepresented by the identifier 'this hashtag' (i.e. #EndMaleGuardianshipSystem) and by female Anti-MGS. Female Pro-MGS suggested that what really represented Saudi women is 'the counter-campaign' and 'its hashtags'.

In the possessive attributive processes, female Pro-MGS identified Saudi women as having 'the lowest rates of harassment and rape in the world'. They also possess 'their rights and great families'. In circumstantial attributive processes, the United States is used as a carrier, such as in the phrase, 'the US busied themselves with Saudi women'. Female Pro-MGS supported their tweets using a collection of screenshots of news headlines and articles showing support from the US towards Saudi women over time. Female Pro-MGS displayed statistics suggesting that Saudi women experienced the lowest rates of various crimes, unlike women in the US, whose problems only the US should confront.

6 Discussion

The findings revealed that different roles were assigned to Saudi women by female Anti-MGS and Pro-MGS. In the female Anti-MGS corpus, Saudi women were frequently passivated and beneficialised through assignments to weak roles. Female Anti-MGS tend to use this representation for Saudi women in order to convey the helplessness and powerlessness of women due to the system. Interestingly, the aggregate representation was used most often; van Leeuwen (2008: 37) explained that 'aggregation is often used to regulate practice'. Hence, the heavy use of aggregation for Saudi women on the part of the female Anti-MGS aimed to regulate the practices of being controlled and abused. Female Pro-MGS, on the other hand, frequently positioned Saudi women in the active role, whereas the passivated role actor was the least used (24 instances) in their corpus. Active representation served their aim of maintaining the system by indicating that Saudi women were capable of participation and involvement in various material processes.

Female Anti-MGS referred to Saudi women as being 'deficient in mind and religion'. This appraisal is borrowed from Islamic discourse and is based on one saying of the Prophet Mohammed. Hence, women being 'deficient in mind' comes from the belief that the testimony of two women equals that of one man. Women are seen to be 'deficient in religion' because they are not required to perform religious duties, such as fasting and praying, during menstruation. The majority of scholars have promoted this saying; however, new voices have attempted to prove its inauthenticity. One of these voices is that of Saudi national Suhaila Hammad, who is a member of Saudi Arabia's National Society for Human Rights. Defending women's rights from an Islamic perspective, she argued that the narrator of this saying was untrustworthy (Hammad 2013). Her research has shown that the idea that women are 'deficient in mind and religion' is not well supported in Islamic literature (Hammad 2013). The idea that the testimony of two female witnesses is equivalent to that of one male is mentioned in only one verse in the Quran, in relation to debt; there are other verses that refer to a woman's testimony being equal to a man's (Fatima/Lakhvi 2015). Using this evidence to justify the mental inadequacy of women seems inaccurate and aimed at embracing masculine power. Moreover, describing women's abstinence from Islamic duties during menstruation as a deficiency in religion is faulty for two reasons. First, women cannot choose to prevent this natural process in order to perform their religious duties. Second, women do not choose to rest during menstruation, rather they are commanded to do so in the verse 222:2 (Itani 2012). If resting during menstruation is part of religion, then it cannot be a deficiency to do so. However, the idea that women are deficient has been widely accepted and generalised.

Saudi women have been represented in various ways; one of which is as *queens*. Alhussein (2018) provided a thorough explanation of the use of such expressions and those who benefit from them. Symbolic language was first used by religious figures in their sermons and publications to justify the proposed limited role of women and to maintain the patriarchal system in Saudi Arabia. In order to normalise domesticity and motivate women to endorse as well as to encourage the community to embrace male dominance, preachers have portrayed women as queens who do not have to earn a living and who are supposed to be served and financially supported by their male relatives. However, female Anti-MGS failed to see how Saudi women could be 'queens' while being controlled under this system.

Female Pro-MGS tended to use the preachers' strategy to justify the male guardianship system by referring to a Saudi woman as a 'queen' or 'pearl'. Thus, in doing so, they were implying that women should be protected by their male guardians. However, preachers had a different meaning for 'pearl' in their sermons, one that was similar to what they meant by 'queen', in that a 'pearl' (i.e. woman) was too precious to be allowed to leave her house and work. This resemblance in persuasive methodology between discourses indicated that female Pro-MGS were influenced heavily by conservative Islamic discourse.

The results have revealed sexist language in the female Pro-MGS corpus. In particular, female Pro-MGS referred to Saudi women as 'daughters of men'. Unlike calling a man a 'woman' or 'woman's son', in Arabic, calling a woman a 'man' or a 'daughter/sister of men' is not an insult. In fact, it is deemed to be a compliment, as a strong woman is seen to have male qualities, such as bravery (Joubin 2013). However, it also means that 'her strength comes from her relationship to men and not from her own person' (Joubin 2013: 198). In the Arabic language, the masculine is viewed 'as the measurement from which the feminine gender is derived' (Aleasa 1996: 5). Consequently, the masculine form implies power, status and authority, whereas the 'feminine form is belittling at best, if not outright derogatory' (Farwaneh 2005: 56). Female Pro-MGS seemed to unconsciously represent Saudi women as a marginalised group through their use of sexist language. Moreover, they represented Saudi women in terms of their religion by, for example, using terms like 'Muslim' and 'veiled women,' and, unlike female Anti-MGS, represented them as unable to exist in society without the help of men.

The analysis of the relational processes has brought out how women in Saudi Arabia can be seen in these opposing ways simultaneously. In the female Anti-MGS corpus, Saudi women were identified as free-women and independent among other identifications. However, in reality, Saudi women have faced strict boundaries in compliance with the male guardianship system and are being undermined (Al-Fassi 2013). Female Anti-MGS also tended to use various persuasive strategies, as identified in the relational processes. For example, they used logical evidence to argue that Saudi women were fully-fledged Saudi citizens who should be treated and recognised as such and given full privileges. To support this argument, Saudi women were represented as having all the qualities necessary to be classified as independent citizens, such as being brave, educated, aware of their rights and so on. Their argument was also supported by comparing the state of Saudi women to their grandmothers who did not have male guardians.

Female Pro-MGS, on the other hand, had different views concerning Saudi women and their rights. To these women, Saudi women are queens and have full rights awarded by Islam; however, this is only the case for women whose guardians fulfil their duties and responsibilities. There was a tendency to highlight the lives of the majority and to marginalise the lives of abused women, who were in the minority. In addition, female Pro-MGS used sexist language to subjugate Saudi women, as they were characterised as ‘mothers of men’ and ‘hero makers’ rather than heroines. Again, there were similarities between the discourse of the female Pro-MGS and the conservative Islamic discourse, which demonstrates how the patriarchal power influenced their portrayal of Saudi women.

7 Conclusion

The study reveals interesting findings about the representation of Saudi women in both female Anti-MGS and Pro-MGS corpora retrieved from the online discourse concerning the #EMGC. The salient social actors were the same for both corpora; besides Saudi women, female Anti-MGS, female Pro-MGS, male guardians and the government were featured. In addition, the social actions undertaken by Saudi women in both corpora were similar i.e. both had predominantly material (i.e. dynamic) and relational (i.e. identification and characteristic) processes. However, the representations of their identities were different. Interestingly, the use of sexist language and the acceptance of the roles assigned to Saudi women were dominant in the female Pro-MGS corpus. On the other hand, in their corpus, female Anti-MGS recognised the degrading role assigned to Saudi women and were campaigning against the system causing such treatment.

This campaign called for signing an online petition to be sent to the king. Although Pro-MGS claimed that the officials would not listen to the Anti-MGS in order to discourage them, the king’s office issued an announcement to amend the regulations relating to the male guardian requirement in April 2017. However, female Anti-MGS have campaigned afterwards to abolish the system completely; in August 2019, a second royal decree was issued easing the guardianship requirements still further. Hence, social media can help publicise a social issue and those seeking solidarity. This effect is not limited to the virtual world but can also be reflected in the real world. Thus, this chapter shows not only the efforts of Saudi women activists to highlight the situation of women within the male guardianship system and promote their demands but also their engagement in a formal demand to those in authority. To what extent this will ultimately lead to *both* cultural and redistributive justice remains to be seen.

References

Admon, Y. 2009. In Response to Calls to Improve Status of Saudi Women, Saudi Princess Launches 'My Guardian Knows What's Best For Me' Campaign. *MEMRI* 559 <https://www.memri.org/reports/response-calls-improve-status-saudi-women-saudi-princess-launches-my-guardian-knows-whats-0>, accessed 12 June 2018.

Al-Asqalani, Ibn Hajar. 2003. *Bulugh al-maram min adillat al-ahkam* [*Attainment of the objective according to the evidence of the ordinance*]. Cairo: Dar Al-Manarah.

Al-Fassi, Hatoon. 2013. Saudi Arabia. In *The Oxford Encyclopedia of Islam and Women.* Oxford: Oxford University Press.

Al-Zuhayli, Wahbah. 1999. *alwjyz fy aswl alfqh* [*The Overview in the Principles of Jurisprudence*]. Damascus: Dar al-Fakar.

Aleasa, Noor Sultan. 1996. Sexist Language in Arabic: The Case of Qatar University Academic and Administrative Staff. *Journal of the Documentation and Humanities Research Center* 8: 1–19.

Alhussein, Eman. 2018. From "Queens" and "Wrapped Candies" to Hashtag Activism [Personal Website] <http://emanalhussein.com/2018/01/04/queens-and-wrapped-candies/>, accessed 20 August 2017.

Anthony, Lawrence 2017. AntConc (version 3.5.0) [Computer Software] < https://www.laurenceanthony.net/software>, accessed 10 February 2017.

Baker, Paul/Gabrielatos, Costas/KhosraviNik, Majid/Krzyżanowski, Michal/McEnery, Tony/Wodak, Ruth. 2008. A Useful Methodological Synergy? Combining Critical Discourse Analysis and Corpus

Linguistics to Examine Discourses of Refugees and Asylum Seekers in the UK Press. *Discourse and Society* 19(3), 273–306.

Blog, Saudi Women's Rights. 2011. Saudi Women's Revolution Statement [Saudi Women's Rights Blog] <https://saudiwomenrights.wordpress.com/2011/05/05/بيان-مجموعة-ثورة-النساء-السعوديات/>, accessed 1 August 2017.

Bloomberg. 2018. Saudi Crown Prince Discusses Trump, Aramco, Arrests., *Bloomberg* 5 October 2018

CBC News. 2018. Saudi Arabia's Heir to the Throne Talks to 60 Minutes. *CBS News* 19-03-2018 <https://www.cbsnews.com/news/saudi-crown-prince-talks-to-60-minutes/>, accessed 25 October 2018.

Commins, David. 2006. *The Wahhabi Mission and Saudi Arabia*. London: I. B. Tauris.

Fairclough, Norman. 2003. *Analysing Discourse: Textual Analysis for Social Research.* London: Routledge.

Fairclough, Norman. 2015. *Language and Power.* 3rd ed. New York: Routledge.

Farwaneh, S. 2005. Asymmetries of Male/Female Representation in Arabic. In Jule, Allyson (ed.) *Gender and the Language of Religion*. London: Palgrave, 41-62.

Fatima, Samira/Lakhvi, Muhammad Hammad. 2015. The Authenticity of Women's Witness in Islam: A Study in the Light of Al- Qur'an. *Al-Qalam* 20(2), 1–16.

Fraser, Nancy. 1995. From Redistribution to Recognition? Dilemmas of Justice in a "Post-Socialist" Age. *New Left Review* 212, 68–93.

Gillespie, Tarleton. 2014. The Relevance of Algorithms. In Gillespie, T./P. J. Boczkowski, P.J./Foot, K.A. (eds.) *Media Technologies: Essays on Communication, Materiality, and Society.* Cambridge: MIT Press, 167–193.

Gries, Stefan T./Newman, John. 2013. Creating and Using Corpora. In Podesva, R.J./Sharma, D. (eds.) *Research Methods in Linguistics.* Cambridge: Cambridge University Press, 257–287.

Halliday, Michael A. K./Matthiessen, Christian. 2014. *Halliday's Introduction to Functional Grammar.* 4th ed. London: Routledge.

Hammad, Suhaila. 2013. *Al-marah wa' algiadh alsiasih: qra'h fi mafhom alwlaih* [*The Woman and Political Leadership: Reading in the Concept of Guardianship*] [Blog] <http://dr-suhaila-z-hammad.blogspot.co.uk/p/blog-page_16.html>, accessed 20 August 2012.

Itani, Talal A., transl.2012. *The Quran*. Dallas: Clear Quran.

Joubin, Rebecca. 2013. *The Politics of Love: Sexuality, Gender, and Marriage in Syrian Television Drama*. Plymouth: Lexington Books.

Lacroix, Stephane. 2015. Understanding Stability and Dissent in the Kingdom: The Double-Edged Role of the jama'at in Saudi Politics. In Haykel, B./Hegghammer, T./Lacroix, S. (eds.) *Saudi Arabia in Transition, Insights on Social, Political, Economic and Religious Change*. Cambridge: Cambridge University Press, 167–180.

Mautner, Gerlinde. 2005. Time to Get Wired: Using Web-Based Corpora in Critical Discourse Analysis. *Discourse and Society* 16(6), 809–828.

Mulderrig, Jane. 2008. Using Keywords Analysis in CDA: Evolving Discourses of the Knowledge Economy in Education. In Jessop, B./Fairclough, Norman/Wodak, Ruth (eds.) *Education and the Knowledge-Based Economy in Europe*. Rotterdam: Sense Publishers, 49–170.

Mulderrig, Jane. 2014. "Enabling" Participatory Governance in Education: A Corpus-Based Critical Analysis of Policy in the United Kingdom. In Smyers, P. et al. (eds.) *International Handbook of Interpretation in Educational Research*. Dordrecht: Springer, 441-470.

Saldana, Johnny. 2013. *The Coding Manual for Qualitative Researchers*. 2nd ed. London: SAGE.

TEI Consortium. 2016. TEI: Text Encoding Initiative <http://www.tei-c.org/index.xml>, accessed 25 December 2017.

Time. 2018. Crown Prince Mohammed bin Salman Talks to TIME About the Middle East, Saudi Arabia's Plans and President Trump. *Time 5-04-2018* <https://time.com/5228006/mohammed-bin-salman-interview-transcript-full/>, accessed January 2019.

Tognini-Bonelli, Elena. 2001. *Corpus Linguistics at Work*. Amsterdam/Philadelphia: John Benjamins.

Unger, Johann W./Wodak, Ruth/KhosraviNik, Majid. 2016. Critical Discourse Studies and Social Media Data. In Silverman, D. (ed.) *Qualitative Research*. London: SAGE, 277–293.

van Leeuwen, Theo. 2008. *Discourse and Practice: New Tools for Critical Discourse Analysis*. Oxford: Oxford University Press.

van Leeuwen, Theo. 2009. Critical Discourse Analysis. In Renkema, J. (ed.) *Discourse, of Course: An Overview of Research in Discourse Studies*. Amsterdam: John Benjamins Publishing Company, 277-292.

Yamani, Maha A. Z. 2008. *Polygamy and Law in Contemporary Saudi Arabia*. Reading: Ithaca Press.

Appendix

Codes used in both corpora

Code	**Stand for**	**Definition**	**Examples from the corpora**
SW	Saudi Woman	Reference to a Saudi woman as a citizen, sister, mother, wife and so forth.	Anti-MGS: 'The traditions control women and their fate' Pro-MGS: 'Their tweets [campaigners] disrespect Saudi women'
WP	Women Proponent	Reference to the women who are campaigning against the system (i.e. Anti-MGS)	Anti-MGS: 'Males abandoned us' Pro-MGS: 'There is disagreement among the campaigners'
WO	Women Opponents	Reference to the women campaigning against #EndMaleGuardianship System and with maintaining the system (i.e. Pro-MGS)	Anti-MGS: 'She is enjoying her life and wants to stop us' Pro-MGS: 'We don't see cases like this in our life'
WN	Woman	Reference to women in general, including Arabic, Western, Muslim woman (i.e. all women other than Saudi)	Anti-MGS: 'Arab women have succeeded in all fields' Pro-MGS: 'We don't want to be like Western women'
MG	Male-Guardian	Indicates the Saudi woman's guardian who is a close male relative	Anti-MGS: 'In our society, woman is controlled by a male' Pro-MGS: 'They insult our fathers'

Codes used in both corpora			
SM	Saudi men	Reference to Saudi men in general	Anti-MGS: 'A Saudi male disrespects your brain' Pro-MGS: 'An electronic army participates in the hashtag to distort Saudi man'
MO	Male Opponents	Indicate the men campaigning against #EndMaleGuardianship System	Anti-MGS: 'The majority of male opponents benefit from this condition where women are under their control' Pro-MGS: 'Male opponents don't participate in this hashtag [#EndMaleGuardianshipSystem]'
MP	Male Proponents	Reference to the men who are campaigning against the system and support WP	Anti-MGS: 'Every male participator in the hashtag is under attack' Pro-MGS: 'The male activists of women's rights have to defend American women'
MN	Men	Reference to men in general, including Arabic, Western, Muslim men (i.e. all men other than Saudi)	Anti-MGS: 'There is no difference between Iranian male and Saudi male' Pro-MGS: 'Half of American men prefer to have baby boys'
PP	Saudi People	Codes Saudi society and people	Anti-MGS: 'A new ideology invades Saudi society' Pro-MGS: 'Saudi women built Saudi society'
GV	Government	Reference to the official representatives	Anti-MGS: 'the society follows the government' Pro-MGS: 'We respect the government'
GU	Gulf people	Reference to Gulf society	Anti-MGS: 'Women in neighbouring Gulf countries have run strong positions' Pro-MGS: 'The trouble reaches Gulf societies'
GO	God	Reference to Allah	Anti-MGS: 'Allah sees and hears us' Pro-MGS: 'Allah, protect our guardians'

Codes used in both corpora			
PR	Prophet	Reference to the Prophet Muhammad	Anti-MGS: 'The prophet commanded you to be kind and considerate to us' Pro-MGS: 'Prophet said: no marriage without *wali*'
FA	Family	Reference to a family	Anti-MGS: 'Girls are married to escape from her abusive family' Pro-MGS: 'They want to separate us from our family'
AD	Addressees	Reference to the readers	Anti-MGS: 'If you wonder why we are demanding, let me tell you' Pro-MGS: 'You only see them in the hashtag'
IS	ISIS	Reference to terrorists and to actors who have radical Islamic fundamentalist views	Anti-MGS: 'ISIS are famous with their hater towards women' Pro-MGS: 'ISIS recruited young men and those recruited young girls'
NO	Nomination	Reference to the social actor's name. (i.e. proper noun)	Anti-MGS: Muhammad bin Salman supports women's rights' Pro-MGS: 'Turki wrote an article explaining how instigators call for violent actions while the country is busy'
AN	Anonymous	Reference to unidentified actors, e.g. no one, someone.	Anti-MGS: 'No one feels your pain' Pro-MGS: 'These are foreign accounts but no one listens'
MS	Muslim Scholars	Reference to Muslim scholars, preachers and Mufti	Anti-MGS: 'The Mufti clarified that guardianship is only in marriage' Pro-MGS: 'Their attempts aim to degrade Muslim scholars'
TR	Tribes	Reference to the tribes in Saudi Arabia	Anti-MGS: 'The backwardness of the tribes ruins our souls' Pro-MGS: 'The nature of tribal society is free and their women are loyal'

Codes used in both corpora			
RP	Religious Police	Reference to the Islamic religious police (i.e. the official force enforcing Sharia law)	Anti-MGS: 'When the religious police were stopped, they said the society was not ready but eventually our society accepted it' Pro-MGS: 'Liberals first demanded to stop the religious police and now they demand to end the guardianship system'
JE	Jews	Reference to the Jew	Anti-MGS: 'This slavery system is borrowed from the Jew' Pro-MGS: 'They defend a Jewish'
EA	Excluded Actor	Reference to the actors who are unknown to the readers and tended to be excluded.	Anti-MGS: 'Your tweets are negatively represented after being photoshopped [by whom]' Pro-MGS: 'Proponents ask [whom?] for support'
Codes only for the female Anti-MGS corpus			
Code	**Stand for**	**Definition**	**Examples from the female Anti-MGS corpus**
GE	Generation	Reference to the generation(s)	'This generation is great and differs from other generations'
PO	Police	Reference to the police force	'For the abused women, call the police'
UNI	University	Reference to the university(ies)	'Universities require a male-guardian's consent to change major ☹'
OT	Others	Reference to others not related to the campaign (e.g. slaves, and an insane person)	'The slaves had been freed'
Codes only for the female Pro-MGS corpus			
Code	**Stand for**	**Definition**	**Examples from the female Pro-MGS corpus**
RE	Rejecters	Reference to rejectors	'Rejectors from Iraq strongly support the campaign'
AT	Atheist	Reference to the atheist.	'You can find atheists participating in this hashtag [#EndMaleGuardianshipSystem]'

Codes used in both corpora			
HO	Homosexuals	Reference to the homosexuals	'The hashtag is trending because of homosexuals who are tweeting every day'
FN	Foreign	Reference to any foreigners or foreign representatives (e.g. foreign media and institutions)	'Foreigners try to threaten our security'
LL	Liberal(s)	Reference to liberals	'A trained network of liberals attacks our religion'
IR	Iran	Reference to Iranian government and people	'As long as Iran and their people support the campaign, we should stand against them'
OO	Others	Reference to strangers, the world, and the West	'The wars and poverty do not concern the West'
HR	Human Rights	Indicate the Human Rights organizations	'The Human Rights organization who is against the Saudi war on Yemen participated in the hashtag'
CH	Christian	Reference to the Christian actors	'Arab Christians aim to damage Saudi women'
ZI	Zionist	Reference to a Zionist actor	'they are following the Zionist by this campaign'

Notes on Contributors

Nouf Alotaibi is a PhD candidate at the *University of Sheffield*. Her interdisciplinary work focuses on discourse analysis, corpus linguistics, Saudi feminism, and social media. Her research currently investigates the online campaign #EndMaleGuardianshipSystem (2016–2019) and the representation of Saudi women by applying a corpus-aided critical discourse analysis.

Helen Baker is a Senior Research Associate at the ESRC Centre for Corpus Approaches to Social Science (CASS) at *Lancaster University*, UK. She has published research on tsarist Russia and, more recently, has focussed on the benefits of using large corpora in the study of the past, particularly in order to explore the ways in which marginalised people were perceived in early modern public discourse.

Leanne Bartley started working in academia in 2008 as a research assistant at the *Universidad de Jaén* in Spain, before moving to the *Universidad de Granada* to work as a Visiting Scholar and complete her PhD in Critical Discourse Analysis (CDA) and Forensic Linguistics in 2017. Since then, she has worked at *Liverpool Hope University* and *Swansea University* in the UK before returning to the *Universidad de Granada* as a Lecturer in English language. More recently, Leanne was awarded a Marie Skłodowska-Curie Global Scholarship, thus allowing her to pursue her main research interests, which are CDA, Corpus Linguistics and Forensic Linguistics, and collaborate with other renowned scholars around the world.

Ana Belén Cabrejas-Peñuelas is an Assistant Lecturer at the *Universitat de València* (Spain), where she teaches diverse subjects related to English Language and Discourse Analysis. She investigates the cognitive processes involved in second or foreign language writing, in particular the revision process and the use of the mother tongue, although she is also concerned with Discourse Analysis, Pragmatics and Systemic Functional Linguistics. Her most important publications deal with L2 writing processes, persuasion in entrepreneurial discourse and also evaluation, metaphors, metonymies and identity construction in political language from a contrastive perspective.

Carmen Dayrell is a research fellow at the ERSC Centre for Corpus Approaches to Social Science (CASS), *Lancaster University* (UK). Her research centres on the use of corpus linguistics methodologies to study language production across many types of public and semi-public language, from a variety of Brazilian and UK contexts. She has undertaken projects on pressing issues such as climate change, social care, racism, drought and water scarcity, immigrants' identity and urban violence.

Rosana Dolón is Associate Professor in the Department of English and German Philology, at the *Universitat de València*. Her main research interests include Critical Discourse Analysis and Sociolinguistics. Her recent publications in *Ibérica (2016), Círculo de Lingüística Aplicada a la Comunicación (CLAC) (2017)* and *Ibérica* (in press) revolve around discursive constructions of privilege in the context of tourism. The first two address issues related to the commodification of 'place' and of abstract values; the latter looks at the construal of what is 'different' versus 'distinct' as eligible consumer choices. Recently, she has turned her attention to political discourse, especially motivated by the Brexit scenario.

Salvador Enguix Oliver bas been a journalist for the newspaper *La Vanguardia* since 1991, and is Associate Professor of Journalism at the *Universitat de València*. His research focuses on framing in political journalism and the impact of digitization on this journalistic specialty. His latest book is *Periodismo politico: fundamentos, práctica, perspectivas* [Political Journalism. Foundations, practices and perspectives] (2015), and, together with Beatriz Gallardo, *Pseudopolítica: el discurso político en las redes sociales* [Pseudopolitics: political discourse on social media].

Miguel Fuster-Márquez is Associate Professor in English Language and Linguistics at the *Universitat de València*, where he teaches Linguistic Subjects in the Department of English and German. Some of his Master courses at the *Universitat de València* deal with methodological and corpus issues. Currently, he is vice-president of AELINCO (Asociación Española de Lingüística de Corpus). Some of his responsibilities

include being in charge of its website (http://www.aelinco.es/en) and coordinating its annual e-bulletin. He is also a member of IULMA-UV (Instituto Universitario de Lenguas Modernas Aplicadas at the *Universitat de València*). As part of his duties, he has been editor-in-chief of IULMA monographs until recently. He is a member of Grup d'Investigació CORPLING: Lingüística de Corpus, Desarrollos y Aplicaciones at the University of Valencia. In his research he has applied corpus approach/methodologies to the study of English lexis and phraseology, discourse analysis, with a particular interest in tourism language discourse. Email: miguel.fuster@uv.es.
His research interests can be followed here:
Web of Science ResearcherID: H-3580–2015,
orcid.org/0000-0003-3813-1770, https://www.researchgate.net/profile/Miguel_Fuster_Marquez

Beatriz Gallardo Paúls is Full Professor of Linguistics at the *Universitat de València*. Her research has always been carried out in the field of pragmatics, and in applied fields such as clinical linguistics (where she directed the Corpus PerLA, Perception, Language and Aphasia, containing conversational samples of speakers with brain damage) and political discourse, in which she has worked mainly on journalistic discourse and social media political discourse. Her latest book is *Tiempos de hipérbole. Inestabilidad e interferencias en el discurso político* [Times of Hyperbole. Instability and interference in political discourse] (2018).

Carmen Gregori-Signes has been Senior lecturer at the Department de Filologia Anglesa i Alemanya since 1991, and a member of IULMA (Instituto Universitario de Lenguas Modernas) since 2005. She completed an MA at the *University of Nottingham* and has been a visiting scholar at several universities (*Birmingham University, Iowa University, Cambridge University, Queen Mary University, George Mason University, Middlebury College*). She is the director of the Research group CORPLING: Lingüística de Corpus, Desarrollos y Aplicaciones at the *Universitat de València*. Her research interests include discourse analysis, pragmatics and applied linguistics. Currently, a great deal of her research is devoted to the analysis of media language using corpus linguistics methodologies.

Anina Kinzel is studying for a PhD in Applied Linguistics at *Swansea University*, where she is also a researcher in the *Developing Resilience against Online Grooming* Project. She has co-authored several articles and book chapters that use Corpus Assisted Discourse Studies to examine cyber-crime.

Nuria Lorenzo-Dus is Professor of Applied Linguistics at *Swansea University*, where she also serves as Director of the *Developing Resilience against Online Grooming* Project. Her research expertise lies at the intersection of Criminology and Corpus-Assisted Discourse Studies. Relevant funded projects she leads include examining ideological grooming online by extreme right and jihadist groups, profiling online sexual groomers' language use, exploring constructions of trust in crypto-drug markets.

Stefania M. Maci (PhD, *Lancaster University*, UK) is Full Professor of English Language and pro Vice-Chancellor (Education) at the *Università di Bergamo*. She is Director of CERLIS (Research Centre on Specialized Languages), and member of CLAVIER (The Corpus and Language Variation in English Research Group), BAAL (British Association of Applied Linguistics), and AELINCO (Spanish Association of Applied Linguistics). She is also member of the executive board of AIA (Associazione Italiana di Anglistica). Her research is focussed on the study of the English language in academic and professional contexts, with particular regard to the analysis of tourism and medical discourses. Recent publications include: the monographs *The MS Digby 133 Mary Magdalene* (2017), *Tourism Discourse: Professional, Promotional and Digital voices* (2013); the co-edited volumes with Maurizio Gotti and Michele Sala *Scholarly Pathways. Knowledge Transfer and Knowledge Exchange in Academia* (2020); with Michele Sala and Cinzia Spinzi *Communicating English in Specialised Domains. A Festschrift for Maurizio Gotti* (2020); and the papers: Parents' narrative about congenital heart diseases: Acquiring knowledge and sharing empathy (2019); Knowledge Dissemination and Evidentiality on Posters. Anatomy of a Condensed Medical Discourse (2019); "The church was built on a basilica plan." Translating and mistranslating Italian churches' panels. (2019); #icantbreathe. Ideology and Consensus: Printed News vs. Twitter (2018).

Sergio Maruenda-Bataller is a senior lecturer in English Language and Linguistics at the *Universitat de València*. His research interests have mainly focused on Corpus-Assisted Discourse Studies (CADS) as applied to gender inequalities in socio-ideological texts. As a member of the research group **Gentext**, he specialises in the critical analysis of gender violence discourses in news media. He has (co-)authored several articles and book chapters on evaluative discourse and the linguistic (cross-cultural) representation of violence against women in news media. He has worked lately on the discursive news values analysis (DNVA) of news reports on gender violence and ethical reporting.

Tony McEnery is Distinguished Professor in the Department of English Language and Linguistics at *Lancaster University*. He has published widely on corpus linguistics and is the author of *Corpus Linguistics: Method, Theory and Practice* (with Andrew Hardie, Cambridge University Press, 2011) and *Corpus Linguistics and 17th Century Prostitution* (Bloomsbury, 2017). He is a fellow and council member of the Academy of Social Sciences. He has served as Director of Research in both the Arts and Humanities Research Council and the Economic and Social Research Council in the UK.

Jane Mulderrig lectures in the School of English, the *University of Sheffield*. Her CDA research interests include the language of public policy, politics, and nudge. Details of her publications can be found here <https://www.sheffield.ac.uk/english/people/academic-staff/jane- mulderrig>

Alan Partington is Professor of English Linguistics at the Department of Interpreters and Translators of the *Università di Bologna* (at Forlì). His research interests include corpus research methodology, corpus-assisted discourse study, particularly into social and political discourses, modern diachronic language studies, evaluation and evaluative prosody, corpus-assisted stylistics, irony, wordplay and metaphor.

Paula Rodríguez-Abruñeiras holds a European Doctorate in Historical Linguistics from the *Universidade de Santiago de Compostela* (January 2015). From August 2013 to May 2015, she was an assistant of Spanish at the Department of Spanish and Portuguese of the *University of Wisconsin-Milwaukee* (USA), where she also completed a two-year

M.A. Degree in Spanish. Between September 2015 and January 2016, Paula held a visiting lecturer position at the Department of English, French and German of the *Universidade de Vigo*, and in February 2016 she joined the Department of English and German at the *Universitat de València*, on a position as Lecturer in English. She has also carried out research at both national (*Vigo* and *Santiago de Compostela*) and international (*Helsinki, Manchester, Freiburg* and *Wisconsin-Milwaukee*) universities, and at the British Library too. She is currently a member of GENTEXT and IULMA, and an affiliated member of LVTC (http://view0.webs.uvigo.es/team/paula-rodriguez-abruneiras). Her research interests are historical linguistics, linguistic variation, new Englishes, corpus linguistics, critical discourse analysis and gender and sexual (in)equality issues.

Alfonso Sánchez-Moya (asanchezmoya@fas.harvard.edu) holds a joint PhD in English Linguistics (Complutense Madrid | VU Amsterdam) and is currently an RCC Postdoctoral Fellow at the Department of Government, *Harvard University*. Embedded within the socio-cognitive approach to critical discourse studies, his research so far has namely focused on online discourse and communication, with an emphasis on social issues dominated by power imbalances and social inequality. His work and *praxis* are methodologically informed by the corpus-assisted approach to discourse analysis. Broadly speaking, his research interests span the interconnectedness of (online) discourse, power and identity and the role these play in the discursive representation of socio-political scenarios.

José Santaemilia is Full Professor of English at the *Universitat de València*, where he teaches legal translation in the Degree in Translation and Interlinguistic Mediation, as well as professional deontology and ethics and introduction to research in the MA in Creative and Humanistic Translation. He has published extensively on gender, sexuality and translation. A few examples are: *Género, lenguaje y traducción* (Valencia, 2003) *Gender, sex and translation: The manipulation of identities* (Manchester, 2005) and *Woman and Translation: Geographies, Voices and Identities* (MONTI 2011, co-edited with Luise von Flotow). Recently (2017) he has edited *Traducir para la igualdad sexual/Translating for Sexual Equality* and co-edited a special issue of the journal *RESLA*

(Revista Española de Lingüística Aplicada), on *Specialised Translation in Spain. Institutional dimensions.* With Dr. Maruenda-Bataller has published several articles on corpus-assisted discourse analyses of the media representation of women in violence against women news reports. He is the coordinator of the GENTEXT research group (http://gentext.blogs.uv.es), on gender and sexual (in)equality issues, and a member of the CORPLING research group (coordinated by Dr. Carmen Gregori-Signes) on corpus linguistics. He was Editor-in-Chief of the journal *MonTI – Monographies on Translation and Interpretation* (https://web.ua.es/monti). Email: jose.santaemilia@uv.es.

Linguistic Insights

Studies in Language and Communication

This series aims to promote specialist language studies in the fields of linguistic theory and applied linguistics, by publishing volumes that focus on specific aspects of language use in one or several languages and provide valuable insights into language and communication research. A cross-disciplinary approach is favoured and most European languages are accepted.

The series includes two types of books:

- Monographs – featuring in-depth studies on special aspects of language theory, language analysis or language teaching.
- Collected papers – assembling papers from workshops, conferences or symposia.

Each volume of the series is subjected to a double peer-reviewing process.

Vol. 1 Maurizio Gotti & Marina Dossena (eds)
Modality in Specialized Texts. Selected Papers of the 1st CERLIS Conference.
421 pages. 2001. ISBN 3-906767-10-8 · US-ISBN 0-8204-5340-4

Vol. 2 Giuseppina Cortese & Philip Riley (eds)
Domain-specific English. Textual Practices across Communities and Classrooms.
420 pages. 2002. ISBN 3-906768-98-8 · US-ISBN 0-8204-5884-8

Vol. 3 Maurizio Gotti, Dorothee Heller & Marina Dossena (eds)
Conflict and Negotiation in Specialized Texts. Selected Papers of the 2nd CERLIS Conference.
470 pages. 2002. ISBN 3-906769-12-7 · US-ISBN 0-8204-5887-2

Vol. 4 Maurizio Gotti, Marina Dossena, Richard Dury, Roberta Facchinetti & Maria Lima
Variation in Central Modals. A Repertoire of Forms and Types of Usage in Middle English and Early Modern English.
364 pages. 2002. ISBN 3-906769-84-4 · US-ISBN 0-8204-5898-8

Editorial address:

Prof. Maurizio Gotti Università di Bergamo, Dipartimento di Lingue, Letterature e Culture Straniere Piazza Rosate 2, 24129 Bergamo, Italy
Fax: +39 035 2052789, E-Mail: m.gotti@unibg.it

Vol. 5 Stefania Nuccorini (ed.)
Phrases and Phraseology. Data and Descriptions.
187 pages. 2002. ISBN 3-906770-08-7 · US-ISBN 0-8204-5933-X

Vol. 6 Vijay Bhatia, Christopher N. Candlin & Maurizio Gotti (eds)
Legal Discourse in Multilingual and Multicultural Contexts.
Arbitration Texts in Europe.
385 pages. 2003. ISBN 3-906770-85-0 · US-ISBN 0-8204-6254-3

Vol. 7 Marina Dossena & Charles Jones (eds)
Insights into Late Modern English. 2nd edition.
378 pages. 2003, 2007.
ISBN 978-3-03911-257-9 · US-ISBN 978-0-8204-8927-8

Vol. 8 Maurizio Gotti
Specialized Discourse. Linguistic Features and Changing Conventions.
351 pages. 2003, 2005.
ISBN 3-03910-606-6 · US-ISBN 0-8204-7000-7

Vol. 9 Alan Partington, John Morley & Louann Haarman (eds)
Corpora and Discourse.
420 pages. 2004. ISBN 3-03910-026-2 · US-ISBN 0-8204-6262-4

Vol. 10 Martina Möllering
The Acquisition of German Modal Particles. A Corpus-Based Approach.
290 pages. 2004. ISBN 3-03910-043-2 · US-ISBN 0-8204-6273-X

Vol. 11 David Hart (ed.)
English Modality in Context. Diachronic Perspectives.
261 pages. 2003. ISBN 3-03910-046-7 · US-ISBN 0-8204-6852-5

Vol. 12 Wendy Swanson
Modes of Co-reference as an Indicator of Genre.
430 pages. 2003. ISBN 3-03910-052-1 · US-ISBN 0-8204-6855-X

Vol. 13 Gina Poncini
Discursive Strategies in Multicultural Business Meetings.
2nd edition. 338 pages. 2004, 2007.
ISBN 978-3-03911-296-8 · US-ISBN 978-0-8204-8937-7

Vol. 14 Christopher N. Candlin & Maurizio Gotti (eds)
Intercultural Aspects of Specialized Communication.
2nd edition. 369 pages. 2004, 2007.
ISBN 978-3-03911-258-6 · US-ISBN 978-0-8204-8926-1

Vol. 15 Gabriella Del Lungo Camiciotti & Elena Tognini Bonelli (eds)
Academic Discourse. New Insights into Evaluation.
234 pages. 2004. ISBN 3-03910-353-9 · US-ISBN 0-8204-7016-3

Vol. 16 Marina Dossena & Roger Lass (eds)
Methods and Data in English Historical Dialectology.
405 pages. 2004. ISBN 3-03910-362-8 · US-ISBN 0-8204-7018-X

Vol. 17 Judy Noguchi
The Science Review Article. An Opportune Genre in
the Construction of Science.
274 pages. 2006. ISBN 3-03910-426-8 · US-ISBN 0-8204-7034-1

Vol. 18 Giuseppina Cortese & Anna Duszak (eds)
Identity, Community, Discourse. English in Intercultural Settings.
495 pages. 2005. ISBN 3-03910-632-5 · US-ISBN 0-8204-7163-1

Vol. 19 Anna Trosborg & Poul Erik Flyvholm Jørgensen (eds)
Business Discourse. Texts and Contexts.
250 pages. 2005. ISBN 3-03910-606-6 · US-ISBN 0-8204-7000-7

Vol. 20 Christopher Williams
Tradition and Change in Legal English. Verbal Constructions in Prescriptive Texts.
2nd revised edition. 216 pages. 2005, 2007. ISBN 978-3-03911-444-3.

Vol. 21 Katarzyna Dziubalska-Kolaczyk & Joanna Przedlacka (eds)
English Pronunciation Models: A Changing Scene.
2nd edition. 476 pages. 2005, 2008. ISBN 978-3-03911-682-9.

Vol. 22 Christián Abello-Contesse, Rubén Chacón-Beltrán, M. Dolores López-Jiménez & M. Mar Torreblanca-López (eds)
Age in L2 Acquisition and Teaching.
214 pages. 2006. ISBN 3-03910-668-6 · US-ISBN 0-8204-7174-7

Vol. 23 Vijay K. Bhatia, Maurizio Gotti, Jan Engberg & Dorothee Heller (eds)
Vagueness in Normative Texts.
474 pages. 2005. ISBN 3-03910-653-8 · US-ISBN 0-8204-7169-0

Vol. 24 Paul Gillaerts & Maurizio Gotti (eds)
Genre Variation in Business Letters. 2nd printing.
407 pages. 2008. ISBN 978-3-03911-681-2.

Vol. 25 Ana María Hornero, María José Luzón & Silvia Murillo (eds)
Corpus Linguistics. Applications for the Study of English.
2nd printing. 526 pages. 2006, 2008. ISBN 978-3-03911-726-0

Vol. 26 J. Lachlan Mackenzie & María de los Ángeles Gómez-González (eds)
Studies in Functional Discourse Grammar.
259 pages. 2005. ISBN 3-03910-696-1 · US-ISBN 0-8204-7558-0

Vol. 27 Debbie G. E. Ho
Classroom Talk. Exploring the Sociocultural Structure of Formal ESL Learning.
2nd edition. 254 pages. 2006, 2007. ISBN 978-3-03911-434-4

Vol. 28 Javier Pérez-Guerra, Dolores González-Álvarez, Jorge L. Bueno-Alonso & Esperanza Rama-Martínez (eds)
'Of Varying Language and Opposing Creed'. New Insights into Late Modern English.
455 pages. 2007. ISBN 978-3-03910-788-9

Vol. 29 Francesca Bargiela-Chiappini & Maurizio Gotti (eds)
Asian Business Discourse(s).
350 pages. 2005. ISBN 3-03910-804-2 · US-ISBN 0-8204-7574-2

Vol. 30 Nicholas Brownlees (ed.)
News Discourse in Early Modern Britain. Selected Papers of CHINED 2004.
300 pages. 2006. ISBN 3-03910-805-0 · US-ISBN 0-8204-8025-8

Vol. 31 Roberta Facchinetti & Matti Rissanen (eds)
Corpus-based Studies of Diachronic English.
300 pages. 2006. ISBN 3-03910-851-4 · US-ISBN 0-8204-8040-1

Vol. 32 Marina Dossena & Susan M. Fitzmaurice (eds)
Business and Official Correspondence. Historical Investigations.
209 pages. 2006. ISBN 3-03910-880-8 · US-ISBN 0-8204-8352-4

Vol. 33 Giuliana Garzone & Srikant Sarangi (eds)
Discourse, Ideology and Specialized Communication.
494 pages. 2007. ISBN 978-3-03910-888-6

Vol. 34 Giuliana Garzone & Cornelia Ilie (eds)
The Use of English in Institutional and Business Settings.
An Intercultural Perspective.
372 pages. 2007. ISBN 978-3-03910-889-3

Vol. 35 Vijay K. Bhatia & Maurizio Gotti (eds)
Explorations in Specialized Genres.
316 pages. 2006. ISBN 3-03910-995-2 · US-ISBN 0-8204-8372-9

Vol. 36 Heribert Picht (ed.)
Modern Approaches to Terminological Theories and Applications.
432 pages. 2006. ISBN 3-03911-156-6 · US-ISBN 0-8204-8380-X

Vol. 37 Anne Wagner & Sophie Cacciaguidi-Fahy (eds)
Legal Language and the Search for Clarity / Le langage juridique et la quête de clarté. Practice and Tools / Pratiques et instruments.
487 pages. 2006. ISBN 3-03911-169-8 · US-ISBN 0-8204-8388-5

Vol. 38 Juan Carlos Palmer-Silveira, Miguel F. Ruiz-Garrido & Inmaculada Fortanet-Gómez (eds)
Intercultural and International Business Communication.
Theory, Research and Teaching.
2nd edition. 343 pages. 2006, 2008. ISBN 978-3-03911-680-5

Vol. 39 Christiane Dalton-Puffer, Dieter Kastovsky, Nikolaus Ritt & Herbert Schendl (eds)
Syntax, Style and Grammatical Norms. English from 1500–2000.
250 pages. 2006. ISBN 3-03911-181-7 · US-ISBN 0-8204-8394-X

Vol. 40 Marina Dossena & Irma Taavitsainen (eds)
Diachronic Perspectives on Domain-Specific English.
280 pages. 2006. ISBN 3-03910-176-0 · US-ISBN 0-8204-8391-5

Vol. 41 John Flowerdew & Maurizio Gotti (eds)
Studies in Specialized Discourse.
293 pages. 2006. ISBN 3-03911-178-7

Vol. 42 Ken Hyland & Marina Bondi (eds)
Academic Discourse Across Disciplines.
320 pages. 2006. ISBN 3-03911-183-3 · US-ISBN 0-8204-8396-6

Vol. 43 Paul Gillaerts & Philip Shaw (eds)
The Map and the Landscape. Norms and Practices in Genre.
256 pages. 2006. ISBN 3-03911-182-5 · US-ISBN 0-8204-8395-4

Vol. 44 Maurizio Gotti & Davide Giannoni (eds)
New Trends in Specialized Discourse Analysis.
301 pages. 2006. ISBN 3-03911-184-1 · US-ISBN 0-8204-8381-8

Vol. 45 Maurizio Gotti & Françoise Salager-Meyer (eds)
Advances in Medical Discourse Analysis. Oral and Written Contexts.
492 pages. 2006. ISBN 3-03911-185-X · US-ISBN 0-8204-8382-6

Vol. 46 Maurizio Gotti & Susan Šarcević (eds)
Insights into Specialized Translation.
396 pages. 2006. ISBN 3-03911-186-8 · US-ISBN 0-8204-8383-4

Vol. 47 Khurshid Ahmad & Margaret Rogers (eds)
Evidence-based LSP. Translation, Text and Terminology.
584 pages. 2007. ISBN 978-3-03911-187-9

Vol. 48 Hao Sun & Dániel Z. Kádár (eds)
It's the Dragon's Turn. Chinese Institutional Discourses.
262 pages. 2008. ISBN 978-3-03911-175-6

Vol. 49 Cristina Suárez-Gómez
Relativization in Early English (950-1250). the Position of Relative Clauses.
149 pages. 2006. ISBN 3-03911-203-1 · US-ISBN 0-8204-8904-2

Vol. 50 Maria Vittoria Calvi & Luisa Chierichetti (eds)
Nuevas tendencias en el discurso de especialidad.
319 pages. 2006. ISBN 978-3-03911-261-6

Vol. 51 Mari Carmen Campoy & María José Luzón (eds)
Spoken Corpora in Applied Linguistics.
274 pages. 2008. ISBN 978-3-03911-275-3

Vol. 52 Konrad Ehlich & Dorothee Heller (Hrsg.)
Die Wissenschaft und ihre Sprachen.
323 pages. 2006. ISBN 978-3-03911-272-2

Vol. 53 Jingyu Zhang
The Semantic Salience Hierarchy Model. The L2 Acquisition of Psych Predicates
273 pages. 2007. ISBN 978-3-03911-300-2

Vol. 54 Norman Fairclough, Giuseppina Cortese & Patrizia Ardizzone (eds)
Discourse and Contemporary Social Change.
555 pages. 2007. ISBN 978-3-03911-276-0

Vol. 55 Jan Engberg, Marianne Grove Ditlevsen, Peter Kastberg & Martin Stegu (eds)
New Directions in LSP Teaching.
331 pages. 2007. ISBN 978-3-03911-433-7

Vol. 56 Dorothee Heller & Konrad Ehlich (Hrsg.)
Studien zur Rechtskommunikation.
322 pages. 2007. ISBN 978-3-03911-436-8

Vol. 57 Teruhiro Ishiguro & Kang-kwong Luke (eds)
Grammar in Cross-Linguistic Perspective.
The Syntax, Semantics, and Pragmatics of Japanese and Chinese.
304 pages. 2012. ISBN 978-3-03911-445-0

Vol. 58 Carmen Frehner
Email – SMS – MMS
294 pages. 2008. ISBN 978-3-03911-451-1

Vol. 59 Isabel Balteiro
The Directionality of Conversion in English. A Dia-Synchronic Study.
276 pages. 2007. ISBN 978-3-03911-241-8

Vol. 60 Maria Milagros Del Saz Rubio
English Discourse Markers of Reformulation.
237 pages. 2007. ISBN 978-3-03911-196-1

Vol. 61 Sally Burgess & Pedro Martín-Martín (eds)
English as an Additional Language in Research Publication and Communication.
259 pages. 2008. ISBN 978-3-03911-462-7

Vol. 62 Sandrine Onillon
Pratiques et représentations de l'écrit.
458 pages. 2008. ISBN 978-3-03911-464-1

Vol. 63 Hugo Bowles & Paul Seedhouse (eds)
Conversation Analysis and Language for Specific Purposes.
2nd edition. 337 pages. 2007, 2009. ISBN 978-3-0343-0045-2

Vol. 64 Vijay K. Bhatia, Christopher N. Candlin & Paola Evangelisti Allori (eds)
Language, Culture and the Law.
The Formulation of Legal Concepts across Systems and Cultures.
342 pages. 2008. ISBN 978-3-03911-470-2

Vol. 65 Jonathan Culpeper & Dániel Z. Kádár (eds)
Historical (Im)politeness.
300 pages. 2010. ISBN 978-3-03911-496-2

Vol. 66 Linda Lombardo (ed.)
Using Corpora to Learn about Language and Discourse.
237 pages. 2009. ISBN 978-3-03911-522-8

Vol. 67 Natsumi Wakamoto
Extroversion/Introversion in Foreign Language Learning.
Interactions with Learner Strategy Use.
159 pages. 2009. ISBN 978-3-03911-596-9

Vol. 68 Eva Alcón-Soler (ed.)
Learning How to Request in an Instructed Language Learning Context.
260 pages. 2008. ISBN 978-3-03911-601-0

Vol. 69 Domenico Pezzini
The Translation of Religious Texts in the Middle Ages.
428 pages. 2008. ISBN 978-3-03911-600-3

Vol. 70 Tomoko Tode
Effects of Frequency in Classroom Second Language Learning.
Quasi-experiment and stimulated-recall analysis.
195 pages. 2008. ISBN 978-3-03911-602-7

Vol. 71 Egor Tsedryk
Fusion symétrique et alternances ditransitives.
211 pages. 2009. ISBN 978-3-03911-609-6

Vol. 72 Cynthia J. Kellett Bidoli & Elana Ochse (eds)
English in International Deaf Communication.
444 pages. 2008. ISBN 978-3-03911-610-2

Vol. 73 Joan C. Beal, Carmela Nocera & Massimo Sturiale (eds)
Perspectives on Prescriptivism.
269 pages. 2008. ISBN 978-3-03911-632-4

Vol. 74 Carol Taylor Torsello, Katherine Ackerley & Erik Castello (eds)
Corpora for University Language Teachers.
308 pages. 2008. ISBN 978-3-03911-639-3

Vol. 88 Kiriko Sato
The Development from Case-Forms to Prepositional Constructions in Old English Prose.
231 pages. 2009. ISBN 978-3-03911-763-5

Vol. 89 Dorothee Heller (Hrsg.)
Formulierungsmuster in deutscher und italienischer Fachkommunikation. Intra- und interlinguale Perspektiven.
315 pages. 2008. ISBN 978-3-03911-778-9

Vol. 90 Henning Bergenholtz, Sandro Nielsen & Sven Tarp (eds)
Lexicography at a Crossroads. Dictionaries and Encyclopedias Today, Lexicographical Tools Tomorrow.
372 pages. 2009. ISBN 978-3-03911-799-4

Vol. 91 Manouchehr Moshtagh Khorasani
The Development of Controversies. From the Early Modern Period to Online Discussion Forums.
317 pages. 2009. ISBN 978-3-3911-711-6

Vol. 92 María Luisa Carrió-Pastor (ed.)
Content and Language Integrated Learning. Cultural Diversity.
178 pages. 2009. ISBN 978-3-3911-818-2

Vol. 93 Roger Berry
Terminology in English Language Teaching. Nature and Use.
262 pages. 2010. ISBN 978-3-0343-0013-1

Vol. 94 Roberto Cagliero & Jennifer Jenkins (eds)
Discourses, Communities, and Global Englishes
240 pages. 2010. ISBN 978-3-0343-0012-4

Vol. 95 Facchinetti Roberta, Crystal David, Seidlhofer Barbara (eds)
From International to Local English – And Back Again.
268 pages. 2010. ISBN 978-3-0343-0011-7

Vol. 96 Cesare Gagliardi & Alan Maley (eds)
EIL, ELF, Global English. Teaching and Learning Issues
376 pages. 2010. ISBN 978-3-0343-0010-0

Vol. 97 Sylvie Hancil (ed.)
The Role of Prosody in Affective Speech.
403 pages. 2009. ISBN 978-3-03911-696-6

Vol. 98 Marina Dossena & Roger Lass (eds)
Studies in English and European Historical Dialectology.
257 pages. 2009. ISBN 978-3-0343-0024-7

Vol. 99 Christine Béal
Les interactions quotidiennes en français et en anglais.
De l'approche comparative à l'analyse des situations interculturelles.
424 pages. 2010. ISBN 978-3-0343-0027-8

Vol. 100 Maurizio Gotti (ed.)
Commonality and Individuality in Academic Discourse.
398 pages. 2009. ISBN 978-3-0343-0023-0

Vol. 101 Javier E. Díaz Vera & Rosario Caballero (eds)
Textual Healing. Studies in Medieval English Medical, Scientific and Technical Texts.
213 pages. 2009. ISBN 978-3-03911-822-9

Vol. 102 Nuria Edo Marzá
The Specialised Lexicographical Approach. A Step further in Dictionary-making.
316 pages. 2009. ISBN 978-3-0343-0043-8

Vol. 103 Carlos Prado-Alonso, Lidia Gómez-García, Iria Pastor-Gómez &
David Tizón-Couto (eds)
New Trends and Methodologies in Applied English Language Research.
Diachronic, Diatopic and Contrastive Studies.
348 pages. 2009. ISBN 978-3-0343-0046-9

Vol. 104 Françoise Salager-Meyer & Beverly A. Lewin
Crossed Words. Criticism in Scholarly Writing?
371 pages. 2011. ISBN 978-3-0343-0049-0.

Vol. 105 Javier Ruano-García
Early Modern Northern English Lexis. A Literary Corpus-Based Study.
611 pages. 2010. ISBN 978-3-0343-0058-2

Vol. 106 Rafael Monroy-Casas
Systems for the Phonetic Transcription of English. Theory and Texts.
280 pages. 2011. ISBN 978-3-0343-0059-9

Vol. 107 Nicola T. Owtram
The Pragmatics of Academic Writing.
A Relevance Approach to the Analysis of Research Article Introductions.
311 pages. 2009. ISBN 978-3-0343-0060-5

Vol. 108 Yolanda Ruiz de Zarobe, Juan Manuel Sierra &
Francisco Gallardo del Puerto (eds)
Content and Foreign Language Integrated Learning.
Contributions to Multilingualism in European Contexts
343 pages. 2011. ISBN 978-3-0343-0074-2

Vol. 109 Ángeles Linde López & Rosalía Crespo Jiménez (eds)
Professional English in the European context. The EHEA challenge.
374 pages. 2010. ISBN 978-3-0343-0088-9

Vol. 110 Rosalía Rodríguez-Vázquez
The Rhythm of Speech, Verse and Vocal Music. A New Theory.
394 pages. 2010. ISBN 978-3-0343-0309-5

Vol. 111 Anastasios Tsangalidis & Roberta Facchinetti (eds)
Studies on English Modality. In Honour of Frank Palmer.
392 pages. 2009. ISBN 978-3-0343-0310-1

Vol. 112 Jing Huang
Autonomy, Agency and Identity in Foreign Language Learning and Teaching.
400 pages. 2013. ISBN 978-3-0343-0370-5

Vol. 113 Mihhail Lotman & Maria-Kristiina Lotman (eds)
Frontiers in Comparative Prosody. In memoriam: Mikhail Gasparov.
426 pages. 2011. ISBN 978-3-0343-0373-6

Vol. 114 Merja Kytö, John Scahill & Harumi Tanabe (eds)
Language Change and Variation from Old English to Late Modern English.
A Festschrift for Minoji Akimoto
422 pages. 2010. ISBN 978-3-0343-0372-9

Vol. 115 Giuliana Garzone & Paola Catenaccio (eds)
Identities across Media and Modes. Discursive Perspectives.
379 pages. 2009. ISBN 978-3-0343-0386-6

Vol. 116 Elena Landone
Los marcadores del discurso y cortesía verbal en español.
390 pages. 2010. ISBN 978-3-0343-0413-9

Vol. 117 Maurizio Gotti & Christopher Williams (eds)
Legal Discourse across Languages and Cultures.
339 pages. 2010. ISBN 978-3-0343-0425-2

Vol. 118 David Hirsh
Academic Vocabulary in Context.
217 pages. 2010. ISBN 978-3-0343-0426-9

Vol. 119 Yvonne Dröschel
Lingua Franca English. The Role of Simplification and Transfer.
358 pages. 2011. ISBN 978-3-0343-0432-0

Vol. 120 Tengku Sepora Tengku Mahadi, Helia Vaezian & Mahmoud Akbari
Corpora in Translation. A Practical Guide.
135 pages. 2010. ISBN 978-3-0343-0434-4

Vol. 121 Davide Simone Giannoni & Celina Frade (eds)
Researching Language and the Law. Textual Features and Translation Issues.
278 pages. 2010. ISBN 978-3-0343-0443-6

Vol. 122 Daniel Madrid & Stephen Hughes (eds)
Studies in Bilingual Education.
472 pages. 2011. ISBN 978-3-0343-0474-0

Vol. 123 Vijay K. Bhatia, Christopher N. Candlin & Maurizio Gotti (eds)
The Discourses of Dispute Resolution.
290 pages. 2010. ISBN 978-3-0343-0476-4

Vol. 124 Davide Simone Giannoni
Mapping Academic Values in the Disciplines. A Corpus-Based Approach.
288 pages. 2010. ISBN 978-3-0343-0488-7

Vol. 125 Giuliana Garzone & James Archibald (eds)
Discourse, Identities and Roles in Specialized Communication.
419 pages. 2010. ISBN 978-3-0343-0494-8

Vol. 126 Iria Pastor-Gómez
The Status and Development of N+N Sequences in
Contemporary English Noun Phrases.
216 pages. 2011. ISBN 978-3-0343-0534-1

Vol. 127 Carlos Prado-Alonso
Full-verb Inversion in Written and Spoken English.
261 pages. 2011. ISBN 978-3-0343-0535-8

Vol. 128 Tony Harris & María Moreno Jaén (eds)
Corpus Linguistics in Language Teaching.
214 pages. 2010. ISBN 978-3-0343-0524-2

Vol. 129 Tetsuji Oda & Hiroyuki Eto (eds)
Multiple Perspectives on English Philology and History of Linguistics.
A Festschrift for Shoichi Watanabe on his 80th Birthday.
378 pages. 2010. ISBN 978-3-0343-0480-1

Vol. 130 Luisa Chierichetti & Giovanni Garofalo (eds)
Lengua y Derecho. líneas de investigación interdisciplinaria.
283 pages. 2010. 978-3-0343-0463-4

Vol. 131 Paola Evangelisti Allori & Giuliana Garzone (eds)
Discourse, Identities and Genres in Corporate Communication.
Sponsorship, Advertising and Organizational Communication.
324 pages. 2011. 978-3-0343-0591-4

Vol. 132 Leyre Ruiz de Zarobe & Yolanda Ruiz de Zarobe (eds)
Speech Acts and Politeness across Languages and Cultures.
402 pages. 2012. 978-3-0343-0611-9

Vol. 133 Thomas Christiansen
Cohesion. A Discourse Perspective.
387 pages. 2011. 978-3-0343-0619-5

Vol. 134 Giuliana Garzone & Maurizio Gotti
Discourse, Communication and the Enterprise. Genres and Trends.
451 pages. 2011. ISBN 978-3-0343-0620-1

Vol. 135 Zsuzsa Hoffmann
Ways of the World's Words.
Language Contact in the Age of Globalization.
334 pages 2011. ISBN 978-3-0343-0673-7

Vol. 136 Cecilia Varcasia (ed.)
Becoming Multilingual.
Language Learning and Language Policy between Attitudes and Identities.
213 pages. 2011. ISBN 978-3-0343-0687-5

Vol. 137 Susy Macqueen
The Emergence of Patterns in Second Language Writing.
A Sociocognitive Exploration of Lexical Trails.
325 pages. 2012. ISBN 978-3-0343-1010-9

Vol. 138 Maria Vittoria Calvi & Giovanna Mapelli (eds)
La lengua del turismo. Géneros discursivos y terminología.
365 pages. 2011. ISBN 978-3-0343-1011-6

Vol. 139 Ken Lau
Learning to Become a Professional in a Textually-Mediated World.
A Text-Oriented Study of Placement Practices.
261 pages. 2012. ISBN 978-3-0343-1016-1

Vol. 140 Sandra Campagna, Giuliana Garzone, Cornelia Ilie & Elizabeth Rowley-Jolivet (eds)
Evolving Genres in Web-mediated Communication.
337 pages. 2012. ISBN 978-3-0343-1013-0

Vol. 141 Edith Esch & Martin Solly (eds)
The Sociolinguistics of Language Education in International Contexts.
263 pages. 2012. ISBN 978-3-0343-1009-3

Vol. 142 Forthcoming.

Vol. 143 David Tizón-Couto
Left Dislocation in English. A Functional-Discoursal Approach.
416 pages. 2012. ISBN 978-3-0343-1037-6

Vol. 144 Margrethe Petersen & Jan Engberg (eds)
Current Trends in LSP Research. Aims and Methods.
323 pages. 2011. ISBN 978-3-0343-1054-3

Vol. 145 David Tizón-Couto, Beatriz Tizón-Couto, Iria Pastor-Gómez & Paula Rodríguez-Puente (eds)
New Trends and Methodologies in Applied English Language Research II. Studies in Language Variation, Meaning and Learning.
283 pages. 2012. ISBN 978-3-0343-1061-1

Vol. 146 Rita Salvi & Hiromasa Tanaka (eds)
Intercultural Interactions in Business and Management.
306 pages. 2011. ISBN 978-3-0343-1039-0

Vol. 147 Francesco Straniero Sergio & Caterina Falbo (eds)
Breaking Ground in Corpus-based Interpreting Studies.
254 pages. 2012. ISBN 978-3-0343-1071-0

Vol. 148 Forthcoming.

Vol. 149 Vijay K. Bhatia & Paola Evangelisti Allori (eds)
Discourse and Identity in the Professions. Legal, Corporate and Institutional Citizenship.
352 pages. 2011. ISBN 978-3-0343-1079-6

Vol. 150 Maurizio Gotti (ed.)
Academic Identity Traits. A Corpus-Based Investigation.
363 pages. 2012. ISBN 978-3-0343-1141-0

Vol. 151 Priscilla Heynderickx, Sylvain Dieltjens, Geert Jacobs, Paul Gillaerts & Elizabeth de Groot (eds)
The Language Factor in International Business. New Perspectives on Research, Teaching and Practice.
320 pages. 2012. ISBN 978-3-0343-1090-1

Vol. 152 Paul Gillaerts, Elizabeth de Groot, Sylvain Dieltjens, Priscilla Heynderickx & Geert Jacobs (eds)
Researching Discourse in Business Genres. Cases and Corpora.
215 pages. 2012. ISBN 978-3-0343-1092-5

Vol. 153 Yongyan Zheng
Dynamic Vocabulary Development in a Foreign Language.
262 pages. 2012. ISBN 978-3-0343-1106-9

Vol. 154 Carmen Argondizzo (ed.)
Creativity and Innovation in Language Education.
357 pages. 2012. ISBN 978-3-0343-1080-2

Vol. 155 David Hirsh (ed.)
Current Perspectives in Second Language Vocabulary Research.
180 pages. 2012. ISBN 978-3-0343-1108-3

Vol. 156 Seiji Shinkawa
Unhistorical Gender Assignment in Lahamon's *Brut*. A Case Study of a Late Stage in the Development of Grammatical Gender toward its Ultimate Loss.
186 pages. 2012. ISBN 978-3-0343-1124-3

Vol. 157 Yeonkwon Jung
Basics of Organizational Writing: A Critical Reading Approach.
151 pages. 2014. ISBN 978-3-0343-1137-3.

Vol. 158 Bárbara Eizaga Rebollar (ed.)
Studies in Linguistics and Cognition.
301 pages. 2012. ISBN 978-3-0343-1138-0

Vol. 159 Giuliana Garzone, Paola Catenaccio, Chiara Degano (eds)
Genre Change in the Contemporary World. Short-term Diachronic Perspectives.
329 pages. 2012. ISBN 978-3-0343-1214-1

Vol. 160 Carol Berkenkotter, Vijay K. Bhatia & Maurizio Gotti (eds)
Insights into Academic Genres.
468 pages. 2012. ISBN 978-3-0343-1211-0

Vol. 161 Beatriz Tizón-Couto
Clausal Complements in Native and Learner Spoken English. A corpus-based study with Lindsei and Vicolse. 357 pages. 2013. ISBN 978-3-0343-1184-7

Vol. 162 Patrizia Anesa
Jury Trials and the Popularization of Legal Language. A Discourse Analytical Approach.
247 pages. 2012. ISBN 978-3-0343-1231-8

Vol. 163 David Hirsh
Endangered Languages, Knowledge Systems and Belief Systems.
153 pages. 2013. ISBN 978-3-0343-1232-5

Vol. 164 Eugenia Sainz (ed.)
De la estructura de la frase al tejido del discurso. Estudios contrastivos español/italiano.
305 pages. 2014. ISBN 978-3-0343-1253-0

Vol. 165 Julia Bamford, Franca Poppi & Davide Mazzi (eds)
Space, Place and the Discursive Construction of Identity.
367 pages. 2014. ISBN 978-3-0343-1249-3

Vol. 166 Rita Salvi & Janet Bowker (eds)
Space, Time and the Construction of Identity.
Discursive Indexicality in Cultural, Institutional and Professional Fields.
324 pages. 2013. ISBN 978-3-0343-1254-7

Vol. 167 Shunji Yamazaki & Robert Sigley (eds)
Approaching Language Variation through Corpora. A Festschrift in Honour of Toshio Saito.
421 pages. 2013. ISBN 978-3-0343-1264-6

Vol. 168 Franca Poppi
Global Interactions in English as a Lingua Franca. How written communication is changing under the influence of electronic media and new contexts of use.
249 pages. 2012. ISBN 978-3-0343-1276-9

Vol. 169 Miguel A. Aijón Oliva & María José Serrano
Style in syntax. Investigating variation in Spanish pronoun subjects.
239 pages. 2013. ISBN 978-3-0343-1244-8

Vol. 170 Inés Olza, Óscar Loureda & Manuel Casado-Velarde (eds)
Language Use in the Public Sphere. Methodological Perspectives and Empirical Applications
564 pages. 2014. ISBN 978-3-0343-1286-8

Vol. 171 Aleksandra Matulewska
Legilinguistic Translatology. A Parametric Approach to Legal Translation.
279 pages. 2013. ISBN 978-3-0343-1287-5

Vol. 172 Maurizio Gotti & Carmen Sancho Guinda (eds)
Narratives in Academic and Professional Genres.
513 pages. 2013. ISBN 978-3-0343-1371-1

Vol. 173 Madalina Chitez
Learner corpus profiles. The case of Romanian Learner English.
244 pages. 2014. ISBN 978-3-0343-1410-7

Vol. 174 Chihiro Inoue
Task Equivalence in Speaking Tests.
251 pages. 2013. ISBN 978-3-0343-1417-6

Vol. 175 Gabriel Quiroz & Pedro Patiño (eds.)
LSP in Colombia: advances and challenges.
339 pages. 2014. ISBN 978-3-0343-1434-3

Vol. 176 Catherine Resche
Economic Terms and Beyond: Capitalising on the Wealth of Notions.
How Researchers in Specialised Varieties of English Can Benefit from Focusing on Terms.
332 pages. 2013. ISBN 978-3-0343-1435-0

Vol. 177 Wei Wang
Media representation of migrant workers in China. Identities and stances
198 pages. 2018. 978-3-0343-1436-7

Vol. 178 Cécile Desoutter & Caroline Mellet (dir.)
Le discours rapporté: approches linguistiques et perspectives didactiques.
270 pages. 2013. ISBN 978-3-0343-1292-9

Vol. 179 Ana Díaz-Negrillo & Francisco Javier Díaz-Pérez (eds)
Specialisation and Variation in Language Corpora.
341 pages. 2014. ISBN 978-3-0343-1316-2

Vol. 180 Pilar Alonso
A Multi-dimensional Approach to Discourse Coherence. From Standardness to Creativity.
247 pages. 2014. ISBN 978-3-0343-1325-4

Vol. 181 Alejandro Alcaraz-Sintes & Salvador Valera-Hernández (eds)
Diachrony and Synchrony in English Corpus Linguistics.
393 pages. 2014. ISBN 978-3-0343-1326-1

Vol. 182 Runhan Zhang
Investigating Linguistic Knowledge of a Second Language.
207 pages. 2015. ISBN 978-3-0343-1330-8

Vol. 183 Hajar Abdul Rahim & Shakila Abdul Manan (eds.)
English in Malaysia. Postcolonial and Beyond.
267 pages. 2014. ISBN 978-3-0343-1341-4

Vol. 184 Virginie Fasel Lauzon
Comprendre et apprendre dans l'interaction. Les séquences d'explication en classe
de français langue seconde.
292 pages. 2014. ISBN 978-3-0343-1451-0

Vol. 185 Forthcoming.

Vol. 186 Wei Ren
L2 Pragmatic Development in Study Abroad Contexts
256 pages. 2015. ISBN 978-3-0343-1358-2

Vol. 187 Marina Bondi & Rosa Lorés Sanz (eds)
Abstracts in Academic Discourse. Variation and Change.
361 pages. 2014. ISBN 978-3-0343-1483-1

Vol. 188 Giuditta Caliendo
Rethinking Community. Discourse, Identity and Citizenship in the European Union.
240 pages. 2017. ISBN 978-3-0343-1561-6

Vol. 189 Paola Evangelisti Allori (ed.)
Identities in and across Cultures.
315 pages. 2014. ISBN 978-3-0343-1458-9

Vol. 190 Erik Castello, Katherine Ackerley & Francesca Coccetta (eds).
Studies in Learner Corpus Linguistics. Research and Applications for Foreign Language Teaching and Assessment.
358 pages. 2015. ISBN 978-3-0343-1506-7

Vol. 191 Ruth Breeze, Maurizio Gotti & Carmen Sancho Guinda (eds)
Interpersonality in Legal Genres.
389 pages. 2014. ISBN 978-3-0343-1524-1

Vol. 192 Paola Evangelisti Allori, John Bateman & Vijay K. Bhatia (eds)
Evolution in Genre. Emergence, Variation, Multimodality.
364 pages. 2014. ISBN 978-3-0343-1533-3

Vol. 193 Jiyeon Kook
Agency in Arzt-Patient-Gesprächen. Zur interaktionistischen Konzeptualisierung von Agency
271 pages. 2015. ISBN 978-3-0343-1666-8

Vol. 194 Susana Nicolás Román & Juan José Torres Núñez (eds)
Drama and CLIL. A new challenge for the teaching approaches in bilingual education.
170 pages. 2015. ISBN 978-3-0343-1629-3

Vol. 195 Alessandra Molino & Serenella Zanotti (eds)
Observing Norm, Observing Usage. Lexis in Dictionaries and in the Media.
430 pages. 2015. ISBN 978-3-0343-1584-5

Vol. 196 Begoña Soneira
A Lexical Description of English for Architecture. A Corpus-based Approach.
267 pages. 2015. ISBN 978-3-0343-1602-6

Vol. 197 M Luisa Roca-Varela
False Friends in Learner Corpora. A corpus-based study of English false friends in the written and spoken production of Spanish learners.
348 pages. 2015. ISBN 978-3-0343-1620-0

Vol. 198 Rahma Al-Mahrooqi & Christopher Denman
Bridging the Gap between Education and Employment. English Language Instruction in EFL Contexts.
416 pages. 2015. ISBN 978-3-0343-1681-1

Vol. 199 Rita Salvi & Janet Bowker (eds)
The Dissemination of Contemporary Knowledge in English. Genres, discourse strategies and professional practices.
171 pages. 2015. ISBN 978-3-0343-1679-8

Vol. 200 Maurizio Gotti & Davide S. Giannoni (eds)
Corpus Analysis for Descriptive and Pedagogical Purposes. ESP Perspectives.
432 pages. 2014. ISBN 978-3-0343-1516-6

Vol. 201 Ida Ruffolo
The Perception of Nature in Travel Promotion Texts. A Corpus-based Discourse Analysis.
148 pages. 2015. ISBN 978-3-0343-1521-0

Vol. 202 Ives Trevian
English suffixes. Stress-assignment properties, productivity, selection and combinatorial processes.
471 pages. 2015. ISBN 978-3-0343-1576-0

Vol. 203 Maurizio Gotti, Stefania Maci & Michele Sala (eds)
Insights into Medical Communication.
422 pages. 2015. ISBN 978-3-0343-1694-1

Vol. 204 Carmen Argondizzo (ed.)
European Projects in University Language Centres. Creativity, Dynamics, Best Practice.
371 pages. 2015. ISBN 978-3-0343-1696-5

Vol. 205 Aura Luz Duffé Montalván (ed.)
Estudios sobre el léxico. Puntos y contrapuntos.
502 pages. 2016. ISBN 978-3-0343-2011-5

Vol. 206 Maria Pavesi, Maicol Formentelli & Elisa Ghia (eds)
The Languages of Dubbing. Mainstream Audiovisual Translation in Italy.
275 pages. 2014. ISBN 978-3-0343-1646-0

Vol. 207 Ruth Breeze & Inés Olza (eds)
Evaluation in media discourse. European perspectives.
268 pages. 2017. ISBN 978-3-0343-2014-6

Vol. 208 Vijay K. Bhatia & Maurizio Gotti (eds)
Arbitration Discourse in Asia.
331 pages. 2015. ISBN 978-3-0343-2032-0

Vol. 209 Sofía Bemposta-Rivas, Carla Bouzada-Jabois, Yolanda Fernández-Pena, Tamara Bouso, Yolanda J. Calvo-Benzies, Iván Tamaredo (eds)
New trends and methodologies in applied English language research III. Synchronic and diachronic studies on discourse, lexis and grammar processing.
280 pages. 2017. ISBN 978-3-0343-2039-9

Vol. 210 Francisco Alonso Almeida, Laura Cruz García & Víctor González Ruiz (eds)
Corpus-based studies on language varieties.
285 pages. 2016. ISBN 978-3-0343-2044-3

Vol. 211 Juan Pedro Rica Peromingo
Aspectos lingüísticos y técnicos de la traducción audiovisual (TAV).
177 pages. 2016. ISBN 978-3-0343-2055-9

Vol. 212 Maria Vender
Disentangling Dyslexia. VenderPhonological and Processing Deficit in Developmental Dyslexia.
338 pages. 2017. ISBN 978-3-0343-2064-1

Vol. 213 Zhilong Xie
Bilingual Advantages. Contributions of Different Bilingual Experiences to Cognitive Control Differences Among Young-adult Bilinguals.
221 pages. 2016. ISBN 978-3-0343-2081-8

Vol. 214 Larissa D'Angelo
Academic posters. A textual and visual metadiscourse analysis.
367 pages. 2016. ISBN 978-3-0343-2083-2

Vol. 215 Evelyne Berger
Prendre la parole en L2. Regard sur la compétence d'interaction en classe de langue.
246 pages. 2016. ISBN 978-3-0343-2084-9

Vol. 216 David Lasagabaster and Aintzane Doiz (eds)
CLIL experiences in secondary and tertiary education: In search of good practices.
262 pages. 2016. ISBN 978-3-0343-2104-4

Vol. 217 Elena Kkese
Identifying Plosives in L2 English: The Case of L1 Cypriot Greek Speakers.
317 pages. 2016. ISBN 978-3-0343-2060-3

Vol. 218 Sandra Campagna, Elana Ochse, Virginia Pulcini & Martin Solly (eds)
Languaging in and across Communities: New Voices, New Identities. Studies in Honour of Giuseppina Cortese.
507 pages. 2016. ISBN 978-3-0343-2073-3

Vol. 219 Adriana Orlandi & Laura Giacomini (ed.)
Defining collocation for lexicographic purposes. From linguistic theory to lexicographic practice.
328 pages. 2016. ISBN 978-3-0343-2054-2

Vol. 220 Pietro Luigi Iaia
Analysing English as a Lingua Franca in Video Games. Linguistic Features, Experiential and Functional Dimensions of Online and Scripted Interactions.
139 pages. 2016. ISBN 978-3-0343-2138-9

Vol. 221 Dimitrinka G. Níkleva (ed.)
La formación de los docentes de español para inmigrantes en distintos contextos educativos.
390 pages. 2017. ISBN 978-3-0343-2135-8

Vol. 222 Katherine Ackerley, Marta Guarda & Francesca Helm (eds)
Sharing Perspectives on English-Medium Instruction.
308 pages. 2017. ISBN 978-3-0343-2537-0

Vol. 223 Juana I. Marín-Arrese, Julia Lavid-López, Marta Carretero, Elena Domínguez Romero, Mª Victoria Martín de la Rosa & María Pérez Blanco (eds)
Evidentiality and Modality in European Languages. Discourse-pragmatic perspectives.
427 pages. 2017. ISBN 978-3-0343-2437-3

Vol. 224 Gilles Col
Construction du sens : un modèle instructionnel pour la sémantique.
292 pages. 2017. ISBN 978-3-0343-2572-1

Vol. 225 Ana Chiquito & Gabriel Quiroz (eds)
Pobreza, Lenguaje y Medios en América Latina.
362 pages. 2017. ISBN 978-3-0343-2142-6

Vol. 226 Xu Zhang
English Quasi-Numeral Classifiers. A Corpus-Based Cognitive-Typological Study.
360 pages. 2017. ISBN 978-3-0343-2818-0

Vol. 227 María Ángeles Orts, Ruth Breeze & Maurizio Gotti (eds)
Power, Persuasion and Manipulation in Specialised Genres. Providing Keys to the Rhetoric of Professional Communities.
368 pages. 2017. ISBN 978-3-0343-3010-7

Vol. 228 Maurizio Gotti, Stefania Maci & Michele Sala (eds)
Ways of Seeing, Ways of Being: Representing the Voices of Tourism.
453 pages. 2017. ISBN 978-3-0343-3031-2

Vol. 229 Dino Selvaggi
Plurilingual Code-Switching between Standard and Local Varieties.
A Socio-Psycholinguistic Approach
371 pages. 2018. ISBN 978-3-0343-2663-6

Vol. 230 Anca-Cristina Sterie
Interprofessional interactions at the hospital. Nurses' requests and reports
of problems in calls with physicians.
371 pages. 2017. ISBN 978-3-0343-2734-3

Vol. 231 Xiaodong Zhang
Understanding Chinese EFL Teachers' Beliefs and Practices in the Textbook-Based Classroom.
189 pages. 2017. ISBN 978-3-0343-3053-4

Vol. 232 Manuela Caterina Moroni & Federica Ricci Garotti (Hrsg.)
Brücken schlagen zwischen Sprachwissenschaft und DaF-Didaktik.
345 pages. 2017. ISBN 978-3-0343-2667-4

Vol. 233 Dimitrinka Georgieva Níkleva
Necesidades y tendencias en la formación del profesorado de español
como lengua extranjera
401 pages. 2017. ISBN 978-3-0343-2946-0

Vol. 234 Juan Santana-Lario & Salvador Valera (Hrsg.)
Competing patterns in English affixation.
272 pages. 2017. ISBN 978-3-0343-2701-5

Vol. 235 Francisco Salgado-Robles
Desarrollo de la competencia sociolingüística por aprendices de español
en un contexto de inmersión en el extranjero
241 pages. 2018. ISBN 978-3-0343-2323-9

Vol. 236 Maria Chiara Janner
Sguardi linguistici sulla marca. Analisi morfosintattica dei nomi commerciali in italiano
345 pages. 2017. ISBN 978-3-0343-2667-4

Vol. 237 Bárbara Herrero Muñoz-Cobo & Otman El Azami Zalachi
La primavera del árabe marroquí.
192 pages. 2017. ISBN 978-3-0343-3104-3

Vol. 238 Consuelo Pascual Escagedo
El papel del oyente en la construcción de la conversación espontánea de estudiantes
italianos en su interlengua y en su lengua materna
295 pages. 2017. ISBN 978-3-0343-3186-9

Vol. 239 Stefania M. Maci
The MS Digby 133 *Mary Magdalene*. Beyond scribal practices:
language, discourse, values and attitudes.
336 pages. 2017. ISBN 978-3-0343-3256-9

Vol. 240 Eliecer Crespo-Fernández
Taboo in Discourse. Studies on Attenuation and Offence in Communication.
326 pages. 2018. ISBN 978-3-0343-3018-3

Vol. 241 Jana Altmanova, Maria Centrella, Katherine E. Russo (eds)
Terminology & Discourse / Terminologie et discours.
424 pages. 2018. ISBN 978-3-0343-2417-5

Vol. 242 Xavier Blanco et Inès Sfar (dir.)
Lexicologie(s) : approches croisées en sémantique lexicale.
442 pages. 2018. ISBN 978-3-0343-3056-5

Vol. 243 Yunfeng Ge
Resolution of Conflict of Interest in Chinese Civil Court Hearings.
A Perspective of Discourse Information Theory.
302 pages. 2018. ISBN 978-3-0343-3313-9

Vol. 244 Carla Vergaro
Illocutionary Shell Nouns in English
322 pages. 2018. ISBN 978-3-0343-3069-5

Vol. 245 Paolo Frassi
L'adjectif en français et sa définition lexicographique.
270 pages. 2018. ISBN 978-3-0343-3394-8

Vol. 246 Suwilai Premsrirat and David Hirsh (eds)
Language Revitalization. Insights from Thailand
328 pages. 2018. ISBN 978-3-0343-3497-6

Vol. 247 Wei Wang
Researching Learning and Learners in Genre-based Academic Writing Instruction
282 pages. 2018. ISBN 978-3-0343-3297-2

Vol. 248 Isusi Alabarte, Alberto & Lahuerta Martínez, Ana Cristina (eds)
La comprensión lectora de lengua extranjera
Estudio de los factores de familiaridad, interés, género y métodos de evaluación
336 pages. 2018. ISBN 978-3-0343-3493-8

Vol. 249 Mercedes Eurrutia Cavero
Approche didactique du langage techno-scientifique
Terminologie et discours
374 pages. 2018. ISBN 978-3-0343-3512-6

Vol. 250 Aurora Ruiz Mezcua (ed.)
Approaches to Telephone Interpretation
Research, Innovation, Teaching and Transference
268 pages. 2018. ISBN 978-3-0343-3330-6

Vol. 251 Morini Massimiliano
A Day in the News
A Stylistic Analysis of Newsspeak
188 pages. 2018. ISBN 978-3-0343-3507-2

Vol. 252 Ignacio Guillén-Galve & Ignacio Vázquez-Orta (eds.)
English as a Lingua Franca and Intercultural Communication
Implications and Applications in the Field of English Language Teaching
414 pages. 2018. ISBN 978-3-0343-2763-3

Vol. 253 Bianca Del Villano
Using the Devil with Courtesy
Shakespeare and the Language of (Im)Politeness
216 pages. 2018. ISBN 978-3-0343-2315-4

Vol. 254 David Hirsh (ed.)
Explorations in Second Language Vocabulary Research
252 pages. 2018. ISBN 978-3-0343-2940-8

Vol. 255 Tania Baumann (ed.)
Reiseführer - Sprach- und Kulturmittlung im Tourismus / Le guide turistiche - mediazione linguistica e culturale in ambito turistico
270 pages. 2018. ISBN 978-3-0343-3402-0

Vol. 256 Ariadna Sánchez-Hernández & Ana Herraiz-Martínez (eds)
Learning second language pragmatics beyond traditional contexts
376 pages. 2018. ISBN 978-3-0343-3437-2

Vol. 257 Albert Bastardas-Boada, Emili Boix-Fuster, Rosa Maria Torrens (eds)
Family Multilingualism in Medium-Sized Linguistic Communities
336 pages. 2019. ISBN 978-3-0343-2536-3

Vol. 258 Yuyang Cai
Examining the Interaction among Components of English for Specific Purposes Ability in Reading. The Triple-Decker Model
296 pages. 2020. 978-3-0343-2913-2

Vol. 259 Catia Nannoni
Participe présent et gérondif dans la presse française contemporaine
176 pages. 2019. ISBN 978-3-0343-3631-4

Vol. 260 Nieves Rodríguez Pérez & Bárbara Heinsch (eds.)
Contextos multilingües. Mediadores interculturales, formación del profesorado de lenguas extranjeras
289 pages. 2019. ISBN 978-3-0343-3768-7

Vol. 261 Giuliana Elena Garzone, Mara Logaldo, Francesca Santulli (eds.)
Investigating Conflict Discourses in the Periodical Press
244 pages. 2020. ISBN 978-3-0343-3668-0

Vol. 262 Laura Nadal
Lingüística experimental y contraargumentación
233 pages. 2019. ISBN 978-3-0343-3791-5

Vol. 263 Claudia Claridge & Merja Kytö (eds.)
Punctuation in Context – Past and Present Perspectives
288 pages. 2019. ISBN 978-3-0343-3790-8

Vol. 264 Maurizio Gotti, Stefania Maci, Michele Sala (eds.)
Scholarly Pathways
530 pages. 2020. ISBN 978-3-0343-3860-8

Vol. 265 Ruth Breeze, Ana M. Fernández Vallejo (eds.)
Politics and populism across modes and media
350 pages. 2020. ISBN 978-3-0343-3707-6

Vol. 266 Jean Marguerite Jimenez
Understanding the Effects of Immediate Electronic Corrective Feedback on Second Language Development
252 pages. 2020. ISBN 978-3-0343-3815-8

Vol. 267 Sergio Rodríguez-Tapia, Adela González-Fernández (eds)
Lenguas y turismo: estudios en torno al discurso, la didáctica y la divulgación
380 pages. 2020. ISBN 978-3-0343-3881-3

Vol. 268 Ana Bocanegra-Valle (ed.)
Applied Linguistics and Knowledge Transfer. Employability, Internationalisation and Social Challenges
344 pages. 2020. ISBN 978-3-0343-3714-4

Vol. 269 Beatrice Garzelli
La traducción audiovisual español-italiano.Películas y cortos entre humor y habla soez
202 pages. 2020. ISBN 978-3-0343-4013-7

Vol. 270 Iván Tamaredo
Complexity, Efficiency, and Language Contact. Pronoun Omission in World Englishes
292 pages. 2020. ISBN 978-3-0343-3902-5

Vol. 271 Silvia Domenica Zollo,
Origine et histoire du vocabulaire des arts de la table. Analyse lexicale et exploitation de corpus textuels
239 pages. 2020. ISBN 978-3-0343-3890-5

Vol. 272 Forthcoming

Vol. 273 María Martínez-Atienza de Dios,
Entre el léxico y la sintaxis: las fases de los eventos
178 pages. 2021. 978-3-0343-4173-8

Vol. 274 Noelia Castro-Chao,
Argument Structure in Flux. The Development of Impersonal Constructions in Middle and Early Modern English, with Special Reference to Verbs of Desire.
300 pages. 2021. 978-3-0343-4189-9

Vol. 275 Gabriella Carobbio, Cécile Desoutter, Aurora Fragonara (eds.)
Macht, Ratio und Emotion: Diskurse im digitalen Zeitalter / Pouvoir, raison et émotion: les discours à l'ère du numérique
246 pages. 2020. 978-3-0343-4184-4

Vol. 276 Miguel Fuster-Márquez, José Santaemilia, Carmen Gregori-Signes, Paula Rodríguez-Abruñeiras (eds.)
Exploring discourse and ideology through corpora
293 pages. 2021. 978-3-0343-3969-8

www.ingramcontent.com/pod-product-compliance
Ingram Content Group UK Ltd.
Pitfield, Milton Keynes, MK11 3LW, UK
UKHW021835100926
8556IPUK00004B/348

9 783034 339698